CHANGING TIMES IN TRIAL COURTS

by

Barry Mahoney

with

Alexander B. Aikman
Pamela Casey
Victor E. Flango
Geoff Gallas

Thomas A. Henderson
Jeanne A. Ito
David C. Steelman
Steven Weller

National Center for State Courts

A project sponsored by the National Institute of Justice
and the Bureau of Justice Assistance

Library of Congress Cataloging-in-Publication Data

Changing times in trial courts.

 "A project sponsored by the National Institute of
Justice and the Bureau of Justice Assistance."
 1. Court congestion and delay—United States.
2. Court administration—United States. I. Mahoney,
Barry. II. National Center for State Courts.
III. National Institute of Justice (U.S.) IV. United
States. Bureau of Justice Assistance.
KF8727.C48   1988   347.73′13   88-15166
ISBN 0-89656-087-2   347.30713

Final report of a research project conducted pursuant to grants to the
National Center for State Courts from the National Institute of Justice
and Bureau of Justice Assistance, United States Department of Justice

Law

Contents

Part III
Dynamics of the Change Process
in Urban Trial Courts

Part IV
Future Directions

Tables and Figures

Foreword

"... trial court delay is not inevitable." Early research suggested that local legal culture largely determined the speed of case processing. However, new evidence reports that local legal culture can be changed and that significant improvement is possible through careful application of management principles. That very encouraging conclusion emerges from this new study of case processing and court delay in 18 urban trial courts. In fact, although the volume of cases in most of these courts increased in the nine years between 1976 and 1985—by as much as 54% in some instances—felony case processing times in some courts were dramatically reduced. Three courts studied cut case processing time by one-half, while two others reduced it by nearly one-third.

This is welcome news. Massive delay in our civil and criminal courts has been a national concern for the past half century. With rising crime in the 1960s and 1970s, court delay reached critical proportions, prompting federal assistance to courts that developed and implemented case processing standards.

The National Center for State Courts, supported by the National Institute of Justice and the Bureau of Justice Assistance, assessed the impact of these efforts in the mid-1970s and gauged the current size and scope of the court delay problem nationwide. The results, published in *Managing the Pace of Justice* and *Justice Delayed*, have brought significant changes in the way courts handle case processing today.

As this current report shows, caseflow management in American urban trial courts has become an important and effective approach to reducing court delay. Successful caseflow management appears to require a comprehensive case processing system that identifies and maintains information on all cases from entry into the process to disposition. Open and regular communication of this information to all participants and sound monitoring of the implementation of the court's caseflow management are also key. Understanding and adoption of the procedures are enhanced by training and special education.

This research gives us a better grasp of the complexities of controlling case processing and reducing delay. Speed must be balanced with fairness. Otherwise, the savings gained by reducing case processing time may only be monetary, and justice may be compromised. Because controlling case processing can also affect the adversary process, it must be carefully developed so it in no way damages this fundamental aspect of our justice system. Caseflow management must also be designed with the needs and concerns of victims and witnesses in mind, as other research attests. Their full cooperation is essential to successful prosecutions.

What ingredients make up success in reducing delay? According to this report, successful courts have strong and attentive leadership at all levels—and their leadership is based on the understanding and cooperation of prosecutors, defense, local bar, and the media. These courts establish and enforce trial time standards. The greater the emphasis on these standards by the leadership, the greater the change in case processing time. A decade ago, very few courts had time standards for civil cases; but by 1985, five of the most successful civil courts did have time standards.

Courts that take the initiative in establishing and maintaining caseflow management programs that attend to the issues and complexities of efficient and fair case processing will realize benefits not only for court operations but the wider community. The task is neither simple nor impossible. It requires decisiveness and determination, qualities that we and everyone who supports court reform encourage and applaud.

The National Institute of Justice and the Bureau of Justice Assistance are pleased to have sponsored this important research by the National Center for State Courts. The field is recognizing the study's contribution to the understanding of caseflow management—a contribution, it is important to note, that would not have been possible without the strong support and cooperation of the staff and judges of the 18 courts that participated in the research.

The past decade has seen major strides in reducing case processing time and court delay. As we look forward to the twenty-first century, we hope that even greater accomplishments will follow from this and other work now in progress.

James K. Stewart
Director
National Institute of Justice

Charles P. Smith
Director
Bureau of Justice Assistance

Preface

This report presents findings from a three-year study of case processing times in 18 general jurisdiction trial courts located in urban areas across the United States. The research has been designed to provide a current picture of the pace of criminal and civil litigation in these courts and to analyze changes that have taken place over the 1976–85 period.

The report is intended primarily to be read and used by persons working in and with trial courts. Trial courts vary widely in the ways they organize themselves to manage their litigation business, and it seems clear from our research that different approaches to management can significantly affect the pace of litigation. Several of the courts participating in the study provide good examples of effective caseflow management in operation, and in preparing this report we have paid particular attention to these courts. Our objective has been to provide a readable and policy-relevant document, with a minimum of the technical jargon of research—one that will be useful in the development of research and action programs designed to improve the functioning of the litigation process.

While this is, in a formal sense, the final report of a research project, it is by no means the last document that will be based upon this research. We have collected a very large amount of data from the courts participating in the study, and have a strong sense that we have only started the analysis. Much more extensive analysis of the data can be undertaken in the future, but is is important to get what we now know (or think we know) into circulation among policymakers, practitioners, and researchers.

As is frequently the case in research, a great many people have been instrumental in conducting this study and helping to prepare this report. It is appropriate to begin by acknowledging special debts of gratitude to three persons—Thomas W. Church, Larry L. Sipes, and Alan Carlson—who were deeply involved in the National Center for State Courts' *Justice Delayed* study. In designing and carrying out that research in 1976–78, they developed data collection methods and analytic approaches that we followed closely in this study. Their work has made possible the beginning of longitudinal analysis in this field. All three of them also contributed to this study in a variety of ways, including providing analysis of caseflow management practices and approaches in specific courts. So, too, did David Neubauer, the principal author of another multijurisdictional study that has been a valuable source of both information and ideas for this project.

Funding for the project was provided by grants to the National Center from two agencies of the U.S. Department of Justice: the Bureau of Justice Assistance and the National Institute of Justice. We very much appreciate the support and encouragement of key officials in those agencies—Jim Swain, Nick Demos, and Jay Marshall of BJA, and Fred Heintzelman, Cheryl Martorana, and Richard Rau of NIJ—throughout the course of the project.

Collecting data about the courts—from court records, questionnaires, interviews and a wide variety of documents—has involved scores of people. A large number of students and court system employees have assisted in the task of collecting data on approximately 50,000 cases. This often tedious work has provided us with the basic data on case processing times in the courts participating in the study. Court administrators, clerks, and presiding judges in the courts participating in the study not only facilitated our access to the court records, but also took the time to describe to us the organization of their courts and their approaches to caseflow management. They completed questionnaires about the courts and, in the jurisdictions where we undertook case studies, they helped arrange interviews with other court staff members, judges, and lawyers.

In addition to the co-authors of this report, a number of present and former National Center staff members have been involved in the project in a variety of ways. Dick Van Duizend and John Greacen helped shape the initial research design. Dan Valluzzi, Mary Elsner Oram, Fred Miller, Dale Sipes, and Don Hardenbergh worked with court personnel to set up the collection of data from court records. Carol Flango, Charles Schober, Doug Schmidt, and Bridget Neary took responsibility for the coding, verification, data entry, and computer programming work that was done in Williamsburg. Administrative and secretarial support was provided by Dawn Mayer, Valerie

Jackson, Vivian Ortega, Alice Larkin, Cheryl Letchworth, and Louise Harris. Anne Friesen organized files, conducted telephone interviews with court administrators, and helped analyze responses to the questionnaires. Jim James (in Wichita), Larry Sipes (in Phoenix), Dale Sipes (in Oakland), and Tom Church (in Detroit Recorder's Court and Newark) conducted interviews and helped with analysis of caseflow management issues in these case study sites. Bill Fishback did the copyediting and layout for the book. Tina Beaven designed the cover and prepared the "box and whisker" charts for Chapter 2. Harvey Solomon, Director of the National Center's Institute for Court Management, and Edward B. McConnell, the President of the National Center, provided ongoing guidance and support, as well as helpful comments on drafts of the manuscript.

A number of persons have had an opportunity to review the manuscript in draft form. The thoughtful and constructive reviews provided by two anonymous reviewers for the National Institute of Justice were very helpful in making final revisions of the report. Valuable comments and suggestions have also been received from Doug Somerlot, David Neubauer, Dick Van Duizend, Holly Bakke, Dan Johnston, Judith Cramer, Ed Kennedy, Jim James, Maureen Solomon, Marlene Thornton, Nancy Maron, and Anne Rankin Mahoney.

Particular note should be made of the roles of the co-authors, all of whom contributed significantly to the project (and to the writing of this report) in several ways. Jeanne Ito was the project methodologist for the first year and a half of the study. She had a major role in the design of the project, in organizing the collection of data from the courts, and in analyzing the 1983 data. Jeanne learned early in 1985 that she had been stricken with cancer, but throughout that year she remained deeply involved in the work of the project. She supervised data collection and analysis work conducted at the National Center's headquarters in Williamsburg, and was a principal co-author of the project's report of preliminary findings presented at the 1985 National Conference on Court Delay Reduction. Her death in December 1985 was a great loss to the project, to the National Center, and to the community of scholars interested in objective action-oriented research. Her courage and dedication remain an inspiration, however, and this report draws heavily on her many contributions to the project.

Gene Flango succeeded Jeanne Ito as the project methodologist, and had primary responsibility for organizing the collection, coding, and computer programming for the 1985 court record data, and for preparing tables analyzing the data. Gene also participated in the case study interviewing in Dayton and Jersey City. Pam Casey worked with Gene in preparing the data tables, and had particular responsibility for analysis of data obtained through the questionnaires completed by presiding judges and court administrators. Steve Weller helped design the questionnaires, participated in analysis of the quantitative data, and was responsible for analysis of the data on court-annexed alternative dispute resolution programs.

The case studies found in Chapters 6–8 draw heavily on materials prepared by Alex Aikman, David Steelman, and Tom Henderson. Alex was deeply involved in the interviewing and analysis of caseflow management and delay reduction programs in Phoenix, while David had similar functions in the Dayton, Jersey City, and Wayne County courts. Tom interviewed policymakers and practitioners at the state and local levels in Kansas and New Jersey, and was a principal draftsman for much of Chapter 8. Geoff Gallas, the Director of Research and Special Services at the National Center, has been a source of very valuable advice and support for the project on an ongoing basis. More than that, Geoff has reviewed successive drafts of this manuscript with painstaking care, providing a great many helpful and constructive suggestions.

For me, the time spent on this study has been enormously rewarding. It has been a wonderful opportunity to work with practitioners in courts all over the United States, as well as with my colleagues at the National Center. I am enormously grateful for the contributions of everyone who has helped with the work of the project and the preparation of this report. At the same time, of course, they are in no way chargeable with responsibility for the presentation and interpretation of the data in the report, or for errors of omission or commission; that responsibility lies with me.

Barry Mahoney
Principal Investigator

Denver, Colorado
June 1988

Part I
Introduction

Interminable and unjustifiable delays in our courts are today compromising the basic legal rights of countless thousands of Americans and, imperceptibly, corroding the very foundations of constitutional government in the United States.

—Chief Justice Earl Warren, 1958[1]

Efficiency must never be the controlling test of criminal justice but the work of the courts can be efficient without jeopardizing basic safeguards. Indeed the delays in trials are often one of the gravest threats to individual rights. Both the accused and the public are entitled to a prompt trial.

—Chief Justice Warren E. Burger, 1970[2]

"Justice delayed is justice denied." Delay devalues judgments, creates anxiety in litigants, and results in loss or deterioration of the evidence upon which rights are determined. Accumulated delay produces backlogs that waste court resources, needlessly increase lawyer fees, and create confusion and conflict in allocating judges' time.

—Commentary, American Bar Association
Standards Relating to Court Delay
Reduction, 1984[3]

Chapter 1
OVERVIEW OF THE RESEARCH

Although court delay has long been a problem in the United States and in other societies, it is only in relatively recent times that the tools of empirical research have been used to examine the dimensions of the problem through a comparative approach.[4] Several multijurisdictional empirical research projects undertaken during the past 12 years, both in federal courts[5] and state courts,[6] have had important practical consequences. They have provided, for the first time, an indication of the range of case processing times across a broad spectrum of courts; have led to revision of some long-held ideas about the causes of court delay and about possible remedies; and have stimulated a number of efforts to address problems of court delay at the federal, state, and local levels.

The research discussed in this report builds directly upon these studies, and has two major objectives. First, it seeks to provide an up-to-date picture of the pace of civil and criminal litigation in urban trial courts, using data collected from 18 state general-jurisdiction trial courts located in metropolitan areas across the United States. Second, through analysis of these data together with data from earlier studies, it is designed to help develop an understanding of the change process in courts—a charting of trends over time, an increased understanding of the dynamics of delay reduction and delay prevention programs, and a sense of the critical elements required for a broad-scale attack upon problems of trial court delay.

We recognize that there are skeptics, both among practitioners and in the academic community, who question whether there is really a "problem" of court delay that warrants significant investment of resources in either research or action programs designed to reduce case processing times.[7] Our view is that court delay is an

3

issue of considerable public importance. It is clear from the results of public opinion surveys that the general public regards court delay as a serious problem[8] and there is ample evidence, from our own research and from earlier studies, that the litigation process in both civil and criminal cases takes a very long time to complete in many courts. While it may be difficult to get agreement on precisely what constitutes unacceptable "delay," either in the abstract or in a specific jurisdiction, we have no difficulty concluding—both from the available quantitative data and from numerous interviews with practitioners—that delay is a problem (and is widely perceived to be a problem) in some courts.

At the same time, it is important to recognize that court delay is not an all-pervasive problem. In their ground-breaking 1976–78 study entitled *Justice Delayed*, researchers at the National Center for State Courts documented wide variations in both civil and criminal case processing times in 21 state general-jurisdiction trial courts.[9] Some of the courts seemed very slow, but others could not be considered delayed by any standard. The time from commencement to disposition of civil litigation was three times longer in the slowest courts than in the fastest, and the differences in the time required to handle criminal cases were even wider. Delay clearly existed in some courts, but when other courts handled their cases very expeditiously it could hardly be said that court delay is ubiquitous or "inevitable."

The sense that trial court delay is an important but not insoluble problem has guided this research from its inception, and has contributed to an action-oriented research strategy. The study has been aimed at developing a base of current knowledge about the dimensions of the problem of trial court delay and about ways to address the problem effectively. The focus of the research, reflected in the way in which this report is organized, has been on two principal sets of questions:

- *The context of the problem.* What is the current pace of litigation in urban trial courts? What is the range of variation in the speed with which cases are handled in these courts, from fast to slow? What factors are associated with relatively speedy (or comparatively slow) case processing times? To what extent do particular types of cases, or particular stages in the litigation process, pose special problems?

- *The dynamics of the change process.* How and to what extent have case processing times in these courts changed in the past decade? Where significant changes have taken place, what factors are associated with swifter (or slower) case processing? Where programs aimed at reducing or preventing delay have been undertaken, what have been the results? What lessons emerge from examining the process of program implementation in these jurisdictions?

The methodology of the study is similar to that employed in the *Justice Delayed* study. Empirical data on case processing times and on a number of structural and procedural characteristics have been collected in 18 different trial courts.[10] At each site, systematic samples were taken of approximately 500 felony cases terminated (by guilty plea, verdict, dismissal, or diversion) in each of three years: 1983, 1984, and 1985. Similar samples were drawn for civil cases terminated in the same three years in the 17 courts that handle civil cases.[11] In all, data have been collected on over 50,000 cases in the participating courts. To supplement the case-specific data acquired through the samples, we have also obtained data on court structure, workloads, and procedures, through questionnaires and from published and unpublished court documents. We have also conducted extensive interviews with judges, lawyers, and court personnel in nine of the jurisdictions.

The 18 courts included in this study are not a randomly selected cross section of American trial courts. Rather, because we are particularly interested in understanding the dynamics of delay reduction efforts over time, we have deliberately selected (a) courts that have been the subject of a prior empirical study of case processing times; and/or (b) courts that have themselves undertaken a significant delay reduction effort within the past decade or are located in a state in which a statewide delay-reduction program has been mounted during this period.

Thirteen of the 18 courts participating in this study were included in the original *Justice Delayed* study, and three of the other five were studied by the American Judicature Society during the 1979–81 period. The 18 courts include some that had in the past processed cases very expeditiously and others that had been relatively slow. For 16 of the courts, systematically collected data on case processing times in the mid- or late 1970s already existed and could provide a baseline for comparison with our own data on case processing times for the 1983–85 period. For the other two courts, we collected data from samples of cases terminated in 1979 as well as in the 1983–85 period.

Initial findings from our research, based principally on analysis of data on cases completed in 1983, were presented at the 1985

National Conference on Court Delay Reduction.[12] The discussion in this report draws on a considerably larger data base, but the main findings and conclusions are essentially consistent with the preliminary findings. Simply put, there are a few key themes.

First, trial court delay is not inevitable. As the tables in Part II show, there are wide variations in the speed with which courts deal with their caseloads. Delay is obviously a problem in some jurisdictions, but it is also clear that a number of American trial courts handle their cases very expeditiously. Second, where backlogs and delays exist, it is possible to reduce them significantly. Part III of this study documents dramatic improvements in civil and/or criminal case processing times made by several courts in recent years. Third, while there is no single model for effective caseflow management and delay reduction, the courts that have been most effective in reducing and preventing delays seem to share a number of characteristics.

These characteristics—most importantly, strong leadership, clear goals, timely and accurate information about caseloads, effective communication mechanisms, and use of a few relatively simple case management techniques—manifest themselves in different ways in different courts. They are found in courts with widely varying structural characteristics and caseload pressures. Some of these courts have become appreciably more efficient in recent years.

Although we have not attempted a systematic analysis of differences in the attitudes and expectations of practitioners in these jurisdictions as compared to others, our non-systematic explorations suggest that these subjective elements of the practice of law are important aspects of the pace of litigation in any trial court. At least equally important, we also find that this local legal culture can be changed. In several jurisdictions in which delay reduction programs have been successfully undertaken in the past decade, there have been major changes in the norms, expectations, and behaviors of both attorneys and judges. The changes will ultimately have important repercussions not only for the time required to deal with cases once they are in court, but for the way law as a profession is practiced and for the way that society organizes institutions to deal with both civil and criminal disputes.

Like many research efforts, this report probably raises more questions than it answers. But some of the questions it does address—such as how long cases take and what can be done to shorten times that seem unnecessarily long—are, we believe, important ones. Our general conclusions are optimistic. We now know much more about the problem of court delay than we did ten years ago, and it is clear that this newly gained knowledge is already being put to effective use in many places. The questions that remain—perhaps most importantly, the nature of the linkages between the pace of litigation in a court and the quality of justice in the jurisdiction— are difficult ones, but valuable progress has been made in addressing a problem long thought to be intractable.

The remainder of this report is organized in three parts. Part II (Chapters 2–4) provides an overview, based on data from cases that reached disposition in 1985, of the pace of litigation in the 18 courts participating in the study. The presentation and analysis of data in these chapters generally follows the same approach as the *Justice Delayed* study, which used data from 1976 dispositions. Part III begins with an overview of changes in workloads and case processing times from 1976 to 1985 (Chapter 5). It then explores the dynamics of the changes that have taken place in seven of these courts, examining both local-level delay reduction and delay prevention programs (Chapters 6 and 7) and state-level initiatives (Chapter 8). Part IV consists of a single chapter that summarizes the study's principal findings and presents recommendations for future research.

ENDNOTES–Chapter 1

1. Earl Warren, Address to the American Bar Association, 1958. Quoted in Maurice Rosenberg, "Court Congestion: Status, Causes, and Proposed Remedies," in Harry W. Jones (ed.), *The Courts, the Public, and the Law Explosion* (Englewood Cliffs, N.J.: Prentice-Hall, Inc., 1965), pp. 29, 31.

2. Warren E. Burger, "The State of the Federal Judiciary," Remarks to the American Bar Association, St. Louis, Missouri, August 10, 1970.

3. ABA National Conference of State Trial Judges, *Standards Relating to Court Delay Reduction* (Chicago: American Bar Association, 1984), p. 5. (Commentary to Sec. 2.50 of the Standards Relating to Trial Courts, as amended in 1984.)

4. Empirical research on trial court delay in the United States goes at least as far back as the 1920s and '30s, but virtually all of the early studies focused solely on problems in a single jurisdiction. See, e.g., Roscoe Pound and Felix Frankfurter, eds., *Criminal Justice in Cleveland: Reports of the Cleveland Foundation Survey of the Administration of Criminal Justice in Cleveland, Ohio* (Cleveland: The Cleveland Foundation, 1922; reprinted, Montclair, NJ: Patterson Smith, 1968); Wayne L. Morse and Ronald H. Beattie, "Survey of the Administration of Criminal Justice in Oregon," *Oregon Law Review*, Vol. 11, No. 4 (Supplement) (June 1932). Later studies of particular note include Hans Zeisel et al., *Delay in the Court* (Boston: Little, Brown and Co., 1959); Maurice Rosenberg and Michael I. Sovern, "Delay and the Dynamics of Personal Injury Litigation," *Columbia Law Review*, Vol. 59 (1959), pp. 1115–89; and A. Leo Levin and E. Woolley, *Dispatch and Delay: A Field Study of Judicial Administration in Pennsylvania* (Philadelphia: Institute of Legal Research, University of Pennsylvania Law School, 1961). For a general review of the pre-1976 literature on the subject, see Thomas W. Church et al., *Pretrial Delay: A Review and Bibliography* (Williamsburg: National Center for State Courts, 1978).

5. Steven Flanders, *Case Management and Court Management in United States District Courts* (Washington, D.C.: Federal Judicial Center, 1977).

6. See, e.g., Thomas W. Church et al., *Justice Delayed: The Pace of Litigation in Urban Trial Courts* (Williamsburg: National Center for State Courts, 1978) [hereafter cited as *Justice Delayed*]; Ernest C. Friesen et al., "Justice in Felony Courts: Report on a Study of Delay in Metropolitan Courts During 1978–79", *Whittier Law Review*, Vol. 2 (1979), pp. 7–60; Larry L. Sipes, et al., *Managing to Reduce Delay* (Williamsburg: National Center for State Courts, 1980); David W. Neubauer et al., *Managing the Pace of Justice: An Evaluation of LEAA's Court Delay Reduction Programs* (Washington, D.C.: National Institute of Justice, 1981).

7. See, e.g., Joel B. Grossman et al., "Measuring the Pace of Civil Litigation in Federal and State Trial Court," *Judicature*, Vol. 65 (1981), pp. 86–87; Austin Sarat, "Understanding Trial Courts: A Critique of Social Science Approaches," *Judicature*, Vol. 61 (1978), p. 324.

8. See, e.g., Yankelovich, Skelly and White, Inc., *The Public Image of Court: Highlights of a National Survey of the General Public, Judges, Lawyers, and Community Leaders* (Williamsburg: National Center for State Courts, 1978); *Citizens Commission to Improve Michigan Courts, Final Report and Recommendations* (Lansing: 1986), esp. Table 7, p. 34 (reporting that 81% of Michigan residents felt that court proceedings take too long).

9. *Justice Delayed*, supra note 3, esp. pp. 1–19.

10. For a detailed description of the study methodology, see *infra*, Appendix A.

11. One of the courts in the study—the Detroit Recorder's Court, in Detroit, Michigan—handles only criminal cases.

12. Barry Mahoney, Larry L. Sipes, and Jeanne A. Ito, *Implementing Delay Reduction and Delay Prevention Programs in Urban Trial Courts: Preliminary Finds from Current Research*. Report Prepared for the National Conference on Delay Reduction, Denver, Colorado, September 1985 (Williamsburg: National Center for State Courts, 1985).

Part II
The Current Picture

Chapter 2
THE PACE OF LITIGATION IN URBAN TRIAL COURTS, 1985

One main objective of this research is to provide a current picture of the pace of litigation in urban general-jurisdiction trial courts. Although the 18 courts involved in this study cannot be regarded as representative of the universe of metropolitan trial courts, we believe the data from these courts will at least roughly reflect the range of variance that exists in metropolitan courts across the United States.[1] This chapter discusses the approach to comparative analysis taken in the study, describes the measures used to compare civil and criminal case processing times across jurisdictions, and sets forth tables and charts showing the times required by each of the 18 courts to deal with civil and criminal cases that reached disposition in 1985.

A. Civil Cases: Measures of Time to Disposition

As the authors of *Justice Delayed* note, construction of cross-comparable civil case processing time measures is made complex by both methodological and conceptual problems.[2] The methodological difficulties arise, in the first instance, from the diversity that exists in local practices and in the composition of caseloads. For example, major events in a civil lawsuit—service, filing, request for trial, pretrial conference, judgment, final order, etc.—mean different things (and are sometimes called by different names) in different jurisdictions. Events that are essential to the progress of a case in some jurisdictions, such as the filing of an "at issue memo" or a "certificate of readiness," never occur at all in others. Moreover, the makeup of civil caseloads varies widely. In some courts, for example, tort cases make up over 80% of the caseload, but in others they make up less than 30%. The balance of the civil caseloads includes many different kinds of cases, including some that are handled in a quasi-administrative fashion.

These methodological problems are compounded by conceptual issues that reflect fundamentally different notions of the functions of courts in the civil litigation process. The traditional view of most lawyers and judges has been that the function of courts is simply to provide trials for litigants who are ready and wish to proceed to trial. Under this view, time consumed in the litigation before the point of lawyer readiness could be regarded as being of no concern to the court. This was the approach taken by Zeisel, Kalven, and Buchholz in their 1959 study, *Delay in the Courts*.[3] Operationally, it is an approach still followed in a number of jurisdictions. Some courts do not even open a file on a case until a certificate of readiness or an at-issue memo is filed. In others, the case may be considered "open" from the time a complaint is filed, but the judges and court staff make no effort to monitor the progress of cases or take other action prior to the filing of a certificate of readiness or similar document.

A competing view of the role of courts with respect to civil litigation began to develop in the 1950s and '60s, focusing not just on the cases ready for trial but on the totality of the litigation business that comes into the court. This view stresses the court's role as a public institution, responsible for the reasonably expeditious resolution of all of the cases that come before it. From this perspective, case processing time would be measured from the date the case first comes into the court (usually through the filing of the complaint) until the date of disposition, for all cases regardless of the mode of disposition. This was the approach followed in the mid-1970s by researchers at the Federal Judicial Center in a groundbreaking study of case processing in six federal district courts. The FJC researchers emphasized that their decision to focus upon the entire caseload and to measure case processing time from filing onward was not accidental: "It reflects the federal courts' widespread assertion that the progress of the whole docket is their responsibility."[4]

Adoption of the broader view of courts' functions does not, of course, preclude a focus on the cases that are ready for trial or that actually go to trial. However, the general orientation of this study—like that of the National Center's *Justice Delayed* study—is toward the view that courts are responsible for expeditious resolution of the totality of the cases that come before them. Our choice of primary measures of case processing times reflects this orientation. Before presenting the data, let us briefly review the four measures that we use and their underlying rationales.

Tort disposition time. This is the principal measure used for comparing civil case processing times in this study, as it was in the *Justice Delayed* study. Because the mix of civil cases varies so widely from one state court to another, there is a strong argument for restricting comparisons to types of cases that are broadly similar to each other and that are common to all courts. The tort disposition time measure assesses the time required to deal with all tort cases in the sample, from filing to disposition, regardless of the method of disposition or the stage of the case at the time of disposition. Tort cases as a class are basically similar from court to court, and make up an important (although widely varying) proportion of the caseload in every court studied. By focusing on tort cases rather than on a wide range of civil cases, it is possible to restrict the analysis to a significant and roughly comparable subset of cases common to all courts.

Even this measure, however, cannot be used for all courts. In some jurisdictions (e.g. New York, Minnesota) it is possible for extensive case activity to take place before the complaint is ever filed with the court. Indeed, in many cases (including many tort cases) in these jurisdictions, no complaint or other document is ever filed, because the lawsuit is settled or abandoned without any court involvement whatsoever. In these jurisdictions it is simply not possible to sample the cases disposed of without any court involvement because there are no court records to be sampled. Thus, there can be no measure of "tort disposition time" in these jurisdictions that is comparable to our measure of tort disposition time in jurisdictions where the formal legal process begins with the filing of the complaint in court. That is a primary reason for use of the second measure.

Trial list disposition time. This measure focuses on cases in which counsel has indicated at least the possibility of trial by filing a certificate of readiness, note of issue, at-issue memo, or similar document to place the case in the pool of cases awaiting trial. It includes all such cases (whether tort, contract, real property, or other category) and measures the time from filing or service of the complaint to filing of the document that officially closes the case at the trial court level. Use of this measure enables us to include jurisdictions such as the Bronx and Minneapolis, where pleadings can be served and discovery can take place prior to the filing of any document, in a multicourt comparative analysis. However, it cannot be used for those jurisdictions (9 of the 17 in our study) that do not use any sort of readiness document procedure.

Time to jury verdict. This measure focuses only on cases that result in a jury verdict. It measures the number of days from filing or service of the complaint to the verdict, and is computed only for cases that were actually tried through to a jury verdict. It reflects the time taken by the cases that, although they constitute only a small percentage of the court's caseload, probably consume the most resources in terms of judge time and courtroom use. The length of time required to complete these cases may also have a bearing on the expectations and behavior of practitioners with respect to other cases, and may thus influence the overall pace of civil litigation in a court. One problem with its use in this study is that, because the percentage of civil case dispositions by jury trial is very low (over 3% in only two of the courts), the number of civil jury trials in our samples is small and generalizations about case processing times in these cases can only be very limited.

These first three measures (tort disposition time, trial list disposition time, and time to jury verdict) are basically the same three measures used to assess case processing times in the *Justice Delayed* study.[5] Using them as key measures of the pace of litigation enables us to make comparisons of similar sets of cases across a number of different courts, using the same starting and ending points. Their use also enables us to make comparisons over time, as we do in Chapter 5—comparing, for example, tort disposition times in the late 1970s with tort disposition times in the mid-1980s for the same courts, to see what changes have taken place.

General civil docket disposition time. Like the first three measures, this measure computes case processing time from filing to disposition. Each of those measures, however, focuses on subsets of cases that, by and large, tend to remain in the court a relatively long time. Use of them tends to disguise the fact that some types of cases that make up a significant part of the civil caseload of many courts (e.g. commercial contract actions, mortgage foreclosures) proceed through the courts very quickly. Though there are good arguments for excluding these types of cases from multijurisdictional analysis, because the diversity of caseload mixes makes comparisons very tricky, it seems even more important to begin to assess the pace of litigation for the totality of courts' caseloads. In this study, we make a start toward this assessment by measuring the pace of litigation for the cases included in our entire general sample of cases. These samples are broad but not all-inclusive; they *exclude* equity, domestic relations, probate, juvenile, and miscellaneous matters such as adoptions, name changes, bar admissions, and the like. The resulting samples still vary considerably from court to court, but they include the main elements of each court's civil caseload and they are more comparable than if we simply accepted each court's definition of what constitutes a civil case. These samples reflect a more comprehensive picture of each court's overall civil caseload than do any of the other measures.

Use of these multiple measures can potentially present a very confusing picture to the reader, especially when a variety of different statistics (e.g. median, 75th percentile, percentage of cases requiring over two years) can be used with each measure. When multiple measures are used, courts may rank in different places on different scales, and there is no single yardstick for measuring efficiency. One way to simplify the picture would be to use a single summary statistic—e.g. median tort disposition time or median time to jury trial—as a sole indicator of case processing time. Alternatively, it is conceivable that different measures could be combined in some fashion to produce a comprehensive single indicator, an "index of case processing time," that could be used to measure comparative effectiveness and assess changes over time. Construction of such an index, while fraught with methodological problems, is not necessarily impossible. Even if such an index could be readily constructed, however, it would not be a totally satisfactory solution to the measurement problems.

Use of either an index or a single summary statistic, without taking account of other measures, poses significant conceptual and policy problems. It is easy to lose sight of meaningful information when several indicators are combined into a single measure (as in an index) or when a single summary statistic is used. Reliance on such summary indicators can sometimes conceal or even misrepresent what may be the most important aspects of the data.[6]

Although dependence upon a single measure can be misleading, it is nevertheless desirable to have one or a few "lead indicators" that provide a basis for first-cut comparisons across courts. We utilize median tort disposition time as our lead indicator of civil case processing time for essentially the same reasons the authors of *Justice Delayed* used it as their principal measure: it enables comparison of case processing times in roughly similar sets of cases that make up a significant portion of every court's civil caseload; it focuses on the times required for all cases in the subset regardless of when and how they reach disposition; and, for the courts in these samples, it is strongly correlated to most other measures of case processing efficiency.[7]

Table 2A shows the medians for each of the four civil case processing time measures for the 17 civil courts involved in the study. As was true in the *Justice Delayed* study, the first three measures are strongly related: although there are some differences, courts tend to rank at approximately the same position on each of the three indices.[8] They also tend to rank in about the same way on the general civil docket disposition time measure, with one major exception. The exception is Wichita, where the general docket moves very quickly (median time of 160 days from filing to disposition) while tort cases move at a considerably slower pace (median time of 406 days). One possible explanation is that torts (which generally take more time than other cases) make up only 20% of the caseload in Wichita— the smallest proportion found in any of our samples.

Interestingly, the differences between the fastest and slowest median times is even greater with respect to general civil docket disposition times than with respect to tort disposition time. Thus, the median tort disposition time in Boston (the slowest court on this measure) is almost three times slower than in Dayton, but median general civil docket time in Boston (the slowest court on this measure, too) is four times slower than in Dayton and six times slower than in Phoenix. In general, the disposition times for the full range of civil cases on the dockets of the courts in the sample were faster than the tort disposition times, and markedly faster in the most efficiently operating courts. There seems to be at least two possible explanations. One possibility is that tort cases may be more complex and more likely to be actively litigated to disposition (or at least through completion of discovery), thus requiring more time than other cases on the docket. A second possibility, not inconsistent with the first, is that the faster courts are organized to take cognizance of incoming cases at an early point after filing and are able to identify and deal quickly with those that do not require much time.

Tables 2B and 2C display additional statistics for tort disposition time and trial list disposition time. The *third quartile* represents the time required for the case that took more time than three-fourths of the cases in the sample. It is a useful indicator of how long the slower cases take to reach disposition. The *90th percentile* focuses on the time required by the longest (or "toughest") cases on the courts' dockets. The *percentage of cases over two years* is an indicator that reflects the case processing time standards adopted by the American Bar Association in 1984, which set two years (from filing) as the outer limit for how long a civil case of any sort should take in the absence of exceptional circumstances.

Table 2A
CIVIL DISPOSITION TIME MEASURES, 1985[a]

	Median Tort Disposition Time[b] (in days)	Median Trial List Disposition Time[c] (in days)	Median Time, Filing To Jury Verdict[d] (in days)	(N)	Median General Civil Docket Disposition Time[e] (in days)
Dayton, OH	279	*	332	(6)	178
Phoenix, AZ	292	505	634	(43)[f]	133
Miami, FL	325	*	295	(9)	186
Cleveland, OH	343	*	551	(55)[f]	298
Portland, OR	389	*	694	(14)	253
Jersey City, NJ	394[g]	*	501	(10)	379[g]
New Orleans, LA	403	560	745	(11)	366
Wichita, KS	411	*	1126	(3)	160
Newark, NJ	624[g]	*	725	(14)	623[g]
Minneapolis, MN	*	603[h]	822[h]	(12)	*
Bronx, NY	*	772[h]	1138[h]	(11)	*
Oakland, CA	637	838	1617	(8)	616
Wayne County, MI	648	*	1314	(22)[f]	624
Pittsburgh, PA	651[i]	694[i]	575	(40)	406[i]
Providence, RI	697	1304	1435	(20)	525
San Diego, CA	719[j]	696	1064	(19)	691[j]
Boston, MA	782	*	1863	(13)	789

*Data unavailable or inapplicable.

[a]Unless indicated to the contrary, on this and the civil tables that follow, courts are listed in order of tort disposition time for cases in the sample of 1985 dispositions. Where that measure is unavailable, the court is placed in order where it seems most appropriate according to the trial list disposition time measure. The footnotes in this table that explain exceptions and special circumstances in the data for individual courts are generally not included in subsequent tables.

[b]Median days from court filing to date of dismissal, settlement, trial verdict, or other action formally concluding the case in the trial court, for all tort cases.

[c]Median days from court filing to date of dismissal, settlement, trial verdict, or other action formally concluding the case in the trial court for all cases in which a "readiness" document was filed signifying that the case should be placed in the pool of cases awaiting trial.

[d]Median days from filing to verdict in cases tried before a jury. The numbers in parentheses under (N) indicates the number of cases tried to a jury verdict that are included in the samples for each court.

[e]Median days from filing to date of dismissal, settlement, trial verdict, or other formal conclusion of the case in the trial court, for all civil cases in the sample.

[f]Includes separate "supplemental" sample of jury trial cases. Such samples were drawn only in the Phoenix, Cleveland, and Wayne County courts. Data from the supplemental samples are used only in computing time from filing to jury verdict in these courts and have not been mixed with data from the general samples for any other purposes.

[g]Does not include cases in which a default judgment, dismissal, or other disposition was reached prior to the filing of an answer.

[h]Measure is from service of the complaint, not filing with the court. By state law, cases may progress to trial readiness prior to the filing of the complaint.

[i]Does not include cases filed directly with the court's civil arbitration program.

[j]Does not include cases that reached disposition prior to filing of certificate of readiness.

Use of these statistics facilitates graphic illustration of the range of key variables to depict differences in case processing time across courts. Figures 2-1 and 2-2 use the "box-and-whisker" technique to illustrate differences in tort disposition time and trial list disposition time across the courts for which it is possible to calculate these

Table 2B
TORT DISPOSITION TIME,[a] 1985

	Median (in days)	Third Quartile (in days)	90th Percentile (in days)	Percent Over Two Years
Dayton, OH	279	445	744	11%
Phoenix, AZ	292	420	636	8%
Miami, FL	325	455	615	6%
Cleveland, OH	343	560	861	15%
Portland, OR	389	632	806	15%
Jersey City, NJ	394	493	607	3%
New Orleans, LA	403	703	1027	23%
Wichita, KS	411	670	786	16%
Newark, NJ	624	699	765	16%
Oakland, CA	637	1050	1427	44%
Wayne County, MI	648	950	1222	45%
Pittsburgh, PA	651	927	1322	37%
Providence, RI	697	1331	1476	48%
San Diego, CA	719	1146	1626	49%
Boston, MA	782	1905	2167	52%

[a]Tort disposition time measures the time from filing to date of dismissal, settlement, trial verdict, or other action formally concluding the case in the trial court, for all tort cases.

Table 2C
TRIAL LIST DISPOSITION TIME,[a] 1985

	Median (in days)	Third Quartile (in days)	90th Percentile (in days)	Percent Over Two Years
Phoenix, AZ	505	733	1203	26%
New Orleans, LA	560	832	1294	32%
Minneapolis, MN[b]	603	861	1083	37%
Pittsburgh, PA	694	1070	1388	45%
San Diego, CA	696	1072	1568	47%
Bronx, NY[b]	772	1183	1178	50%
Oakland, CA	838	1217	1659	57%
Providence, RI	1304	1408	1597	70%

[a]Trial list disposition time measures the time from filing to date of dismissal, settlement, trial verdict, or other action formally concluding the case in the trial court, for all cases in which a "readiness" document was filed signifying that the case should be placed in the pool of cases awaiting trial.
[b]Measure is from service of the complaint, not filing with the court.

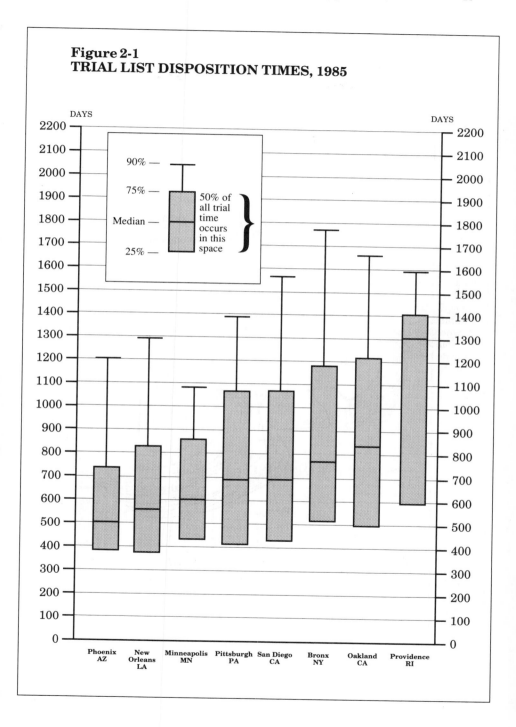

Figure 2-1
TRIAL LIST DISPOSITION TIMES, 1985

Figure 2-2
TORT DISPOSITION TIMES, 1985

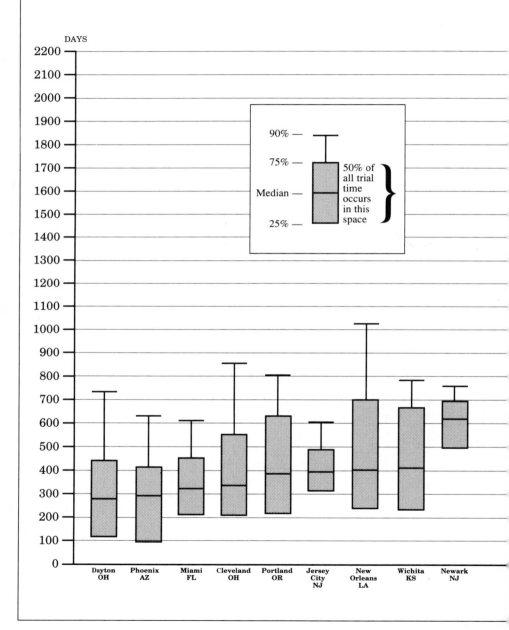

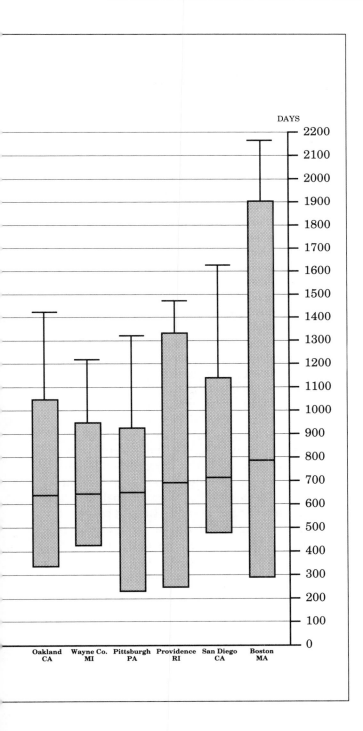

measures. The box contains half of the cases in the sample for each court and is a visual summary of the "middle" range—the greater the range, the larger the box. The 75th and 25th percentiles form the top and bottom lines of the box, while the median—shown as a horizontal line in the box—gives the center of the distribution. The whiskers, shown by lines, indicate the tails of the distribution, up to the 90th percentile.

As both the tables and the figures indicate, the courts range in roughly the same order from fast to slow with respect to the subsidiary indicators—third quartile, 90th percentile, and percentage of cases over two years—as with respect to the median times.[9] However, there are some notable exceptions that reflect important differences among courts and indicate why it is important to avoid relying on a single indicator such as the median. For example, the median tort disposition time in New Orleans is relatively fast (403 days) but the 75th and 90th percentile cases take considerably longer in the New Orleans court. Conversely, the data indicate that two New Jersey courts, Jersey City and Newark, handle the great bulk of their litigation faster than their median times alone would suggest. While Jersey City shows the sixth fastest median tort disposition time, it ranks first in the speed with which it handles the 90th percentile cases and has the lowest percentage of cases requiring over two years. Newark's median tort disposition time is ninth but its 90th percentile time is fourth and only 16% of its tort cases required over two years. (These times would be even faster, it should be noted, if the Jersey City and Newark samples had included cases that reached disposition prior to the filing of an answer.)

Table 2D and Figure 2-3 present statistics on general civil docket disposition times. These data should be viewed with particular caution because the caseload mix varies so widely from court to court, but they nevertheless provide a valuable picture of each court's ability to handle its total caseload expeditiously. As with respect to the other measures of time from filing to disposition, there are strong correlations across the different statistics—courts that show a fast median time also rank well on the other indicators and vice versa. Data on the percentage of cases requiring over one year and over two years are included in order to enable comparison with the ABA time standards, which call for completion of 90% of a court's civil cases within one year, 98% within 18 months, and 100% within two years.

The data in Table 2D and Figure 2-3 indicate that several of the courts in this study come very close to meeting the standards of timely disposition adopted by the ABA. None of them complete 90%

Table 2D
GENERAL CIVIL DOCKET DISPOSITION TIME,[a] 1985

	Median (in days)	Third Quartile (in days)	90th Percentile (in days)	Percent Cases Over One Year	Percent Cases Over Two Years
Phoenix, AZ	133	400	527	30%	6%
Wichita, KS	160	308	632	21%	6%
Dayton, OH	178	357	628	24%	7%
Miami, FL	186	354	490	23%	2%
Portland, OR	253	465	702	36%	9%
Cleveland, OH	298	520	834	41%	14%
New Orleans, LA	366	699	1133	50%	22%
Jersey City, NJ	379	489	609	55%	4%
Pittsburgh, PA	406	717	1138	51%	23%
Providence, RI	525	1325	1459	58%	42%
Oakland, CA	616	1039	1428	70%	41%
Newark, NJ	623	686	762	87%	15%
Wayne County, MI	624	943	1264	88%	44%
San Diego, CA	691	1072	1553	81%	46%
Boston, MA	789	1930	2170	67%	53%

[a]Median days from filing to date of dismissal, settlement, trial verdict, or other formal conclusion of the case in the trial court, for all civil cases in the sample.

of their civil cases within a year, but four (Wichita, Miami, Dayton, and Phoenix) dispose of at least 70% within the first 12 months. Those four and two others, Jersey City and Portland, are able to complete work on at least 90% of their cases within two years. The Miami court has an extraordinary record, completing 98% of its civil cases within two years of filing.

B. Criminal Cases: Measures of Time to Disposition

Measuring criminal case processing time in general jurisdiction trial courts presents methodological problems similar in many ways to those that exist with respect to civil litigation. As on the civil side, there is considerable diversity in nomenclature, local practices, and caseload composition. Terms such as felony and misdemeanor, for example, carry different meanings in different places, cases are commenced in different ways, and caseload mixes vary widely. While most of the courts in the study deal almost exclusively with felony

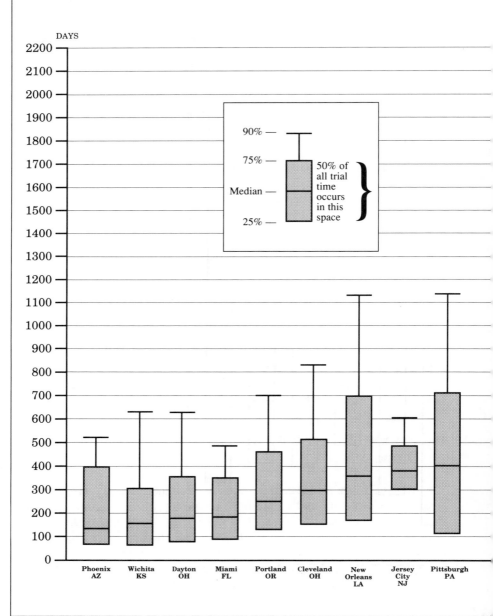

Figure 2-3
GENERAL CIVIL DOCKET DISPOSITION TIMES, 1985

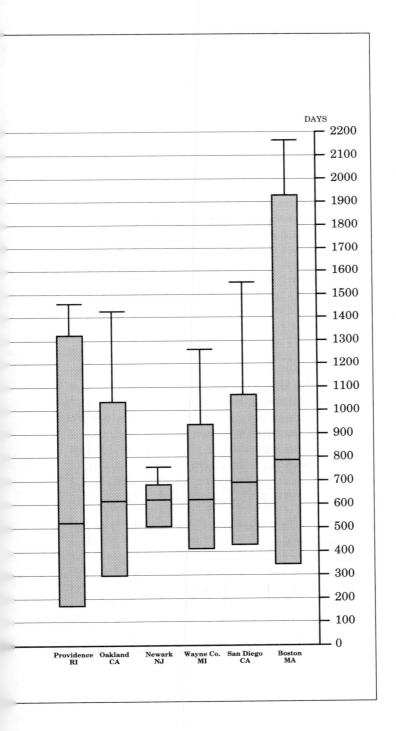

cases in which the sentence can be a year or more in prison, some of them also handle misdemeanors and other relatively minor offenses.

These methodological difficulties are exacerbated by differences in court structure that significantly affect the criminal litigation process and raise conceptual issues concerning appropriate measurement points. Case processing in the great majority of jurisdictions reflects the two-tier trial court structure that exists in most states. In this framework, limited jurisdiction courts—usually county courts or municipal courts, often simply called "lower courts"—handle relatively minor matters (e.g. misdemeanors, traffic offenses) and also deal with the initial stages of more serious cases. Their functions typically include advising defendants of their rights, setting bail amounts, and conducting preliminary examinations to determine whether there are grounds to hold the defendant for further proceedings. General jurisdiction trial courts ("upper courts") generally handle only the more serious cases, typically becoming involved only after an accusatory instrument (usually an indictment or information) has been filed. In some states, however, different structures exist and different procedures are followed. For example, 2 of our 18 courts, those in Minneapolis and Wichita, are "unitary" trial courts. These two general jurisdiction trial courts deal with all of the cases in which the prosecutor files a document charging the defendant with violation of the criminal law; there is no lower court to handle the initial stages of criminal proceedings.

In this study, we have sought to limit the scope of our inquiry to cases in which the highest charge in the accusatory instrument filed in the general jurisdiction trial court could result in imprisonment for a year or more. The nomenclature varies, but these cases are generally categorized as felonies. Focusing on them enables us to compare the way different courts deal with roughly similar groups of criminal cases.

Even when the scope of the inquiry is thus limited and the problem of comparability in caseloads thereby minimized to some extent, tricky questions of measurement remain. In particular, what are the most appropriate starting points and ending points for measuring case processing time? Should the inquiry focus only on the time required by the general jurisdiction trial court, ignoring time between arrest (or other start of the proceedings) and the filing of an indictment or information? Or should it measure from the arrest, the initial lower court complaint, or some other event occurring at the outset of the criminal proceedings? And how should "disposition" be defined? Where a defendant has pleaded guilty, for example, should the disposition date be the date of the plea or the date the sentence is imposed? Finally, how should we deal with cases in which case processing time is affected by factors over which the court has little or no control, such as delays caused by a defendant's failure to appear when on bail or the need for psychiatric examination of a defendant to determine his competency to stand trial?

There are no fully satisfactory answers to these questions, and in developing measures to assess the pace of criminal litigation we have sought to take account of competing views as to what is most important to measure. We use three principal measures of felony case processing time.

Total disposition time. This is the time from the date of arrest (or, where the court record data did not indicate arrest date, the date the complaint charging the defendant with a crime was first filed in any court) to the date of disposition. "Disposition" for this purpose means verdict, guilty plea, dismissal or nolle prosequi, or formal determination of entry into a diversion program. It does *not* mean sentence. (The date of sentence is, however, included in the data base for cases in which the disposition was a guilty verdict or guilty plea, and can be used in constructing secondary measures of felony case processing time.) From the perspective of the public, total disposition time is probably the most important measure. However, because of the bifurcated structure of criminal case processing in most jurisdictions, the general jurisdiction trial courts (which are the primary subjects of our research) often have little control over the speed with which cases move through the lower courts prior to the filing of an information or indictment. For some types of analysis, it is more appropriate to use our second measure.

Upper court disposition time. This is the time from the filing of the indictment or information in the general jurisdiction court to the date of disposition. It measures time during which the general jurisdiction court clearly has authority over the case, and is especially appropriate for analysis that focuses on structural, procedural, and resource variables in these courts. For the two jurisdictions in which there is no lower court (Minneapolis and Wichita), upper court time will be the same as total time.

Upper court time in jury trial cases. This is the number of days from the filing of the indictment or information to the date of verdict for cases resolved by jury verdict. It is a useful indicator of how long the most seriously contested cases can be expected to take.

All of these measures were also used to gauge criminal case processing times in the *Justice Delayed* study,[10] thus enabling comparisons over time between that study and this. In computing them, we have used all of the cases in our samples, and have not attempted to make any adjustments for cases in which defendants skipped bail or required psychiatric exams. As with respect to civil cases, our primary focus is on the full complement of cases entering the courts, not on those that result in a trial.

In our choice of a lead indicator, we depart somewhat from the approach taken in *Justice Delayed*, which used median upper court disposition time as the primary index of criminal case processing speed. We will use upper court time as our principal measure where it seems most appropriate (e.g., in comparing the time consumed by upper courts that have different types of calendaring systems), but our primary measure will be total disposition time. Use of this measure focuses attention on the entire period from arrest to disposition. Like tort disposition time, which measures civil case processing from the point at which a court's jurisdiction is first invoked, the arrest-to-disposition measure reflects a consumer's perspective—the perspective of a victim, witness, defendant, or other interested citizen. From that perspective, the concern is not so much which court (upper or lower) has responsibility for particular stages of a case as how long the whole process takes, from start to finish.

Table 2E shows the medians for each of the three principal measures of criminal case processing time for the 18 courts included in the study. The courts tend to rank in approximately the same position on all three measures.[11] When a jurisdiction's overall arrest-to-disposition process is expeditious, the upper court is usually handling its business efficiently and even the cases requiring a jury trial move swiftly through the system. Not always, however. For example, both Providence and Bronx County have a median arrest-to-disposition time of about four months, but it takes the upper courts in those jurisdictions approximately a year to handle jury trial cases.

Tables 2F and 2G provide additional data on total disposition time and upper court disposition times—third quartile, 90th percentile, and percentage of cases exceeding specific times (180 days for total disposition time and 150 days for upper court disposition time). The additional statistics are strongly correlated with the median times,[12] but again there are some exceptions. For example, Oakland has relatively speedy median times (87 days total time, 57 days upper court time), but the third quartile and 90th percentile cases move relatively slowly in that court. Pittsburgh, by contrast,

Table 2E
FELONY CASE DISPOSITION TIME MEASURES,[a] 1985

	Median Total Disposition Time[b] (in days)	Median Upper Court Disposition Time[c] (in days)	Median Upper Court Time in Jury Trial Cases[d] (in days)	(N)
Portland, OR	55	56	69	(33)
Detroit Rec Ct, MI	58[e]	31	106	(35)
Dayton, OH	61	47	112	(28)
San Diego, CA	77[f]	49[f]	91	(77)
Phoenix, AZ	78	58	114	(6)
New Orleans, LA	83	48	110	(24)
Oakland, CA	87[f]	57[f]	118	(22)
Minneapolis, MN	88[g]	88	134	(31)
Wichita, KS	115[h]	115	118	(36)
Cleveland, OH	121	90	137	(72)[i]
Bronx, NY	121[j]	152[j]	318	(45)
Providence, RI	122	63	375	(12)
Miami, FL	123	108	169	(17)
Wayne County, MI	133[e]	64	165	(36)
Pittsburgh, PA	149[e]	120	160	(14)
Jersey City, NJ	163[e]	115	145	(19)
Newark, NJ	300[e]	124	208	(52)
Boston, MA	*[k]	332	332	(53)

*Data unavailable or inapplicable.

[a]This and all subsequent criminal tables are based on samples of cases disposed of in the general jurisdiction trial court, following the filing of an indictment, information, or other formal accusatory instrument. On this and most of the remaining tables, courts are listed in order of total disposition time. Explanatory footnotes in this table are generally not included in subsequent tables.

[b]Median days from arrest or filing of lower court complaint (when arrest date is unavailable) to date of guilty plea, trial verdict, dismissal, or formal determination of entry into diversion program. Unless otherwise indicated, the starting point for this measure is date of arrest.

[c]Median days from filing of indictment or information in the general jurisdiction trial court to date of guilty plea, trial verdict, dismissal, or formal determination of entry into diversion program.

[d]Median days from filing of indictment or information in the general jurisdiction trial court to date of verdict in cases tried before a jury. Numbers in parentheses under (N) indicate the number of cases tried to a jury verdict that are included in the samples for each court.

[e]Measure is from date lower court complaint or warrant is filed, not date of arrest.

[f]In San Diego and Oakland it is possible for pleas to felony charges to be entered in the Municipal Court, with an information subsequently filed in the Superior Court and the defendant sentenced in the Superior Court. Cases disposed of in this fashion have been included in the calculation of total disposition time but *not* in the calculation of upper court disposition time.

[g]There is no lower court stage in Minneapolis. The starting point for measuring both total disposition time and upper court disposition time is the filing of the complaint in the District Court (general jurisdiction trial court), which ordinarily takes place within 48 hours following arrest of the defendant.

[h]Wichita has no lower court. The starting point for measuring total disposition time is the arrest date. The starting point for measuring upper court time is the filing of the complaint in the District Court (general jurisdiction trial court), which ordinarily takes place within 24 hours following arrest of the defendant. (continued on page 32)

Table 2F
TOTAL DISPOSITION TIME IN FELONY CASES,[a] 1985

	Median (in days)	Third Quartile (in days)	90th Percentile (in days)	Percent Cases Over 180 days
Portland, OR	55	89	162	9%
Detroit Rec Ct, MI	58	109	183	10%
Dayton, OH	61	101	190	11%
San Diego, CA	77	132	217	14%
Phoenix, AZ	78	125	198	12%
New Orleans, LA	83	142	254	19%
Oakland, CA	87	211	436	28%
Minneapolis, MN	88	162	289	22%
Wichita, KS	115	156	205	16%
Cleveland, OH	121	207	398	28%
Bronx, NY	121	256	407	37%
Providence, RI	122	224	511	30%
Miami, FL	123	241	477	35%
Wayne County, MI	133	296	481	39%
Pittsburgh, PA	149	202	380	29%
Jersey City, NJ	163	264	664	42%
Newark, NJ	300	486	882	74%
Boston, MA	*	*	*	*

*Data unavailable or not applicable.

[a]Total disposition time measures time from arrest (or, for court where arrest date is unavailable, from first filing of a complaint against the defendant) to date of guilty plea, trial verdict, dismissal, or formal determination of entry into a diversion program.

shows comparatively lengthy median times (149 days total time, 120 days upper court time), but its third quartile and 90th percentile cases proceed with greater dispatch than those in several courts with faster median times.

Figures 2-4 and 2-5 are "box-and-whisker" charts that graphically illustrate the range of arrest-to-disposition and upper court

---

[i]Includes cases in supplemental trial samples drawn for the Cleveland and San Diego courts. Data from the supplemental samples have been used only in computing times to jury verdict in these courts and have not been mixed with data from the general samples for any other purpose.

[j]In Bronx County, most felony cases are prosecuted under an indictment. However, it is possible to proceed under an information in certain circumstances. In these cases, a plea agreement has usually been reached while the case was in the lower court, and the proceedings in the Supreme Court (the general jurisdiction trial court) typically involve only the formal entry of the plea and the imposition of sentence. Cases disposed of in this fashion have been included in the calculation of total disposition time but *not* in the calculation of upper court disposition time.

[k]It was not possible to obtain data on either date of arrest or date of filing of lower court complaint from records of the general jurisdiction trial court in Boston.

Table 2G
UPPER COURT DISPOSITION TIME
IN CRIMINAL CASES,[a] 1985

	Median (in days)	Third Quartile (in days)	90th Percentile (in days)	Percent Cases Over 150 days
Detroit Rec Ct, MI	31	80	141	8%
Dayton, OH	47	85	171	13%
New Orleans, LA	48	105	200	16%
San Diego, CA	49	72	118	4%
Portland, OR	56	108	240	16%
Oakland, CA	57	144	396	23%
Phoenix, AZ	58	105	168	12%
Providence, RI	63	175	443	28%
Wayne County, MI	64	158	390	27%
Minneapolis, MN	88	162	289	22%
Cleveland, OH	90	185	377	31%
Miami, FL	108	257	567	40%
Wichita, KS	115	156	201	28%
Jersey City, NJ	115	234	1201	38%
Pittsburgh, PA	120	165	328	31%
Newark, NJ	124	294	592	42%
Bronx, NY	152	277	392	50%
Boston, MA	332	665	1395	82%

[a]Upper court disposition time measures time from filing of indictment or information in the general jurisdiction trial court to date of guilty plea, trial verdict, dismissal, or formal determination of entry into diversion program.

processing times across all of the courts using the data in Tables 2F and 2G. As these charts show, the faster courts (Portland, Detroit Recorder's Court, Dayton, San Diego, Phoenix) deal with the great bulk of their felony cases within a relatively short time period. By comparison with virtually all of the slower courts (Pittsburgh is the major exception in this respect), there is a greater homogenization of case treatment in the faster courts. As we shall see in subsequent chapters, the faster felony courts have well-established time standards and routine procedures that are designed to enable *all* cases to be dealt with in an expeditious fashion.

One way of measuring a jurisdiction's efficiency in dealing with its felony caseload is to compare its case processing times with the time standards adopted by the American Bar Association in 1984. Those standards provide that 90% of all felony cases should be adjudicated or otherwise concluded within 120 days from the date of

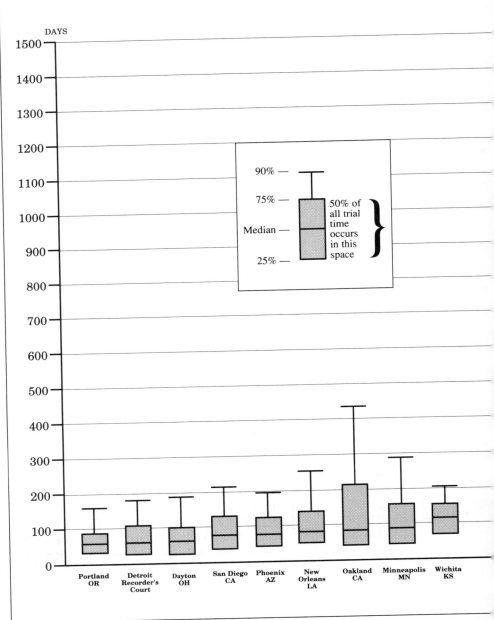

Figure 2-4
TOTAL DISPOSITION TIME IN FELONY CASES, 1985

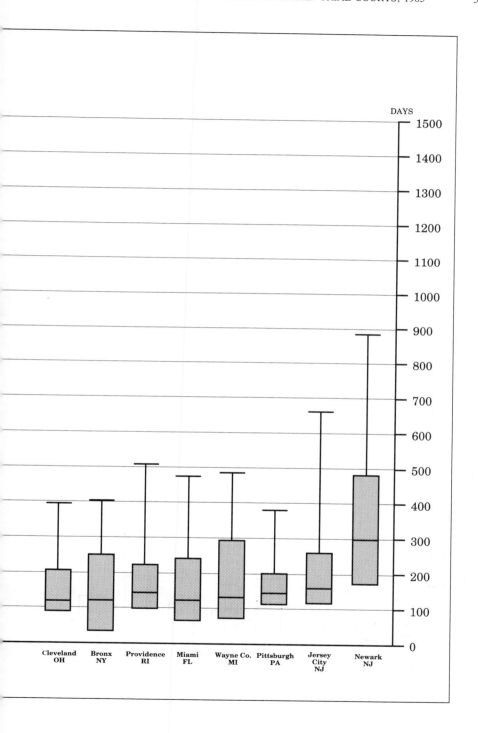

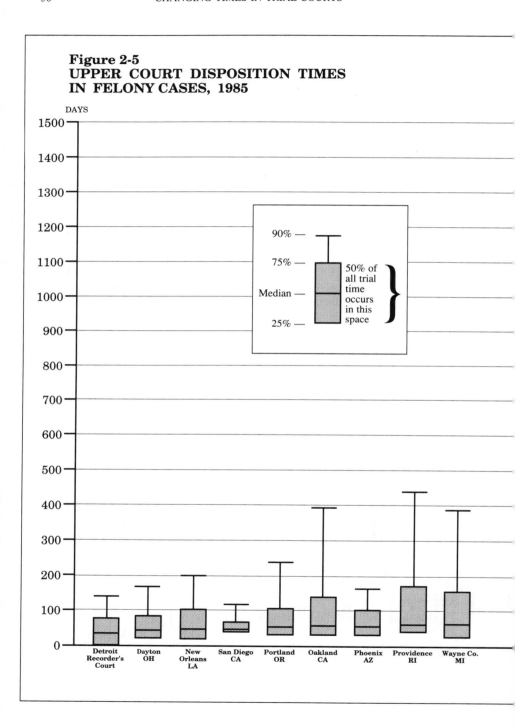

Figure 2-5
UPPER COURT DISPOSITION TIMES
IN FELONY CASES, 1985

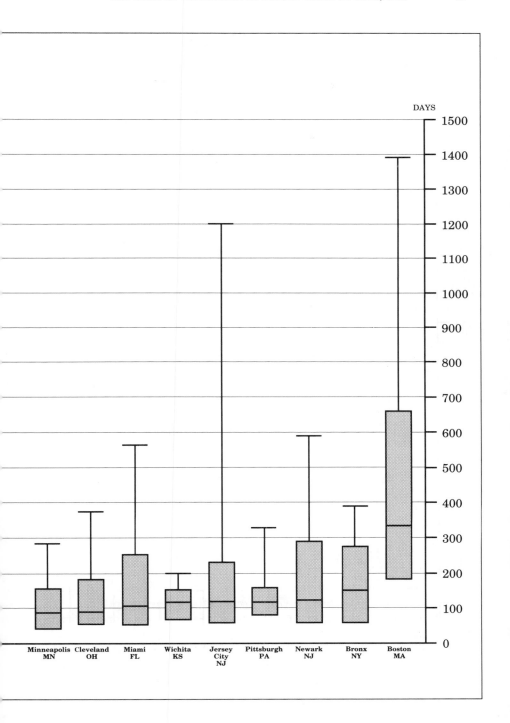

Table 2H
FELONY CASE PROCESSING TIMES OF
PARTICIPATING COURTS IN RELATION
TO ABA TIME STANDARDS

	Percent Completed in 120 days or Less (Standard—90%)	Percent Completed in 180 Days or Less (Standard—98%)	Percent Completed in One Year or Less (Standard—100%)
Portland, OR	85%	91%	96%
Dayton, OH	81%	89%	96%
Detroit Rec Ct, MI	78%	90%	99%
Phoenix, AZ	73%	88%	97%
San Diego, CA	71%	86%	97%
New Orleans, LA	68%	81%	94%
Minneapolis, MN	64%	78%	93%
Oakland, CA	60%	72%	88%
Wichita, KS	58%	84%	97%
Bronx, NY	50%	63%	85%
Cleveland, OH	49%	72%	89%
Miami, FL	49%	65%	84%
Providence, RI	49%	70%	83%
Wayne County, MI	47%	61%	80%
Pittsburgh, PA	43%	71%	91%
Jersey City, NJ	29%	58%	83%
Newark, NJ	13%	26%	63%

Note: The percentages in this table are based on times from arrest (or, for courts where arrest date is unavailable, from first filing of a complaint against the defendant) to date of guilty plea, trial verdict, dismissal or formal determination of entry into a diversion program.

arrest; 98% within 180 days, and 100% within one year. Table 2H shows how each of the courts involved in this study performs in relation to these standards.

None of the courts complete 90% of their cases within 120 days, but three of them (Portland, Dayton, and Detroit Recorder's court) complete over 75% within 4 months of arrest. Those three, as well as two others (Phoenix and San Diego), complete at least 85% within six months. All of the courts except for Newark and Boston complete at least 80% of their cases within a year after their inception.

One of the most common reasons for lengthy case processing time (and a possible reason why some courts fall short of meeting the ABA standards) is defendants' failure to appear in court when scheduled, whether inadvertant or deliberate. Data in Tables 2I and 2J indicate that defendants' failure to appear is something of a

Table 2I
COMPARISON OF MEDIAN TOTAL FELONY CASE DISPOSITION TIMES IN CASES WHERE BENCH WARRANT WAS ISSUED WITH CASES WHERE NO BENCH WARRANT WAS ISSUED, 1985

	Median Time, No Bench Warrant Issued (in days)	Median Time, Bench Warrant Was Issued (in days)	(N)	Median Time, All Cases (in days)	Percent of Cases in Which Bench Warrant Was Issued
Portland, OR	54	71	(76)	55	16%
Detroit Rec Ct, MI	54	92	(48)	58	10%
Dayton, OH	56	132	(61)	61	15%
Phoenix, AZ	73	121	(64)	78	16%
San Diego, CA	75	132	(35)	77	8%
New Orleans, LA	78	125	(52)	83	12%
Minneapolis, MN	79	164	(73)	88	12%
Miami, FL	107	199	(118)	123	31%
Wichita, KS	110	180	(58)	115	12%
Bronx, NY	112	213	(80)	121	14%
Cleveland, OH	112	230	(45)	121	13%
Providence, RI	115	194	(86)	122	23%
Wayne County, MI	119	317	(82)	133	14%
Jersey City, NJ	147	425	(138)	163	30%
Newark, NJ	269	378	(151)	300	32%

problem in all of these urban courts. Bench warrants were issued in at least 8% of the cases in every court, but four of the courts— Miami, Jersey City, Newark, and Boston, all with bench warrants issued in between 31 and 36% of their cases—seem to have particular problems.

Interestingly, when cases involving bench warrants are subtracted from the samples, there are virtually no changes in the rank order of the jurisdictions' median total time to disposition (Table 2I) or median upper court time (Table 2J). It is also worth noting that the median times for cases in which bench warrants were issued in the faster courts (e.g. Detroit Recorder's Court, San Diego, Portland) are faster than the median times for cases with *no* bench warrant in several of the other courts. To some extent, this may reflect different court policies with respect to circumstances under which warrants are issued, but it may also reflect stronger overall management controls and a more active concern about tracking down missing

Table 2J

COMPARISON OF MEDIAN UPPER COURT TIMES IN FELONY CASES WHERE BENCH WARRANT WAS ISSUED WITH CASES WHERE NO BENCH WARRANT WAS ISSUED, 1985

	Median Upper Court Time, No Bench Warrant Issued (in days)	Median Upper Court Time, Bench Warrant Issued (in days)	(N)	Median Upper Court Time, All Cases (in days)	Percent of Cases in Which Bench Warrant Was Issued
Detroit Rec Ct, MI	31	21	(48)	31	9%
Dayton, OH	40	115	(82)	47	17%
New Orleans, LA	42	87	(54)	48	12%
San Diego, CA	48	57	(35)	49	12%
Phoenix, AZ	54	101	(65)	58	18%
Portland, OR	55	71	(80)	56	16%
Providence, RI	56	154	(108)	63	22%
Wayne County, MI	58	258	(81)	64	15%
Minneapolis, MN	79	164	(73)	88	12%
Cleveland, OH	82	228	(64)	90	14%
Miami, FL	89	168	(142)	108	36%
Jersey City, NJ	91	391	(150)	115	31%
Wichita, KS	110	180	(58)	115	12%
Newark, NJ	111	156	(145)	124	34%
Bronx, NY	145	251	(60)	152	15%
Boston, MA	268	525	(136)	332	32%

defendants in the courts that handle their felony case business most efficiently.

C. Summary

The most striking feature of the data on case processing times presented in this chapter is the wide variability that exists across courts. The slowest courts take more than twice as long to deal with their civil cases as do the fastest courts. On the criminal side, the variations are even greater, although there are fewer courts at the slow end of the tables.

The data make it clear that trial court delay is not inevitable. A number of courts in the study came very close to meeting the ambitious case processing time standards established by the American Bar Association. By virtually every measure of case processing time, these courts operate expeditiously. It is equally clear, however, that some courts fall far short of these standards.

The box-and-whisker charts are particularly useful in illustrating the disparities in the speed with which different courts deal with their caseloads. To help gain an understanding of the reasons for the wide disparities, the next two chapters examine the courts' civil and criminal case processing times in light of a number of structural, procedural, and attitudinal variables.

ENDNOTES–Chapter 2

1. The approach to selecting courts for inclusion in the study is described in Appendix A. As the description of the methodology indicates, the selection of sites was purposive, not random. Statistically, it is thus possible that relationships that appear in the tables in this report may be artifacts of the non-random way that the courts were chosen for inclusion in the study.

2. *Justice Delayed*, p. 7. See also Thomas W. Church et al., *Pretrial Delay: A Review and Bibliography* (Williamsburg: National Center for State Courts, 1978), pp. 3–5.

3. Hans Zeisel, Harry Kalven, Jr., and Bernard Buchholz, *Delay in the Court* (Boston: Little, Brown and Co., 1959).

4. Steven Flanders, *Case Management and Court Management in U.S. District Courts* (Washington, D.C: Federal Judicial Center, 1977), pp. 5–6.

5. See *Justice Delayed*, pp. 7–12. It should be noted that our measure of time to jury verdict is slightly different from the time to start of jury trial measure employed in *Justice Delayed*. Trials are typically several days in duration, so the time to jury verdict will result in slightly longer time periods than the time to start of trial.

6. See Federick Hartwig and Brian Dearing, *Exploratory Data Analysis* (Beverly Hills: Sage Publications, 1975), p. 9. For an early discussion of the need for multiple measures (and the potential for erroneous analysis that can result from reliance on a single measure) in the context of civil litigation, see Maurice Rosenberg, "Court Congestion: Status, Causes, and Proposed Remedies," in Harry W. Jones (ed.), *The Courts, the Public, and the Law Explosion* (Englewood Cliffs, N.J.: Prentice-Hall, Inc., 1965), pp. 29, 32–35.

7. *Justice Delayed*, pp. 8–9.

8. As in the *Justice Delayed* study, the primary statistic used for relating these variables is the correlation coefficient, or Pearson's r. See H. Blalock, Jr., *Social Statistics*, 2d ed. (New York: McGraw-Hill Book Company, Inc., 1972), pp. 408–413. Correlation analysis measures the strength of relationship between two variables, or the extent to which they "track." The correlation coefficient always varies from 1.0 (indicating a perfect "fit" between the two variables) through 0 (indicating no relationship) to -1.0 (indicating a perfect inverse relationship).

Table 2A, for example, depicts four indices of processing time for civil cases that are positively correlated. The correlation coefficient between tort disposition time and general civil docket disposition time is .92; between tort disposition time and trial-list disposition time is .65; between trial-list disposition time and time to jury verdict is .73; and between tort-disposition time and time to jury verdict is .77. These are relatively high correlations since in most social research a correlation coefficient above .6 (or below $-.6$) indicates a fairly strong relationship. These high correlations indicate that if a court is fast by one measure, it will tend to be fast by the others.

One additional statistic is useful in evaluating the relationship described by the correlation coefficient. This is the significance level, or p. The significance level indicates the probability that the relationship described by the correlation coefficient could have occurred by chance. A significance level of $p = .01$ indicates only 1 chance in 100 that the variables examined are unrelated and the correlation observed occurred by chance. Correlations derived above .7 from Table 2A are significant at $p = .01$.

9. For tort disposition time, the correlation between the median and third quartile is .88; between the median and 90th percentile is .86; and between the median and the percentage of cases over two years is .90. The correlations are significant at $p = .001$.

10. See *Justice Delayed*, pp. 12–19. As on the civil side, we measure time to verdict, which will be slightly longer than the time to start of jury trial measures used in the *Justice Delayed* study.

11. The correlation coefficients among felony case disposition time measures contained in Table 2E are as follows: Between total disposition time and upper court disposition time .65; between total disposition time and upper court time in jury trial cases .40; and between upper court disposition time and upper court time in jury trial cases .61. Given 17 sites, correlation coefficients above .60 are significant at $p = .01$. Although these correlation coefficients are fairly strong, they are not nearly as strong as was found in the *Justice Delayed* study. The weaker the relationship between these case processing time variables, the more important it is to look at them separately; they measure different dimensions of case processing times.

12. For total disposition time, the correlation between median and third quartile times is .94; between median and 90th percentile is .90; and between median and percent over 180 days is .90. For upper court disposition time, the correlation between median and third quartile time is .97; between median and 90th percentile is .79; and between median and percentage of cases over 150 days is .90. The correlations are statistically significant at the $p = .001$ level.

Chapter 3
STRUCTURAL FACTORS AND CASE PROCESSING TIMES

Prior to the mid-1970s, most writing on the subject of court delay, by both scholars and practitioners, focused principally on perceived needs for more resources, reduced workloads, and/or more efficacious court procedures.[1] The existence of a causal link between workload and delay was taken for granted. Thus, for example, Hans Zeisel and his colleagues wrote in 1959 that "while study is indispensable for disclosing the exact additional judge power needed to cure delay, it takes no ghost come from the grave to tell us that delay can be cured by adding more judges."[2]

Research conducted during the past decade has produced a more complex definition of the problem and has suggested the need for a broader range of vision in devising remedies for delay. The new conventional wisdom does not reject the idea that resources, workloads, and formal rules and procedures can significantly affect the pace of litigation, but it emphasizes that these factors operate through complex systems of practitioner attitudes and practices. In this model, the informal norms, expectations, behaviors, and relationships of judges, attorneys, and staff in a trial court—the "local legal culture"—are regarded as being as important as the formal structural and procedural factors in understanding the problem of delay and developing realistic solutions.[3]

In this study, we have attempted to take account of both sets of factors. The research strategy is similar to that employed in the *Justice Delayed* study: we compare courts with widely varying paces of litigation, and attempt to determine whether any particular factors tend to differentiate faster courts from slower ones. This chapter deals with a number of different structural factors that have been hypothesized as contributing to court delay, examining them in light of the 1985 case processing times for the full range of courts participating in the study.

A. Size of Court

One of the commonly held maxims about court delay is that it is primarily a problem in large urban areas. Although the courts involved in this study are all in relatively populous metropolitan areas, the jurisdictions vary considerably in the size of their populations and in the volume of cases handled by the courts.

As Table 3A indicates, there seems to be no relationship between size (whether measured in terms of the jurisdiction's population, the total number of judges on the court, or the number of judges assigned to hear felony cases) and the speed with which felony cases are handled in the jurisdiction. Table 3B shows a lack of any relationship between size and civil case processing times. On both tables, the top half dozen courts include three of the largest and three of the smallest courts in the study. The slower courts include both some that are large and some that are small.

The data in these tables are consistent with findings of the *Justice Delayed* study with respect to the effects of court size on the pace of litigation: by itself, size is irrelevant.[4] Both large courts and small ones are capable of handling caseloads expeditiously.

B. Caseload Mix

It is possible that some courts may be slower than others because their caseload includes a large number of serious or complex cases. Such cases would presumably require more judge time and other court resources than would more "routine" cases.

On the criminal side, it is possible to identify some kinds of cases that are "serious" by any standard. Table 3C presents data on upper court felony case processing times for all cases in the samples and then for two subgroups: (1) cases in which the defendant was charged in the general jurisdiction trial court with homicide, rape, or robbery ("serious cases")[5]; and (2) cases in which the highest charge in the indictment or information was for some other felony offense. The tables also show the percentage of serious cases in each court's total caseload.

The three courts with the highest percentage of serious cases (Newark, Bronx County, and Boston) are also the three slowest.

Table 3A
FELONY CASE PROCESSING TIMES
AND COURT SIZE, 1985

	Median Total Disposition Time (in days)	Median Upper Court Disposition Time (in days)	1980 Population (in thousands)	Total Judges[a]	Felony Judges[b]
Portland, OR	55	56	562	21	*
Detroit Rec Ct, MI	58	31	1,203[c]	29	29
Dayton, OH	61	47	571	13	*
San Diego, CA	77	49	1,861	48	12
Phoenix, AZ	78	58	1,509	50	13.5
New Orleans, LA	83	48	557	*	16
Oakland, CA	87	57	1,105	35	12
Minneapolis, MN	88	88	941	42	8
Wichita, KS	115	115	366	22	7
Cleveland, OH	121	90	1,498	33	*
Bronx, NY	121	152	1,168	44	36
Providence, RI	122	63	571	13	6
Miami, FL	123	108	1,625	58	18
Wayne County, MI	133	64	1,134[c]	35	8
Pittsburgh, PA	149	120	1,456	47	20
Jersey City, NJ	163	115	556	22	7
Newark, NJ	300	124	851	46	19
Boston, MA	*	332	650	*	8

*Data unavailable or inapplicable.

[a]Total number of full-time or "full-time equivalent" judges in the entire court during 1985. Source: questionnaires answered by trial court administrators.

[b]Total number of full-time or "full-time equivalent" judges assigned to handle felony charge cases. Source: questionnaire answered by trial court administrators.

[c]The total 1980 census population in Wayne County was 2,337,000. The population figures shown in this table for Detroit Recorder's Court are the population figures for the city of Detroit. The population shown for Wayne County Circuit Court (which in 1985 handled all felony charge cases originating in Wayne County outside the city of Detroit) is the Wayne County population less the population of Detroit.

Aside from these three jurisdictions, however, there is little relationship between seriousness of the caseload and median time to disposition. For the other courts in the study, the proportion of serious cases ranges between 7% and 16%, and the distribution is similar at the top and bottom of the table. At least for these 15 courts, the speed with which cases are handled seems to be largely independent of the proportion of especially serious offenses in the caseload.

Table 3B
CIVIL CASE PROCESSING TIMES AND
COURT SIZE, 1985

	Median Tort Disposition Time (in days)	Median Trial List Disposition Time (in days)	1980 Population (in thousands)	Total Judges	General Civil Judges
Dayton, OH	279	*	571	13	*
Phoenix, AZ	292	505	1,509	50	22.5
Miami, FL	325	*	1,625	58	30
Cleveland, OH	343	*	1,498	33	*
Portland, OR	389	*	562	21	*
Jersey City, NJ	394	*	556	22	5
New Orleans, LA	403	560	557	12	10
Wichita, KS	411	*	366	22	9
Newark, NJ	624	*	851	46	11
Minneapolis, MN	*	603	941	42	10
Bronx, NY	*	772	1,168	44	8
Oakland, CA	637	838	1,105	35	11
Wayne County, MI	648	*	2,337	35	27
Pittsburgh, PA	651	694	1,456	47	15
Providence, RI	697	1,304	571	13	7
San Diego, CA	719	696	1,861	48	24
Boston, MA	782	*	650	16	8

*Data unavailable or inapplicable.

As in the *Justice Delayed* study, the courts tend to rank in virtually the same order when the median times for handling the more serious and less serious offenses are compared.[6] The serious cases take longer, in every court except Wichita, than do the less serious ones. However, the fast courts usually deal with both their more serious cases and their less serious ones relatively quickly, while courts that are comparatively slow in dealing with the most serious cases are also slow in dealing with the less serious ones. There are, however, two exceptions to this general pattern: both New Orleans and Providence deal swiftly with the great bulk of their cases but take considerably longer to deal with the more serious ones.

Assessing the effects of different caseload mixes is more difficult on the civil side, because our data base does not include reliable indicators of the seriousness or complexity of civil cases. Conceivably, case type might be a factor: tort cases tend to reach disposition

Table 3C
UPPER COURT DISPOSITION TIMES
AND PROPORTION OF "SERIOUS" FELONY CASES
IN COURT CASELOADS, 1985

	Median Upper Court Time, All Cases (in days)	Median Upper Court Time, Serious Cases[a] (in days)	Median Upper Court Time, Less Serious Cases[b] (in days)	Percentage of Serious Cases in Sample
Detroit Rec Ct, MI	31	80	21	11%
Dayton, OH	47	60	42	16%
New Orleans, LA	48	130	45	9%
San Diego, CA	49	56	48	9%
Portland, OR	56	64	53	14%
Oakland, CA	57	74	56	15%
Phoenix, AZ	58	66	56	9%
Providence, RI	63	323	62	7%
Wayne County, MI	64	121	61	12%
Minneapolis, MN	88	103	68	16%
Cleveland, OH	90	118	83	15%
Miami, FL	108	155	105	9%
Wichita, KS	115	84	117	10%
Jersey City, NJ	115	143	110	14%
Pittsburgh, PA	120	141	122	8%
Newark, NJ	124	167	117	20%
Bronx, NY	152	187	135	33%
Boston, MA	332	328	332	32%

[a]Cases in which the defendant was charged with homicide, rape, or robbery.
[b]Felony cases exclusive of homicide, rape, and robbery.

more slowly than contract cases (the other major case type in our samples), and the presence of a high proportion of torts in a court's caseload might help account for slow case processing times.

Table 3D indicates that several of the courts with speedy tort disposition time have a comparatively small percentage of tort cases in their overall caseload (e.g. Phoenix, Miami, Portland). However, two of the faster courts (Jersey City and New Orleans) have very high proportions of tort cases (69 and 72%, respectively). By contrast, the percentage of torts in the caseloads of the five slowest courts ranges between 34 and 61%.

Overall, the data on caseload composition are inconclusive. They certainly do not establish that caseload mix is a clear determinant of case processing time, but they do suggest that this is an area that

Table 3D
CIVIL CASE PROCESSING TIMES AND CASELOAD COMPOSITION, 1985

	Median Tort Disposition Time (in days)	Median General Civil Disposition Time (in days)	Percentage of Tort Cases in Sample
Dayton, OH	279	178	43%
Phoenix, AZ	292	133	30%
Miami, FL	325	186	20%
Cleveland, OH	343	298	49%
Portland, OR	389	253	32%
Jersey City, NJ	394	379	69%
New Orleans, LA	403	366	72%
Wichita, KS	411	160	20%
Newark, NJ	624	623	83%
Oakland, CA	637	616	89%
Wayne County, MI	648	624	56%
Pittsburgh, PA	651	406	34%
Providence, RI	697	525	54%
San Diego, CA	719	691	61%
Boston, MA	782	789	48%

warrants further inquiry. For such an inquiry to be productive, however, it would be necessary to develop considerably more extensive data on case characteristics than it has been possible to collect in this study.[7]

C. Trials and Trial Rates

Cases that result in a trial generally take longer than cases disposed of by other means (see, e.g., Tables 2A and 2E), and in the process they often consume considerable amounts of judge time and courtroom resources. One of the common tenets of the old conventional wisdom about court delay was that courts could dispose of more cases, and deal with them more quickly, if the number of trials could be minimized. On the criminal side, the need to process cases speedily has often been used as a rationale to justify (or at least explain) the prevalence of plea bargaining practices. On the civil side, techniques such as mandatory settlement conferences and "crash" settlement programs have been used to reduce the number of cases

Table 3E
JURY TRIAL UTILIZATION RATES, FELONY CASE PROCESSING TIMES AND PER-JUDGE DISPOSITIONS, 1985

	Jury Trial Utilization Rate	Median Total Court Disposition Time (in days)	Median Upper Court Disposition Time (in days)	Upper Court Dispositions per Felony Judge[a]
Phoenix,AZ	2%	78	58	653
Providence, RI	2%	122	63	447
Miami, FL	4%	123	108	*
Pittsburgh, PA	4%	149	120	*
Jersey City, NJ	4%	163	115	355
San Diego, CA	5%	77	49	568
Oakland, CA	5%	87	57	330
Minneapolis, MN	5%	88	88	412
Cleveland, OH	5%	121	90	*
New Orleans, LA	6%	83	48	273
Wayne County, MI	6%	133	64	540
Portland, OR	7%	55	56	633
Detroit Rec Ct, MI	7%	58	31	365
Wichita, KS	7%	115	115	263
Dayton, OH	8%	61	47	*
Bronx, NY	8%	121	152	169
Newark, NJ	11%	300	124	344
Boston, MA	12%	*	332	179

*Data unavailable or inapplicable.

[a]Measure obtained by dividing total 1985 felony dispositions by the number of judges assigned to handle felony cases in the general jurisdiction trial court.

requiring jury trial on the assumption that this will speed the disposition process.

Findings from the *Justice Delayed* study cast doubt on the proposition that high trial rates lead to longer case processing times;[8] and findings from this study raise similar doubts. Tables 3E and 3F show the proportion of felony cases and civil cases that result in a jury verdict in the courts participating in the study. It is readily apparent from these tables that courts vary widely in the proportion of cases that go to jury trial. On the criminal side, there does appear to be some correlation between trial rates and case processing at one extreme: the two courts with the highest jury trial rates (Boston

Table 3F
JURY TRIAL UTILIZATION RATES,
TORT CASE PROCESSING TIMES, AND
PER-JUDGE TORT DISPOSITIONS, 1985

	Jury Trial Utilization Rate in Tort Cases	Jury Trial Utilization Rate, All Civil Cases	Median Tort Disposition Time (in days)	1985 Tort Dispositions per Civil Judge	1985 Total Civil Dispositions per Civil Judge[a]
Oakland, CA	1%	2%	637	273	724
Dayton, OH	2%	1%	279	*	*
Cleveland, OH	2%	2%	343	*	*
Jersey City, NJ	2%	2%	394	554	1,074
Wayne County, MI	2%	1%	648	442	815
Phoenix, AZ	3%	1%	292	315	1,461
New Orleans, LA	3%	2%	403	*	*
Wichita, KS	3%	1%	411	93	1,571
San Diego, CA	5%	4%	719	145	1,252
Boston, MA	5%	3%	782	*	1,354
Providence, RI	6%	4%	697	113	236
Portland, OR	7%	3%	389	*	*
Miami, FL	8%	2%	325	230	1,035
Pittsburgh, PA	11%	8%	651	89	225

*Data unavailable or inapplicable.

[a]Because of significant differences in caseload composition and statistical procedures used to count filings and dispositions in these courts, the figures in this column are non-comparable.

and Newark) are also the two slowest courts in total disposition time. However, three courts with relatively high felony jury trial rates—Detroit Recorder's Court, Dayton, and Portland, all with 7 or 8% jury trial rates—are among the fastest courts in the study in terms of both total time and upper court time. At the other end of the scale, the courts with low jury trial rates include some that are fast and some that are comparatively slow.

There are some indications in Table 3E that felony jury trial rates may be associated with variance in judicial productivity, but the patterns are not clear. The two felony courts with the lowest jury trial rates, Phoenix and Providence, both show a relatively high number of dispositions per judge, while the court with highest jury trial rate (Boston) disposes of relatively few cases per judge. However, the Newark court, with an 11% jury trial rate, disposes of more than twice as many cases per judge as Boston. Portland and San Diego, both with relatively high jury trial rates, are also very speedy and very productive in terms of dispositions per judge.

On the civil side, the percentage of tort cases resulting in jury trials also seems unrelated to tort case processing time. As Table 3F shows, some of the courts with low trial rates are fast, but others are relatively slow. And two of the courts with a high percentage of tort cases going to jury trial (Portland and Miami) are among the fastest courts in handling their tort cases. The data on trial rates in relation to dispositions per judge, while much less extensive, show no clear linkages.

D. Case Volume and Backlogs

Although inadequate judicial resources in relation to workload is commonly asserted to be a primary cause of court delay, recent empirical research has challenged the validity of this assertion. The *Justice Delayed* study found no relationship between the pace of litigation and either annual filings per judge or cases pending per judge.

Tables 3G and 3H point to the same conclusion. As Table 3G shows, some of the fastest felony courts (e.g. San Diego, Phoenix) have among the highest numbers of filings per judge, while the slowest court (Boston) has the lowest number of filings per judge. Indeed, San Diego and Phoenix both had more than four times as many filings per judge in 1985 as Boston. A perusal of the columns showing pending cases and total annual felony case workload shows the same lack of a clear association between workload (as measured by number of cases) and case processing time: some fast courts have light per-judge caseloads, but others have heavy ones. Similar wide variations are found among the slower courts.

The data are sketchier with respect to civil case workloads. However, Table 3H indicates a lack of any pattern of strong correlations between speed of case processing and per-judge filings, per-judge pending caseloads, or overall per-judge annual workloads. Both the faster courts and the slower ones vary widely on all of these dimensions.

The data on workloads are, to be sure, very crude. They address only per-judge filings and pending caseloads, do not take account of staff resources within the court, and do not take account of case volume pressures faced by institutions such as the prosecutor's office, public defender's office, and private law firms. At a minimum, however, they tend to refute the notion that problems can be cured simply by adding more judges.

Table 3G
FELONY CASE PROCESSING TIMES AND
PER-JUDGE WORKLOADS, 1985

	Median Total Disposition Time (in days)	Median Upper Court Disposition Time (in days)	1985 Felony Filings per Judge	Felony Cases Pending per Judge 1/1/85	Total 1985 Felony Case Workload per Judge[a]
Portland, OR	55	56	*	*	*
Detroit Rec Ct, MI	58	31	351	64	415
Dayton, OH	61	47	*	*	*
San Diego, CA	77	49	619	*	*
Phoenix, AZ	78	58	725	253	978
New Orleans, LA	83	48	274	26	300
Oakland, CA	87	57	373	62	435
Minneapolis, MN	88	88	376	100	476
Wichita, KS	115	115	241	124	365
Cleveland, OH	121	90	*	*	*
Bronx, NY	121	152	186	57	243
Providence, RI	122	63	533	275	807
Miami, FL	123	108	804	*	*
Wayne County, MI	133	64	521	100	621
Pittsburgh, PA	149	120	*	*	*
Jersey City, NJ	163	115	318	280	598
Newark, NJ	300	124	367	371	738
Boston, MA	*	332	151	194	345

*Data unavailable or inapplicable.

[a]Measure obtained by adding number of felony cases pending in the general jurisdiction trial court on 1/1/85 plus the number of filings during 1985, and dividing that total by the number of judges assigned to handle felony cases in the general jurisdiction trial court.

The data on pending caseloads are of particular interest. It is clear from Tables 3G and 3H that on both the criminal and civil sides some of the faster courts had relatively high per-judge pending caseloads at the start of 1985. In these courts, the judges were able to deal with their large inventories quite expeditiously. Other courts, however, were not able to deal with high pending caseloads nearly as quickly. This suggests that, as others have observed, a pending caseload is not necessarily the same thing as a case "backlog."[9]

Researchers in the *Justice Delayed* study found that analysis of a court's pending caseload in relation to its total dispositions per year was useful in understanding variations in case processing time across courts. They utilized a "backlog index": the number

Table 3H
TORT DISPOSITION TIMES AND
PER-JUDGE WORKLOADS, 1985

	Median Tort Disposition Time (in days)	Tort Cases Pending per Civil Judge	1985 Tort Filings per Civil Judge	Total 1985 Tort Case Workload per Civil Judge[a]
Dayton, OH	279	*	*	*
Phoenix, AZ	292	326	332	658
Miami, FL	325	362	253	615
Cleveland, OH	343	*	*	*
Portland, OR	389	298	*	*
Jersey City, NJ	394	468	524	992
New Orleans, LA	403	*	*	*
Wichita, KS	411	95	84	179
Newark, NJ	624	*	*	*
Bronx, NY	*	204[b]	441[b]	645[b]
Oakland, CA	637	62[b]	*	*
Wayne County, MI	648	704	402	1106
Pittsburgh, PA	651	122[b]	101[b]	223[b]
Providence, RI	697	*	*	*
San Diego, CA	719	*	753	*
Boston, MA	782	*	*	*

*Data unavailable or inapplicable.

[a]Measure obtained by adding the number of tort cases pending on 1/1/85 plus the number of tort filings during 1985, and dividing that total number by the number of judges assigned to handle civil cases.

[b]Includes only tort cases in which a readiness document has been filed.

of cases pending in a court at the start of a year divided by that year's dispositions. The higher the backlog index, the more pending cases a court has in relation to its yearly productivity. In the *Justice Delayed* study, this index was a good indicator of delay: the higher a court's backlog index, the lengthier its 1976 case processing time.[10]

Problems of divergent caseload composition and data unavailability make construction of the backlog index difficult, especially for civil cases. Despite these difficulties, the backlog index again appears to be a useful indicator and diagnostic tool in assessing case processing times, particularly for criminal cases. In Table 3I, which ranks the felony courts by 1985 median upper court disposition time, the slowest courts are the ones with the highest backlog indices. The same general pattern holds with respect to civil case dispostion times: the higher the backlog index,

Table 3I
FELONY CASE PROCESSING TIMES
AND CASE BACKLOG, 1985

	Median Upper Court Disposition Time (in days)	Median Total Disposition Time (in days)	Felony Case Backlog Index[a]
Detroit Rec Ct, MI	31	58	.17
Dayton, OH	47	61	.18
New Orleans, LA	48	83	.09
Portland, OR	56	55	.36
Oakland, CA	57	87	.19
Phoenix, AZ	58	78	.39
Providence, RI	63	122	.61
Wayne County, MI	64	133	.19
Minneapolis, MN	88	88	.24
Cleveland, OH	90	121	.24
Wichita, KS	115	115	.47
Jersey City, NJ	115	163	.79
Newark, NJ	124	300	1.08
Bronx, NY	152	121	.34
Boston, MA	332	*	1.08

*Data unavailable or inapplicable.

[a]Felony cases pending as of 1/1/85 divided by 1985 felony dispositions.

the lengthier a court's tort and general civil case processing times (Table 3J). The slower courts are backlogged courts: they have a relatively small number of dispositions per year in relation to their pending caseloads.

There is one particularly interesting exception to this pattern. The Bronx court has a relatively low felony case backlog index (.34), despite having the second slowest median upper court disposition time. The explanation seems to lie in the dynamics of the change process. During 1985, the Bronx court was involved in a delay reduction program that had begun several years earlier. Although its 1985 disposition times were slower than most of the other courts in the study, these times were markedly faster than they had been in 1976 or even in 1983. As part of the delay reduction program, the Bronx court focused on reducing the size of its pending caseload (by disposing of substantially more cases than were filed) during 1983–84, and the results are reflected in the lower backlog index.

Table 3J
TORT CASE PROCESSING TIMES
AND CASE BACKLOG, 1985

	Median Tort Disposition Time (in days)	Tort Case Backlog Index[a]	Median General Civil Docket Disposition Time (in days)	General Civil Case Backlog Index[b]
Dayton, OH	279	.97	178	.65
Phoenix, AZ	292	1.04	133	.69
Miami, FL	325	1.57	186	1.07
Cleveland, OH	343	.99	298	.82
Portland, OR	389	.89	253	.72
Jersey City, NJ	394	.85	379	.76
New Orleans, LA	403	*	366	*
Wichita, KS	411	1.01	160	.30
Newark, NJ	624	*	623	.93
Wayne County, MI	648	1.59	624	1.42
Pittsburgh, PA	651	1.38	406	1.39
Providence, RI	697	*	525	2.83
Boston, MA	782	*	789	2.13

*Data unavailable or not applicable.

[a]Tort cases pending 1/1/85 divided by 1985 tort dispositions.

[b]Total civil cases pending 1/1/85 divided by 1985 civil case dispositions.

E. Charging Process (Criminal Cases)

It is widely believed that jurisdictions that use a grand jury process to charge a defendant with a felony by indictment take longer to handle their felony caseloads than do jurisdictions where the charging process is based on the filing of an information by the prosecutor. Data from the *Justice Delayed* project supported this proposition, with information-based systems taking less time from arrest to filing in the upper court and less time from arrest to dispostion.[11]

Data from our current study present a similar picture. As Table 3K indicates, the 1985 median times from arrest to upper court filing and from arrest to disposition are again faster in most of the jurisdictions that use a prosecutor's information. However, one jurisdiction that uses a grand jury indictment system (Dayton) is one of the fastest courts in handling felony cases. In Dayton, prosecutions typically proceed along one of two tracks, both of which call for rapid

Table 3K
FELONY CASE PROCESSING TIMES AND TYPE OF CHARGING PROCESS

	Information-Based Systems			Indictment-Based Systems	
	Median Time Arrest to Upper Court Filing (in days)	Median Total Disposition Time (in days)		Median Time Arrest to Upper Court Filing (in days)	Median Total Disposition Time (in days)
Detroit Rec Ct, MI	21	58	Dayton, OH*	0	61
San Diego, CA	42	77	Bronx, NJ	20	121
Phoenix, AZ	15	78	Cleveland, OH	36	121
New Orleans, LA	28	83	Jersey City, NJ	54	163
Oakland, CA	32	87	Newark, NJ	168	300
Minneapolis, MN	0	88			
Wichita, KS	0	115			
Wayne County, MI	30	133			
Pittsburgh, PA	23	149			
MEAN	21	96	MEAN	56	153
			MEAN, EXCLUDING NEWARK	28	116

*In Dayton, the prosecutor's office often uses a direct indictment procedure, under which a defendant is not formally arrested until after the indictment has been filed. Frequently, however, the defendant has been questioned and released by the police prior to the indictment. The period between initial police questioning and the filing of the indictment is not reflected in the data.

screening of cases in which the police have charged a defendant with a felony. In the first track, a preliminary hearing will be held within 7–10 days of the arrest. If probable cause is found, the case will be bound over for action by the grand jury, which usually acts within a week. The second track involves direct presentation of cases to the grand jury, which will be done within 24–48 hours if the defendant is in custody. If the defendant is not in custody, the process takes longer but is usually concluded within a month. In these cases, the defendant is often not arrested until the indictment is filed. Portland, a speedy jurisdiction that previously used an information-based system, recently adopted a direct indictment system and initial indications are that case processing time has not been adversely affected.

The Dayton and Portland examples indicate that the type of charging process used by a jurisdiction is not an insuperable barrier to expeditious case processing. They also reinforce the notion that practitioner attitudes and practices are at least as important as structural factors in determining the pace of litigation. The prosecutors in Portland and Dayton have been concerned about the problem of delay and have taken steps, in cooperation with the court, to expedite the process. By contrast, there was recurrent conflict over administrative issues between the prosecutor and the court in Newark during this period, and the problem of pre-indictment delay steadily worsened. The median time from arrest to indictment, which had stood at 79 days in 1976, slipped to 135 days in 1983 and to 168 days in 1985.

Differences in case processing times among courts with different types of charging systems may not be attributable as much to the type of system (i.e. indictment or information) as to the way in which any type of charging system is run. The prosecutor's role is especially important. In several of the faster courts, experienced prosecutors review the charges and the available evidence at a point very shortly after the arrest, decide which cases warrant full-scale prosecution as felonies in the general jurisdiction trial court, and arrange for the witnesses and paperwork to move quickly to the next stage of the process. The next stage may be the filing of an information and subsequent arraignment on the information in the upper court, or it may be a grand jury presentation to be held the same day or within a week. Either way, the case moves quickly and it arrives in the upper court at a point where the events are still fresh in the minds of the witnesses.

F. Speedy Trial Laws and Case Processing Time Standards

One of the striking differences between civil and criminal case processing is the extent to which the latter is subject to some type of speedy trial statute or rule of criminal procedure that establishes limits on the amount of time allowed for bringing a criminal case to trial or other disposition. On the civil side, although jurisdictions commonly have some time limits for certain steps in the litigation process (e.g., the time allowed by statute for the defendant to file an answer to the complaint), such limits are typically lengthy and can ordinarily be extended by stipulation of counsel. There are rarely limitations on the amount of time allowed for bringing a civil case to trial.

Criminal speedy trial statutes and rules are typically designed to give effect to the defendant's right to a speedy trial, a right guaranteed by the constitutions of most states. These provisions are

Table 3L
1985 CIVIL CASE PROCESSING TIMES IN RELATION TO TIME STANDARDS

Court	Source and Type of Standard	Time(s) Allowed	Median General Civil Dispo. Time	Percent General Civil Cases Over 2 Years	Median Tort Dispo. Time (in days)	Median Time To Jury Trial (in days)	(N)
Phoenix, AZ	No State Standards as of 1985 Local Standards: Phoenix Civil Case Management Plan, Local Rules of Practice	270 days from filing to complete discovery and file Certificate of Readiness. Trial date set within 90 days after Certificate of Readiness is filed.	133	6%	292	634	(43)
Wichita, KS	State Supreme Court (General Principles and Guidelines for the District Courts)	50% within 180 days of filing. 100% within 2 years of filing.	160	6%	411	1126	(3)
Dayton, OH	State Supreme Court (Rules of Superintendence)	Personal injury—24 months from filing. Appropriations—6 months from filing. Other civil cases—12 months from filing.	178	7%	279	332	(6)
	Local Standards Dayton Civil Case Management Plan	Med Malpractice—360 days. Personal Injury—270 days. Appropriation—180 days. Mortgage Foreclosure—120 days. Other Civil Cases—150 days.					
Miami, FL	State Supreme Court (Administrative Order of Chief Justice, adopting standards recommended by Judicial Council of Florida).	Jury cases—18 months, filing to trial. Non-jury cases—12 months, filing to final disposition. Summary civil—60 days, filing to final disposition.	186	2%	325	295	(9)

City	Standard-Setting Authority	Time Standard					
Portland, OR	None as of 1985	Personal Injury—24 months from filing. Appropriations—6 months from filing.	253	9%	389	694	(14)
Cleveland, OH	State Supreme Court (Rules of Superintendence)		298	14%	343	551	(55)
New Orleans, LA	None as of 1985		366	22%	403	745	(11)
Jersey City, NJ	"Informal" State AOC Guidelines	12 months from filing.	379	4%	394	501	(10)
Pittsburgh, PA	None as of 1985		406	23%	651	575	(40)
Providence, RI	Chief Judges of Statewide Courts	18 months, docketing to disposition.	525	42%	697	1435	(20)
Minneapolis, MN	None as of 1985		*	*	*	822	(12)
Bronx, NY	Administrative Board of the Courts/Chief Administrative Judge	15 months, trial readiness certificate to disposition.	*	*	*	1138	(11)
Oakland, CA	No standards as of 1985, but CA Code of Civil Procedure provides outside limits	CA Code of Civil Procedure sec 583.360—mandatory dismissal after 5 years from filing, if trial not held.	616	41%	637	1617	(8)
Newark, NJ	"Informal" State AOC Guidelines	12 months from filing.	623	15%	624	725	(14)
Wayne Co, MI	None as of 1985		624	44%	648	1314	(22)
San Diego, CA	No standards as of 1985, but CA Code of Civil Procedure provides outside limits	CA Code of Civil Procedure sec. 583.360—mandatory dismissal after 5 years from filing, if trial not held.	691	46%	719	1064	(19)
Boston, MA	None as of 1985		789	53%	782	1863	(13)

phrased in many different ways, but usually require that the defendant be tried within a specific period of time following arrest, following filing of an indictment or information in the general jurisdiction trial court, or (in a few instances) following the defendant's demand for a speedy trial. The statutes and rules provide rights for the defendant (e.g., dismissal of the case if the time limit is exceeded), but do not create rights for anyone else, nor are they intended to enforce a public interest in speedy prosecution. They frequently come into operation only if the defendant moves for a speedy trial and usually allow for "excludable time" for a variety of reasons including defense requests for a continuance. Almost always, the right to be brought to trial within the allowable time can be waived by the defendant. Unless the speedy trial rule is invoked by the defendant (and defendants in criminal cases often have good reasons for not wanting to have a prosecution proceed expeditiously), it creates no independent obligation on the court to bring a case to disposition quickly.

As concern about the problem of trial court delay has increased during the 1970s and '80s, one of the main developments has been the formulation and adoption of case processing time standards. Time standards are essentially statements of court or court system goals for managing total caseloads—e.g., disposition of all felony cases within 180 days of arrest or of all civil cases within two years of filing.[12] They are typically developed through a broad-based consultative process at either the state or local level (sometimes both) and ideally will reflect a consensus as to what is both desirable and achievable with respect to case processing in the jurisdiction. Unlike speedy trial statutes or rules, time standards establish no rights for anyone, and there are no sanctions for failure to meet the standards in an individual case. They do, however, provide guidelines for judges and others in the handling of their cases.

Ohio, which adopted time standards as part of a major court reorganization and delay reduction initiative in the early 1970s,[13] was the first state court system to do so. In 1983–84, sets of model standards were developed by major national organizations—notably the Conference of State Court Administrators, Conference of Chief Justices, and the American Bar Association—and these efforts helped spur attention to the issue in individual states. By 1985, 14 states had adopted both criminal and civil case processing time standards,[14] and by 1987 more than 20 states had statewide standards.

There are some indications that the existence of civil case processing time standards is associated with a relatively speedy pace of litigation. On the civil side, as Table 3L shows, five of the six courts that dealt most expeditiously with their civil caseloads in 1985 had some type of civil case processing time standards in place. Four of the courts (Wichita, Dayton, Miami, and Cleveland) are located in states that have such standards, and the Dayton court has also adopted standards of its own, which are more stringent than the state standards. The Phoenix court, which is at the top of this ranking, adopted its own time standards (together with local rules designed to implement the standards) in 1980, as part of a locally initiated civil case management plan. These five are the only courts in the study that, as of 1985, had formal time standards that covered the time period from filing (or service of the complaint) to disposition.

On the criminal side, while every court was subject to some type of speedy trial statute or rule that could be invoked by defendants, only half of them operated under any type of case processing time standard. Neither the speedy trial laws nor the time standards are clearly correlated with speedy felony case processing times.

Given the fact that time standards are still in a very early stage of development in most jurisdictions, it may simply be too early to tell what effect they will have on the pace of litigation. The limited experience to date provides strong indications that time standards, *by themselves*, are not a panacea, but that they can be an important part of a comprehensive program to reduce or prevent delays. First, they express an important concept: that timely disposition of the court's business is a responsibility of the judiciary. Second, they provide goals for the court and the participants in the litigation process to seek to achieve, both in managing their total caseloads and in handling individual cases. Third, they can lead directly to the development of systems for monitoring caseload status and the progress of individual cases, as participants in the process seek to manage their dockets more effectively in order to achieve their goals.

G. Alternative Dispute Resolution Programs

During the past 15 years, there has been a proliferation of programs that provide alternatives to conventional civil litigation. In some courts the decision to send a case to an alternative dispute resolution (ADR) program is voluntary, made with the agreement of the parties to the case. However, a growing number of courts have adopted mandatory programs, usually involving initial arbitration with the opportunity for a trial de novo on appeal, for some portion of their civil caseloads. An underlying premise of many of the programs has been that removing a significant volume of particular

Table 3M
1985 CIVIL CASE PROCESSING TIMES AND ALTERNATIVE DISPUTE RESOLUTION PROGRAMS

Court	Median General Civil Disposition Time	Median Tort Disposition Time	Types of ADR Programs	Point of Entry for Mandatory ADR Programs
Phoenix, AZ	133	292	Mandatory—all cases up to $15,000 Voluntary—medical malpractice claims up to $50,000	9–11 months after filing (when readiness certificate is due)
Wichita, KS	160	411	None	
Dayton, OH	178	279	Mandatory—all cases up to $10,000 except personal injury, plus all medical malpractice Voluntary—Other civil cases	60–90 days after filing (upon review by judge)
Miami, FL	186	325	Voluntary	
Portland, OR	253	389	Mandatory—all cases up to $15,000	30–60 days after filing (after all parties have entered appearances)
Cleveland, OH	298	343	Mandatory—all cases up to $20,000	8–14 months (after discovery is complete)
New Orleans, LA	366	403	None	

Jersey City, NJ	379	394	Mandatory—Auto accident cases up to $15,000 or $2,500 in medical expense claims	After answer filed
Pittsburgh, PA	406	651	Mandatory—All cases up to $20,000	Filed directly into Arbitration program (Note: case processing times reported in this study do *not* include these cases.)
Providence, RI	525	697	None	
Oakland, CA	616	637	Mandatory—All cases up to $25,000 Voluntary—Other cases, by agreement of parties (Early Disposition Program)	Approximately 26 months (after at-issue memo filed)
Newark, NJ	623	624	None	
Wayne Co., MI	624	648	Mandatory	16–26 months (after completion of discovery)
San Diego, CA	691	719	Mandatory—All cases up to $25,000 Voluntary—Other cases, by agreement of parties	Approximately 24 months (after at-issue memo filed)
Boston, MA	789	782	Voluntary—Civil Mediation Project	

types of cases from the courts would help reduce backlogs and improve the speed with which the remaining cases are processed.[15]

All but 5 of the 17 civil courts participating in this study utilized some form of alternative dispute resolution mechanism during 1985, and 9 of them had mandatory arbitration for at least part of their civil caseloads. Table 3M shows the types of programs that were operating in (or in conjunction with) these courts, with the courts ranked in order of their median general civil docket disposition times. It is clear from this table that simply the existence of an alternative dispute resolution program, whether mandatory or voluntary, is not correlated with speedy civil case processing. ADR programs exist both in fast courts and slow ones.

Nor does mandatory referral to an arbitration program appear to make a major difference. Two of the fastest courts, Wichita and Miami, do not have mandatory programs, and Wichita has no alternative dispute resolution program at all. On the other hand, three of the five slowest courts have mandatory arbitration, and two of those, Oakland and San Diego, send a large percentage of their caseloads into arbitration. Overall, the courts with mandatory arbitration programs are fairly evenly dispersed across the spectrum of fast, medium, and slow courts.

For the courts with mandatory arbitration programs, the variable that separates fast courts from slow courts is the point at which cases are diverted into the arbitration program from the regular civil docket. Early referral—within a short time after an answer is due—correlates with speedy overall case processing. Care must be taken, however, not to infer unwarranted causal relationships from the very preliminary data presented here. While the courts that divert cases to arbitration at an early stage in the process are among the faster courts in total civil case processing time, this does not mean that the arbitration program can be credited with the speediness of the court. It may be that early diversion in these courts is merely one part of early control over the entire civil caseload. Courts that refer cases to the arbitration program only after they reach the stage of trial readiness obviously build delay into the process. One possible advantage gained by waiting until discovery has been completed and cases are trial-ready is that it is easier at that point to assess real value of the claims, thus making it more difficult for plaintiffs to use inflated claims to avoid arbitration. If waiting until trial readiness is coupled with strong control of the caseload to move cases to trial readiness quickly, as is done in Phoenix, the disadvantage of some built-in delay may be reduced.

Three of the courts in our sample divert cases into arbitration at very early stages of the civil litigation process. In Pittsburgh, cases meeting the jurisdictional limit are filed directly into the arbitration program, and our data base does not include those cases. In Dayton and Portland, cases are sent to arbitration when the pleading stage is complete. While these two courts are among the faster civil courts in our sample, attributing their relative speed to the arbitration program would clearly not be justified from our data. In both courts only a relatively limited portion of the caseload is eligible for arbitration (because of jurisdictional limits), and in fact, both send a relatively small percentage of their cases to arbitration.

At the other extreme, Oakland and San Diego do not send cases into arbitration until the case is at issue and exert little control over the progress of cases prior to that time. Those two courts are among the slower civil courts in our sample despite diverting a relatively large percentage of cases to arbitration.

Overall, while our data clearly indicate that an ADR program will not in and of itself turn a slow court into a fast one, this does not mean that alternative dispute resolution mechanisms have no effect on reducing delay. It is still very possible that such a program can help turn a slow court into a somewhat faster one. What does seem clear is that the way an ADR program fits into the entire civil caseflow process is as important as the existence of the program.

The experiences of the courts in Phoenix, Dayton, Portland, and Cleveland—all of them speedily operating courts that have arbitration programs for cases involving relatively low claim amounts—indicate that court-annexed programs can be useful components of an overall delay reduction or prevention effort, provided other elements of case management are present. However, the fact that alternative dispute resolution programs also exist in some of the slowest courts strongly suggests that, by itself, establishment of an ADR program will not provide a "quick fix" for problems of delay.

H. Summary

Our review of aspects of court structure that might conceivably affect case processing times leads to conclusions that are essentially similar to those of the authors of *Justice Delayed*: although structural factors are not irrelevant, they do not appear to be the primary determinants of case processing times. In particular, per-judge filings seem to have little relation to the pace of litigation.

Two structural factors do seem to be associated with speed of case processing. First, backlogs, defined as the ratio of pending cases to yearly terminations, clearly are associated with delays. This finding, which is consistent with conclusions in the *Justice Delayed* study, has important policy implications: while backlog may not be a cause of delay in itself, one element of a successful delay reduction program must be a reduction in the size and age of the pending caseload. Second, although this is clearly an area in which further research is necessary, it appears that time standards that establish guidelines for civil case processing from the inception of a lawsuit until its disposition are associated with a speedy pace of litigation.

It is conceivable that some of the factors examined separately in this chapter could, in combination, affect the pace of litigation in a court. Thus, for example, it is possible that the combination of high case volume, an unusually large proportion of serious or complex cases, and a high jury trial rate could lead to delays. The extent to which this sort of combination exists, and how it may affect case processing time, warrants further inquiry but will require more detailed knowledge of caseload characteristics than our data base will permit. Any such analysis should, however, also take account of the set of factors to which we turn our attention in the next chapter—the sets of operational procedures, case management practices, and practitioner norms and attitudes that exist in each local trial court.

ENDNOTES–Chapter 3

1. See, e.g., Hans Zeisel, Harry Kalven, Jr., and Bernard Buchholz, *Delay in the Court* (Boston: Little, Brown and Co., 1959); John P. Frank, *American Law: The Case of Radical Reform* (New York: Macmillan, 1969); Laura Banfield and C.D. Anderson, "Continuances in Cook County Criminal Court," *University of Chicago Law Review*, Vol. 35 (1968), p. 256.

2. Zeisel, Kalven, and Buchholz, *Delay in the Court*, p. 8.

3. Thomas W. Church, "The 'Old and the New' Conventional Wisdom of Court Delay," *Justice System Journal*, Vol. 7 (1982), pp. 395, 396–401. See also Ernest C. Friesen et al., "Justice in Felony Courts: Report on a Study of Delay in Metropolitan Courts During 1978–1979," *Whittier Law Review*, Vol. 2 (1979), pp. 7, 34–46; David W. Neubauer et al., *Managing the Pace of Justice: An Evaluation of LEAA's Court Delay-Reduction Programs* (Washington, D.C.: National Institute of Justice, 1981), esp. pp. 10–11, 78–115, 422–29; *Justice Delayed*, pp. 53–62, 79–84.

4. See *Justice Delayed*, pp. 21–24. There is considerable evidence from other sources that small (three- or four-judge) courts vary widely in their case processing times, with some of them taking very lengthy periods. See, e.g., David C. Steelman et al., *Civil and Criminal Case Processing in the Northumberland County (PA) Court of Common Pleas* (North Andover, Mass.: Northeastern Regional Office of the National Center for State Courts, 1986). Similar variations unrelated to the size of the court, were found in a nine-court study of criminal case processing. See Roy B. Flemming, Peter F. Nardulli, and James Eisenstein, "The Timing of Justice in Felony Trial Courts," in *Law & Policy*, Vol. 9, No. 2 (April 1987), pp. 179, 190–91.

5. By characterizing these cases as "serious," we do not mean to imply that other felony charges are not serious. Indeed, particularly when a defendant has a prior record of felony convictions, any felony charge can be regarded as serious. But homicide, rape, and robbery all involve violent offenses for which severe sentences are commonplace. The same three categories of offenses were used to analyze case processing time by seriousness of caseload in earlier National Center research. See *Justice Delayed*, pp. 29–31.

6. *Justice Delayed*, pp. 29–31.

7. At least two multijurisdictional studies of criminal case processing time have collected much more extensive data on the characteristics of specific cases (including defendant characteristics) than we have attempted to do in this research. See Neubauer et al., *Managing the Pace of Justice*, esp. pp. 34–43; also James Eisenstein, Peter F. Nardulli, and Roy B. Flemming, *Explaining and Assessing Criminal Case Dispositions: A Comparative Study of Nine Counties* (Final Report submitted to the National Institute of Justice, 1982). Given finite resources, the choice is between breadth of coverage and depth of detail. To achieve the objectives of this study, which are primarily descriptive and exploratory, our decision was to obtain court record data samples from a broad range of courts, collecting data on a relatively small number of variables.

8. *Justice Delayed*, pp. 31–36.

9. See, e.g., Friesen et al., "Justice in Felony Courts," *Whittier Law Review*, Vol. 2, pp. 7, 14–18. Friesen defines backlog as "the number of cases in any significant category which cannot be disposed of by the court within tolerable delays" (*ibid.*, pp. 15–16). If, for example, a court had a standard that all felony cases should be completed within 90 days of the filing of an indictment, any cases pending more than 90 days would be "backlog" cases.

10. *Justice Delayed*, pp. 24–29.

11. *Justice Delayed*, pp. 46–49.

12. See J. Denis Moran, "Stating the Case for Timely Justice," *State Court Journal*, Vol. 8, No. 4 (Fall 1984), p. 24; Howard P. Schwartz, "Monitoring Delay Reduction Efforts," *1985 Court Management Journal*, p. 4.

13. See Chapter 8, infra.

14. Schwartz, supra note 12, pp. 4, 7.

15. See, e.g., Elizabeth Rolph, *Introducing Court-Annexed Arbitration: A Policymaker's Guide* (Santa Monica: The RAND Corporation, 1984), esp. pp. 3–9.

Chapter 4
CASEFLOW MANAGEMENT PRACTICES
AND ATTITUDES

Writing in 1978, the authors of *Justice Delayed* commented that probably the greatest observable difference between criminal and civil case processing was in the area of case management. Nearly every court that they examined controlled the pace of criminal litigation to some extent, but management of civil case progress was seldom exercised.[1]

A decade later, it is clear that the judges and staff in some courts are now much more involved in the management of their civil dockets. In others, however, the situation has remained much the same as it was ten years ago. The differences in approach reflect differing philosophies about the role of courts in the litigation process, and they can have important consequences for the speed with which cases reach disposition in the courts.

In this chapter, we examine practices and attitudes toward both civil and criminal caseflow management that we found in the courts participating in the study. Our primary focus is on the impacts of different approaches to case management upon case processing times. To what extent do different approaches have different results in terms of the speed with which civil and criminal cases reach resolution? Secondarily, how do differing sets of practitioners' attitudes toward issues of court delay and caseflow management relate to speed of case processing?

A. Calendaring/Case Assignment Systems

One of the long-standing controversies in the field of judicial administration involves the relative advantages and disadvantages of two markedly different approaches to the allocation of work on cases in a multijudge court—the individual calendar (or individual assignment) system and the master calendar (or central assignment) system. In a "pure" individual calendar (IC) system, a case is assigned to one of the judges at the time of initial filing, usually on the basis of a random "blind-draw" procedure. The case remains on that judge's docket until it is concluded, with the IC judge hearing all motions, conducting pretrial conferences, and presiding over the trial if one is held. In an individual calendar system, the judges in a multijudge court operate essentially independently in managing their caseloads, can become familiar with the cases, have responsibility for their disposition, and can be held accountable for the size and age of their pending caseloads.[2]

In a master calendar system, cases go into a pool (or onto a "master calendar") when they are filed, and are then assigned to a particular judge as action is needed—e.g., to rule on a motion, to conduct a pretrial conference, or to preside over a trial. The advantages claimed for this system include maximizing the use of judge time on any particular day, increasing the likelihood that a case will be reached on the assigned trial date, providing more uniform application of court policies regarding continuances and trial preparation, and enabling overall monitoring of the court's total caseload by a single individual (the master calendar judge).[3]

In practice, there are few "pure" individual or master calendar systems. For example, in many courts that use an individual calendar system there is provision for "back-up" assistance when the IC judge finds that there is a conflict between two or more trial-ready cases on the trial date. And in some courts using a master calendar system special arrangements may be made so that a single judge handles all of the pretrial motions and conferences, as well as the trial (if there is one) in particularly complex cases. Sometimes the two approaches are combined in such a way that a court's calendaring system can best be described as a hybrid, perhaps looking more like one or the other of the two basic systems.

The roles of staff in the two types of systems are different in important ways. In an individual calendar system, judges often utilize their personal staff—e.g., secretary, bailiff, courtroom clerk, law clerk—to help schedule cases, monitor the status of the docket, and contact the attorneys involved in cases set for trial. Central staff in an individual calendar court generally have relatively little responsibility for case scheduling, but often have important coordinating functions and responsibilities for data collection, analysis, and dissemination of information. In a master calendar court, the individual judges' secretaries, bailiffs, and clerks are less likely to be involved in scheduling and case management, and the burden of performing these functions either falls on central staff or is left essentially to the lawyers.

When the *Justice Delayed* researchers examined case processing times in light of courts' calendaring systems, they found no strong correlation between speed of felony case processing and the type of calendaring system used. For civil courts, however, there was a striking difference: civil courts using the individual calendar system dealt with their cases substantially faster than did courts using some variant of the master calendar system. On the average, courts using the IC system disposed of their tort cases about 200 days faster than did the master calendar courts.[4]

Our factual findings in the current study are very similar with respect to associations between calendaring systems and case processing times. Table 4A shows the type of calendaring system used in the 18 felony courts in this study, ranked by median upper court disposition time. It indicates that neither the IC system nor the master calendar system is appreciably more effective than the other in minimizing felony case delays. The mean of the median upper court disposition times for the IC courts is 84 days compared to 109 days for the master calendar courts, but if the one extraordinarily slow master calendar court (Boston) is excluded from the analysis, the mean for the master calendar courts drops to 71 days.

On the civil side, as Table 4B shows, the individual calendar courts cluster at the top of the rankings, the master calendar courts at the bottom. The four fastest courts, in terms of median tort disposition time, all use the individual calendar system. The mean of the median tort disposition times for the IC courts is 328 days (about 11 months) compared to 589 days (approximately 20 months) for the master calendar courts—a difference of about nine months.

Despite these differences, we are hesitant to conclude that use of an individual calendar system will consistently produce faster civil case processing. The fact that several master calendar courts— e.g. Portland, Jersey City, Wichita—handle their civil caseloads very expeditiously makes it clear that a master calendar court *can* deal with its business in an efficient manner. It is worth noting that in these courts the judge in charge of the master calendar is also either the chief judge or the administrative judge for the civil division. In all three courts, this is a permanent position that does not rotate frequently. The master calendar judge in the Portland, Jersey City, and Wichita courts can thus be held accountable for the court's performance with respect to civil case processing, in much the same

Table 4A
COURT CALENDARING SYSTEMS AND FELONY CASE
PROCESSING TIMES, 1985

	Median Upper Court Disposition Time (in days)	Median Total Disposition Time (in days)	Type of Calendaring System
Detroit Rec Ct, MI	31	58	Hybrid(IC)
Dayton, OH	47	61	IC
New Orleans, LA	48	83	IC
San Diego, CA	49	77	Master
Portland, OR	56	55	Master
Oakland, CA	57	87	Master
Phoenix, AZ	58	78	IC
Providence, RI	63	122	Master
Wayne County, MI	64	133	Hybrid(IC)
Minneapolis, MN	88	88	Master
Cleveland, OH	90	121	IC
Miami, FL	108	123	IC
Wichita, KS	115	115	Master
Jersey City, NJ	115	163	IC
Pittsburgh, PA	120	149	IC
Newark, NJ	124	300	Hybrid(IC)
Bronx, NY	152	121	Hybrid(M)
Boston, MA	332	*	Master

*Data unavailable or inapplicable.

way that individual calendar judges can be held accountable for the progress of cases on their calendars. By contrast, rotation of the "calendar judge" position is common in some of the slower courts. The master calendar judges in the faster courts also have staff support that they utilize to help monitor the progress of pending cases.

B. Point of Judicial Intervention (Civil Cases)

Differences in civil case processing time between the IC and master calendar courts may have less to do with the type of calendaring system than with the point at which the court (or the individual judge) becomes involved in monitoring and, in a sense, managing the progress of cases. In courts using the individual calendar system, judges commonly become involved in case manage-

Table 4B
COURT CALENDARING SYSTEMS AND CIVIL CASE PROCESSING TIMES, 1985

	Median Tort Disposition Time (in days)	Median Trial List Disposition Time (in days)	Type of Calendaring System
Dayton, OH	279	*	IC
Phoenix, AZ	292	505	IC
Miami, FL	325	*	IC
Cleveland, OH	343	*	IC
Portland, OR	389	*	Master
Jersey City, NJ	394	*	Master
New Orleans, LA	403	560	IC
Wichita, KS	411	*	Master
Newark, NJ	624	*	Master
Minneapolis, MN	*	603	*a
Bronx, NY	*	772	Hybrid(M)
Oakland, CA	637	838	Master
Wayne County, MI	648	*	Hybrid(M)
Pittsburgh, PA	651	694	Master
Providence, RI	697	1304	Master
San Diego, CA	719	696	Master
Boston, MA	782	*	Master

*Data unavailable or inapplicable.

aThe Minneapolis court was in the process of changing from a master to an individual calendar system in 1985.

ment within two to four months after the complaint is filed. They oversee case progress and (in consultation with the attorneys) establish deadlines for completion of discovery and set dates for trials and for pretrial conferences. This is also done to some extent in the faster master calendar courts, but not in most of the slower ones. In those courts the progress of the case is left entirely to the parties, at least until a certificate of readiness, at-issue memo, or similar document is filed by the attorneys (or one of them) signifying that the case is ready to be placed on the trial calendar.

One of the fundamental precepts of those who advocate strong management by courts in civil cases is that courts must take control of incoming cases at the earliest possible time—ideally, at the point the complaint is filed. The rationale is simple: for management purposes, the earlier the potential caseload is recognized and accounted for, the better prepared the court will be to deal with it.[5] "Taking control," as used in this sense, does not mean that the court must become actively involved in managing case progress or scheduling intervening events at this initial point. But simply organizing filing and record keeping systems to account for every case, from the point of its inception as a civil lawsuit until its conclusion, can enable the court to have a full picture of its caseload and thus to monitor both the status of the overall caseload and the progress of individual cases. With such information, the court is in a position to act upon problems as they arise and to make early decisions about case scheduling so as to allocate resources effectively and avoid or minimize delays.

Two of the civil courts in this study (Minneapolis and Bronx County) cannot take cognizance of all of their potential caseload at an early stage, because in those jurisdictions there is no requirement that civil complaints be filed with the court. Those two courts do not even know that there is a case until one of the lawyers requests the intervention of the court to rule on a motion or (most often) to set the case for trial. The other civil courts have no such barrier to taking control of a case from filing onward, but their actual practices vary widely.

By and large, the courts that occupy the bottom half of the civil case time-to-disposition tables are ones that exercise virtually no control at all over the pace of civil litigation and have little or no knowledge about the relative complexity of different cases prior to the point of trial readiness. In some of these courts, cases are simply placed at the bottom of a master trial calendar either when the answer is filed or when a certificate of readiness or similar document is filed. They gradually rise toward the top of the calendar as the cases ahead of them reach disposition. In these courts, there is often no contact between the court and the lawyers for the parties and no other examination by the court of what the case is about and what judicial resources it might require until the case is at or near the top of the trial calender. This approach involves virtually no exercise of management responsibility by the court other than providing a courtroom and judge for cases in which the parties are ready for a trial.

For practical purposes, the Oakland and San Diego courts have until very recently operated essentially the same way as do the Bronx and Minneapolis courts. Although complaints in civil cases are filed in these courts at the outset of the case, the California courts have historically defined their "active inventory" as only those cases in which an at-issue memorandum has been filed signifying

Table 4C
TRIAL LIST DISPOSITION TIMES IN COURTS USING A
CERTIFICATE OF READINESS PROCEDURE

	Median Time, Filing/ Service to Disposition	Median Time, Filing/ Service to Readiness	Median Time, Readiness to Disposition
Phoenix, AZ	505	303	210
New Orleans, LA	560	210	288
Minneapolis, MN	603	392	190
Pittsburgh, PA	694	142	438
San Diego, CA	696	371	261
Bronx, NY	772	586	142
Oakland, CA	838	305	420
Providence, RI	1304	86	914

that the case is ready to be scheduled for trial.[6] Essentially the same procedure is followed in Pittsburgh, where the court begins its management of cases only after a praecipe is filed indicating that the case is at issue. As Table 4C indicates, the times from filing to readiness and readiness to disposition can be lengthy in these courts.

Although use of a certificate of readiness procedure is generally associated with a laissez-faire attitude by the court toward the lawyers' handling of the initial stages of litigation, there is one notable exception. The court in Phoenix has imposed a time requirement—330 days from the filing of the complaint—for filing the certificate of readiness, which indicates that discovery has been completed. Extensions of this time period can be obtained, but only on a showing of good cause, and failure to file the certificate within the allowable period will result in dismissal of the case. Once the certificate has been filed, the judge to whom the case is assigned will ordinarily set it for a trial to begin within 90 days. A continuance of the trial date can be obtained for good cause, but multiple continuances are not common.[7]

The Phoenix system is an example of an approach that combines a rule putting short outside limits on the discovery period (with allowance for exceptions where clearly warranted) plus strong case management by the court beginning at the point where discovery is expected to be completed. The approach has the effect of placing some of the responsibility for managing the pretrial stage on the parties, especially the plaintiff's lawyer, but it gives the court a substantial degree of control over the pace of litigation. In contrast to the systems in most other jurisdictions that use a readiness certificate or similar procedure, the Phoenix system is closed-ended. The filing of the complaint is a meaningful event for management purposes, and the court treats the 330-day discovery period seriously. Although extensions can be obtained for good cause, discovery cannot go on endlessly and the lawyers must allocate their time and resources to comply with the deadlines.

Several of the courts in this study take an active managerial approach that begins at a much earlier stage in the process. The types of managerial activities undertaken in these early stages are difficult to catalogue neatly; they vary widely by type of case and by individual judge, even within the same court. In a large multi-judge court that has an individual calendar system, such as Miami, there may be as many different managerial approaches as there are judges handling civil cases. There are, however, a few basic minimum functions that usually take place at an initial screening in a court where there is active civil case management. These typically include a check to see whether an answer has been filed (if not, a default judgment may be in order), an assessment of the complexity of the case based on the nature of the claims and defenses, and a determination about the case's eligibility for referral to an alternative dispute resolution program. In the courts that are most committed to the concept of strong management, the initial screening may also involve a conference with the attorneys to set a schedule for future events in the case.

The Montgomery County Court of Common Pleas, in Dayton, Ohio, provides a good example of a court that has organized itself to manage its civil caseload effectively, using an individual calendar system in which judges begin to monitor case progress at an early stage. The Dayton court takes the position that once a complaint is filed, it is the court's responsibility to monitor case progress, take steps to ensure that the case does not linger dormant, and—in consultation with the lawyers—set schedules for completion of the case. Each judge still has some distinctive docket management practices of his own, but the basic approach is consistent. Every civil case file will be examined at some point within the first three months after a complaint is filed. For cases in which an answer has been filed, a scheduling conference will be held either at the court or by telephone. At the scheduling conference, discovery issues will be reviewed, schedules will be agreed upon for completion of discovery, and a trial date will be set. The Dayton plan creates a structure and process that forces both the court and the lawyers to take a hard look at the case at a relatively early stage of the litigation—generally between two and four months after the lawsuit has been started. Estimates about time and resources likely to be needed in the future are made at that time, and cases that require little or no discovery can be scheduled for arbitration or early trial. In the more complicated cases, discovery issues can be identified (and perhaps resolved) and a schedule acceptable to the parties can be arranged.

C. Early Control in Felony Cases

In contrast to civil litigation, where there are generally a great many lawyers involved in the litigation process, there are usually two important institutional litigants in criminal litigation: the prosecutor's office and (in most urban courts) a public defender's office. The effective exercise of early case management in felony cases is shaped to a considerable degree by the policies of these institutional litigants and by the type of working relationship that exists between each of them and the court.

In the 18 jurisdictions in this study, the prosecutor's office is involved in virtually every felony case from an early point, and at least theoretically has a responsibility to ensure expeditious handling of all cases. By contrast, the general jurisidiction trial court— the "upper court" in most states—typically has formal authority over the case only after an indictment or information is filed. It is the prosecutor who has the responsibility for pulling together the evidence necessary to obtain an indictment or file an information. No matter how committed a prosecutor's office may be to expeditious case processing (and in the jurisdictions in this study, the extent of such a commitment varies widely), there will almost inevitably be some situations in which a prosecutor's office will not want to see an individual case proceed rapidly. For example, an arrest or indictment in one case may provide leads to other (sometimes more serious) cases in which an investigation or prosecution could be compromised if the defendant in the first case was brought to trial speedily. Other times, the prosecution case is simply a weak one, and the assistant prosecutor responsible for it is not anxious to bring it to trial or other resolution.

If a court is concerned about expeditious felony case processing, there is an inherent potential for conflict with the prosecutor's office, especially with respect to case progress during the stages between arrest and the filing of an indictment or information. This potential for conflict is dealt with in different ways, and with different consequences for felony case processing times, in the jurisdictions participating in this study. In some, the prosecutor clearly has the dominant role, and in a few such places (e.g. New Orleans, San Diego) the prosecutor's strong commitment to sound management and expeditious resolution of cases has resulted in speedy case processing times. Elsewhere, however, the prosecutor's office has had other priorities and the court has not been able to develop an effective caseflow management system.

Four of the courts in this study—Dayton, Detroit Recorder's Court, Phoenix, and Portland—provide particularly good models of effective working relationships in the context of a local criminal justice system. In each of these jurisdictions there is a strong management-oriented prosecutor's office and the court has both good management capability and a strong commitment to expeditious case processing. And in each jurisdiction, the chief judge has taken initiatives to develop and maintain communications with the prosecutor's office, the public defender's office, the private defense bar, and other relevant actors.

Each of these jurisdictions has organized its felony case processing system somewhat differently, but each has placed heavy emphasis on effective early decisionmaking. The prosecutor's office in each jurisdiction is organized to enable early screening of incoming cases (to determine which should be prosecuted as felonies and what evidence will be essential), rapid action to obtain an indictment or file an information once the decision is made to prosecute the case as a felony, and "open-file" discovery that generally allows defense attorneys to know the prosecution's case at an early stage. With efficient notification to the defendant and the upper court about the filing of an indictment or information, it is then possible for the upper court to "take control" of each case at an early point—usually when the defendant is arraigned on the indictment or information. Since discovery is rarely an issue in these jurisdictions, both prosecutor and defense counsel can focus from the outset on the central issues relevant to disposition of the case. The court itself can then obtain basic knowledge about the complexity of the case and the likelihood of a nontrial disposition at an early point, and can schedule future events (e.g. motion hearing, pretrial conference, trial) within relatively short time frames and on the basis of realistic estimates of the amount of time that will be required.

D. Case Scheduling and Continuance Policies

Previous research has provided strong evidence that the overall pace of litigation in a court is affected significantly by court and attorney practices regarding scheduled trial dates and the granting of continuances. Courts with relatively speedy case processing times have generally been those with early first scheduled trial dates and a high proportion of cases commencing trial near that date.[8] Those findings are consistent with comments of numerous judges and practicing trial lawyers to the effect that nothing is more likely to produce a settlement in a case then the imminent and unavoidable prospect of actually going to trial.[9]

From the standpoint of the court (or of each judge in an individual calendar court) the problem in ensuring a "firm" trial date for a case is that there are almost always more cases that could theoretically go to trial than it is possible to actually try. Almost always, courts "overset" their trial calendars, scheduling more cases for trial on a given day or week than they could possibly try if some did not settle. There are, however, wide variations among courts (and, in individual calendar courts, among judges in the same court) with respect to the extent of the over-setting. There are also significant variations with respect to the point in the process at which the scheduling takes place (both in relation to the inception of the case and in relation to the date for which the trial is scheduled) and in the degree of knowledge that the scheduler has about the likelihood that cases scheduled for a particular day or week will settle or result in a trial. Courts and judges also differ in the extent to which they make provisions to hold trials on the scheduled date, i.e., to provide a meaningful "firm trial date."

We have not attempted to undertake a comprehensive quantitative examination of the trial setting and continuance policies of the courts involved in this study, because it is extremely difficult to obtain reliable data on practices in these areas from court records. Table 4D does, however, provide some data on trial scheduling and on continuances of trial dates in cases that actually resulted in a jury trial. The table shows that two courts—Detroit Recorder's Court and Dayton, two of the fastest courts in the study—had a remarkably high percentage of trials starting on the scheduled date. Two other relatively speedy courts, San Diego and Portland, have high percentages of trials beginning within two weeks of the originally scheduled trial date. At the other end of the spectrum, the Bronx and Boston courts begin only a small proportion of their trials on the

Table 4D

TRIAL SCHEDULING PRACTICES AND UPPER COURT TIME IN FELONY JURY TRIAL CASES

	Median Upper Court Disposition Time (in days)	Median Upper Court Time in Jury Trial Cases (in days)	Percentage of Trials Beginning				(N)
			On Day Scheduled	In 7 Days	In 14 Days	Over 14 Days	
Detroit Rec Ct, MI	31	106	79%	3%	—	17%	(29)
Dayton, OH	47	112	78%	—	4%	18%	(27)
New Orleans, LA	48	110	23%	5%	5%	68%	(22)
San Diego, CA	49	70	—	29%	24%	47%	(17)
Portland, OR	56	69	21%	42%	5%	32%	(19)
Phoenix, AZ	58	114	—	—	—	100%	(7)
Providence, RI	63	375	17%	8%	8%	67%	(12)
Wayne County, MI	64	165	25%	3%	3%	69%	(36)
Minneapolis, MN	88	134	42%	10%	6%	42%	(31)
Cleveland, OH	90	129	17%	13%	4%	67%	(24)
Wichita, KS	115	118	8%	22%	—	69%	(36)
Jersey City, NJ	115	145	42%	21%	—	37%	(19)
Newark, NJ	124	208	43%	2%	2%	53%	(44)
Bronx, NY	152	318	6%	—	3%	91%	(34)
Boston, MA	332	332	3%	8%	8%	82%	(40)

*Data unavailable or inapplicable.

scheduled date or within 14 days thereafter. Although fragmentary, these data are consistent with the notion that a court's capacity to ensure a firm trial date is an important element of effective caseflow management. Setting an early date for a trial is a useful management device only if the lawyers in the case know that the court is serious about holding trials on or near the scheduled date.

The techniques used by the Dayton court to help ensure firm trial dates in civil cases are particularly worth noting. In this court, the trial date is initially set at a scheduling conference held three or four months after the complaint is filed. In June 1986, the Dayton judges were typically setting trials for weeks between October and February—four to eight months after the scheduling conference. At the time a trial is set, the judge's calendar may show as many as seven or eight other trials scheduled for the same week. Experience has shown, however, that as the parties complete discovery and the trial date draws near, settlements are likely to occur. To help catalyze settlements, many (though not all) of the Dayton judges will schedule a "final" pretrial conference to be held approximately two weeks before the trial date.[10]

E. Information Systems and Monitoring Practices

In a world awash with information, a lack of data about how quickly or slowly cases progress through the courts is puzzling. But as recently as 1976, when the National Center for State Courts began its research into the causes of pretrial delay in state trial courts, it was necessary to deploy researchers and data gatherers in every one of the 21 sites participating in the *Justice Delayed* study in order to obtain accurate measurement of the pace of litigation. While this effort was also essential in order to ensure cross-court comparability of the data sets, the fact is that not one of these courts regularly measured and reported its overall pace of litigation from commencement to disposition.

In the ten years that have passed since the National Center began its *Justice Delayed* study, a number of urban courts have developed information systems—many of them computer-based— that provide information from which a profile of the pace of litigation can be constructed. More importantly, some of the courts have developed both the capacity to obtain such information and the ability to use it to manage their caseloads effectively. At this point, the key issue is not so much the availability of information (in most courts, the requisite information is available or can be obtained easily), as how the available information is used.

Virtually all of the courts participating in this study have some type of information system that produces statistical data for management information purposes. As Tables 4E and 4F indicate, most of the courts collect data on a monthly basis on filings, dispositions and total number of cases pending. A smaller percentage (but more than half) also have data on the age of cases at disposition and on the number and percentage of cases pending more than a specified period of time—e.g., criminal cases pending more than 120 days or civil cases pending more than a year. In comparing the faster civil courts with the slower ones in terms of the availability of basic data essential for caseflow management, there seems to be one major difference—the courts at the top of the tables are much more likely to have information on cases pending more than specified periods of time. The six fastest civil courts all collect such data on a monthly basis. Only three of the six slowest courts collect such data on a monthly basis, and one of them (Oakland) measures the age of case only from the filing of the at-issue memorandum (Table 4E). On the criminal side, no clear patterns emerge.

Interestingly, having an automated information system rather than a manual one does not seem to be a distinguishing factor in terms of speed of case processing. On both the civil and criminal sides, several of the slowest courts report having automated systems, while several of the faster ones have systems that are completely or partially manual. One possible explanation is the age of the automated systems. Several of the courts with automated information systems began their systems development work over 15 years ago, at a time when there was less focus on issues of caseflow management and delay reduction. Some of the newer automated systems such as those in Dayton (civil) and Detroit Recorder's Court (criminal) have been designed with a view to facilitating caseflow management and minimizing delays, whereas many of the earlier ones were not.

Information by itself does not solve caseflow management problems or even necessarily pinpoint them. It is critical for court managers—especially the presiding judge and the senior administrators—to use the information to (1) identify the problem areas; and (2) in consultation with others involved in the litigation process, develop effective solutions to the problems that are identified. One of the most striking characteristics of courts with speedy case processsing times is the extent to which the court's leaders use information as a key tool in on-going management.

Table 4E
CIVIL CASE PROCESSING TIMES AND COLLECTION OF MANAGEMENT INFORMATION, 1985

Courts	Median Tort Disposition Time	Type of Management Information System	Frequency With Which Information Is Collected			
			Total Cases Pending	Total Cases Disposed	Age of Cases at Disposition	Number of Cases Pending Over Specified Age
Dayton, OH	279	Auto	monthly	monthly	*	monthly
Phoenix, AZ	292	Mixed	monthly	monthly	bi-weekly	monthly
Miami, FL	325	Mixed[a]	monthly	monthly	not collected	monthly
Cleveland, OH	343	Auto	monthly	monthly	monthly	monthly
Portland, OR	389	Auto	monthly	monthly	monthly	monthly
Jersey City, NJ	394	Manual	monthly	monthly	monthly	monthly
New Orleans, LA	403	*	*	*	*	*
Wichita, KS	411	Mixed	quarterly	quarterly	quarterly	quarterly
Newark, NJ	624	Manual	monthly	monthly	not collected	monthly
Minneapolis, MN	*	Manual	monthly[b]	monthly	monthly	not collected
Bronx, NY	*	Auto	weekly[b]	weekly	weekly	weekly[e]
Oakland, CA	637	Manual	monthly[b]	not collected	monthly	monthly[e]
Wayne County, MI	648	Auto	monthly	monthly	monthly[c]	monthly
Pittsburgh, PA	651	Auto	monthly[b]	monthly	monthly	not collected[e]
Providence, RI	697	Auto	monthly	monthly	monthly[d]	quarterly
San Diego, CA	719	Mixed	not collected	monthly	monthly[d]	not collected
Boston, MA	782	Auto	monthly	monthly	monthly	monthly

*Data not reported on questionnaire sent to trial court administrators.

[a]Automation of management information system in progress in 1985.
[b]Includes only cases for which at-issue memo or other readiness document has been filed.
[c]Age at disposition measured only for cases disposed of by trial.
[d]Age at disposition measured from filing of at-issue memo.
[e]Age of pending cases measured from filing at-issue memo or other readiness document.

Table 4F

FELONY CASE PROCESSING TIMES AND COLLECTION
OF MANAGEMENT INFORMATION, 1985

	Median Total Disposition Time	Median Upper Court Disposition Time	Type of Management Information System	Total Cases Pending	Total Cases Disposed	Age at Disposition	Number of Cases Pending Over Specified Age
Portland, OR	55	56	Auto	monthly	monthly	monthly	monthly
Detroit Rec Ct, MI	58	31	Auto	weekly	monthly	semi-annually	weekly
Dayton, OH	61	47	Manual	monthly	monthly	monthly	monthly
San Diego, CA	77	49	*	*	monthly	*	*
Phoenix, AZ	78	58	Mixed	monthly	monthly	monthly	monthly
New Orleans, LA	83	48	*	*	*	*	*
Oakland, CA	87	57	Mixed	monthly	monthly	monthly	monthly
Minneapolis, MN	88	88	Auto	monthly	monthly	not collected	not collected
Wichita, KS	115	115	Mixed	quarterly	quarterly	quarterly	quarterly
Cleveland, OH	121	90	Auto	monthly	monthly	monthly	monthly
Bronx, NY	121	152	Auto	weekly	weekly	weekly	weekly
Providence, RI	122	63	Mixed	monthly	weekly	not collected	periodically
Miami, FL	123	108	Mixed	weekly	monthly	monthly	weekly
Wayne County, MI	133	64	Auto	weekly	monthly	monthly	monthly
Pittsburgh, PA	149	120	Auto	monthly	monthly	monthly	*
Jersey City, NJ	163	115	Auto	monthly	monthly	quarterly	monthly
Newark, NJ	300	124	Mixed	monthly	monthly	not collected	monthly
Boston, MA	*	332	Manual	monthly	monthly	monthly	monthly

*Data not reported on questionnaire sent to trial court administrators.

In Detroit Recorder's Court, for example, a five-person docket control center collects and analyzes a large amount of data on the caseloads and performances of each judge and of the entire court. Some of the information is generated by the court's computer, but a number of key items are collected manually, from each of the courtrooms in the 29-judge court. The docket control center produces a number of different management reports, including weekly reports on the status of each judge's docket and on continuances granted and pleas accepted on the scheduled trial date. The court's chief judge meets regularly with the court administrator and docket control manager to review these reports and they are a primary subject of discussion at meetings of the judges. The Dayton court, with only ten judges, relies less on the computer and more on manually collected data, but follows essentially the same approach.

F. Practitioner Attitudes and Expectations

One of the central concepts of the "new" conventional wisdom about court delay is that the norms, expectations, and relationships of practitioners in a local trial court—what the authors of *Justice Delayed* called the "local legal culture"—have a very substantial impact on the pace of litigation in the court.[11] Although it is difficult to test the relationship of legal culture to case processing times, there is at least some empirical support for the hypothesis.

In this study, we have not attempted to systematically assess the linkage between practitioner attitudes and case processing times. However, the responses to a questionnaire sent to all of the trial court administrators do provide some interesting insights into the perceptions of the administrators with respect to problems of delay. One of the questions presented a list of 25 factors, asking the administrators to indicate which factors were most important in contributing to delay in their courts. As Table 4G indicates, the administrators from civil case processing in both fast courts and slow courts responded that high case volume was a very important factor. With respect to other factors, however, there was considerable divergence of opinion. On the average, the administrators from the faster courts did not give any of the other factors a rating greater than 1.8 on a 3-point scale, while the administrators from the slower courts gave 14 other factors an average importance rating of 2.0 or better.

Table 4G

COMPARATIVE ASSESSMENT OF IMPORTANCE OF VARIOUS FACTORS POSSIBLY CONTRIBUTING TO CIVIL CASE DELAY, BY ADMINISTRATORS FROM FASTER AND SLOWER COURTS

Causes of Delay	Mean Rating Faster Courts (N = 5)	Mean Rating Slower Courts (N = 5)
High volume of cases	2.6	2.6
Too few judges	1.8	2.2
Lack of case processing time standards or goals	1.4	2.4
Lack of effective "firm trial date" policy	1.6	2.4
Lack of systems for monitoring caseload status	1.2	1.2
Lack of data on case processing times	1.2	1.4
Too many continuances granted by judges	1.6	2.4
Extensive use of delaying tactics by lawyers	1.6	2.4
Unprepared lawyers	1.8	1.8
Lawyers take on too many cases, with resulting schedule conflicts	1.8	2.0
Frivolous cases filed by attorneys	1.8	2.0
Too little emphasis on settlement by some judges	1.8	1.8
Too much emphasis on settlement by some judges	1.4	1.2
Lack of concern about delay by local bar	1.4	2.0
Lack of concern about delay by judges in your court	1.2	1.8
Inefficient use of time by some judges	1.6	2.0
Lack of leadership at the state level	1.6	1.4
Inadequately trained personal staff of judges	1.2	1.2
Inadequate communication about case processing problems	1.0	1.6
Not enough courtrooms	1.2	2.0
Resistance of bar to court efforts to manage caseflow	1.0	2.2
Large backlog of pending cases	1.4	2.6
Inability to obtain "back-up" judicial resources	1.2	2.2
Calendaring/judge assignment system is inefficient	1.2	2.0

NOTE: Importance was rated on a scale of 1 (not important) to 3 (very important).

The factors on which the ratings of the administrators from the fast and slow courts had the greatest discrepancies (.6 or greater) cluster in four main areas:

(1) *Workloads/Resources*
   - Large backlogs of pending cases
   - Not enough courtrooms
   - Inability to obtain "back-up" judicial resources

(2) *Time Standards*
   - Lack of processing time standards or goals

(3) *Calendaring/Case Scheduling/Continuances*
   - Lack of effective "firm trial date" policies
   - Too many continuances granted by judges
   - Extensive use of delaying tactics by lawyers
   - Calendaring/judge assignment system is inefficient

(4) *Bench-Bar Relationships*
   - Lack of concern about delay by local bar
   - Lack of concern about delay by judges in the court
   - Inadequate communication about case processing problems
   - Resistance of bar to court efforts to manage caseflow

While these patterns of responses provide only fragmentary data about practitioner attitudes and behaviors, they suggest the existence of strikingly different attitudes and behavior patterns in the slower courts by comparison to the faster ones. The administrators in the faster civil courts, which are the ones most likely to be involved in active management of their civil caseloads, seem to believe that their courts are functioning well and that the bar is not strongly resisting the court's efforts to manage its caseloads. By contrast, the responses of the administrators in the slower courts paint a picture of courts facing multiple problems: severe workload pressures, resource constraints, lack of effective case scheduling policies, lack of concern (on the part of both judges and lawyers) about problems of delay, and resistance by the bar to any efforts by the court to take control over what has been a lawyer-dominated system.

The responses to this question reinforce the notion that there are significant differences across courts—particularly between relatively fast and relatively slow courts—with respect to the attitudes, expectations, and behavior patterns of those involved in the trial court litigation process. They suggest rather strongly that there are differing local legal cultures in the courts participating in this study, and on some highly relevant dimensions the differences appear to be related to differences in the pace of litigation.

G. Summary

Our review of case management practices and attitudes as of 1985–86 generally reinforces the findings of other research of the past 15 years. In particular, the concepts of early control, on-going monitoring of caseloads and individual case progress, and emphasis on ensuring firm trial dates appear to have major impact when they are put into operation by courts that are committed to managing their caseload and minimizing delays.

From this analysis, the particular type of calendaring or case assignment system used by a court seems less important than how the system actually works in practice. The stage in the process at which the court becomes involved is important—the earlier the better, if the court is concerned with minimizing delays.

Linkages with the bar also emerge as important with respect to both civil and criminal case processing time. The questionnaire data, although sketchy, indicate that there is better bench-bar communication, greater concern about delay, and less resistance to court efforts to manage caseflow in the courts that deal with their cases expeditiously than in the slower courts.

ENDNOTES–Chapter 4

1. *Justice Delayed*, p. 39.

2. See Maureen Solomon, *Caseflow Management in the Trial Court* (Chicago: American Bar Association, 1973), pp. 23–26.

3. *Ibid.*, pp. 26–29.

4. *Justice Delayed*, pp. 36–39.

5. Ernest C. Friesen, "Cures for Court Congestion," *Judges Journal*, Vol. 23, No. 1 (Winter 1984), pp. 4, 7; also Friesen et al., *Arrest to Trial in Forty-Five Days* (Los Angeles: Whittier College School of Law, 1978), p. 58.

6. A recently enacted California statute, the Trial Court Delay Reduction Act of 1986 (California Government Code sec. 68600 et seq.), has given considerable impetus to management innovation in trial courts in that state. Pursuant to the legislation, the California Judicial Council adopted case processing time standards modeled on the ABA standards. The legislation also provides for the Judicial Council to establish "exemplary" delay reduction programs in nine superior courts in the state. The San Diego and Oakland courts are two of those that will be involved in this effort, and as of 1987 both have begun implementing programs aimed at reducing backlogs and delays. As part of these programs, both courts have begun taking cognizance of cases at the initial filing of the complaint and have instituted procedures that will enable them to exercise control over case scheduling from an early point.

7. There are a number of articles discussing the Phoenix program and its evolution. See, e.g., Robert C. Broomfield (with Howard Schwartz), "Delay: How Kansas and Phoenix are Making it Disappear," *Judges Journal*, Vol. 23, No. 1 (Winter 1984), p. 23; Bonnie Dicus, "Phoenix Revisited," *State Court Journal*, Vol. 10, No. 1 (Winter 1986), p. 24; Noel Fidel, "Why the Court Measures Delay from Commencement," *State Court Journal*, Vol. 10, No. 3 (Summer 1986); also Larry L. Sipes et al., *Managing to Reduce Delay* (Williamsburg: National Center for State Courts, 1980) pp. 6–12, 41–55. For further detail, see the discussion in Chapter 6, infra.

8. See, e.g., Maureen Solomon, *Caseflow Management in the Trial Court*, supra note 2; *Justice Delayed*, pp. 40–42, 69.

9. See, e.g., Larry L. Sipes et al., *Managing to Reduce Delay* (Williamsburg: National Center for State Courts, 1980), pp. 12–13; Anthony J. Langdon, *The New Jersey Delay Reduction Program* (Denver: Institute for Court Management, 1983), p. 106.

10. See Chapter 6, infra, for more detailed discussion of the techniques used by the Dayton court to help ensure a firm trial date.

11. See *Justice Delayed*, pp. 54–62, 83–84; Thomas W. Church, "The 'Old' and 'New' Conventional Wisdom of Court Delay," *Justice System Journal*, Vol. 7 (1982), pp. 395, 398–404.

Part III
Dynamics of the Change Process in Urban Trial Courts

Chapter 5
PATTERNS OF CHANGE

A. Justice Delayed and Its Progeny: Ferment and Change in State Courts

The publication of *Justice Delayed* in 1978 had significant impact on thinking and behavior with respect to pretrial delay in state trial courts. Prior to its publication, there had been virtually no knowledge about the dimensions of the problem or the extent of the variation among courts in the speed with which they dealt with cases. *Justice Delayed* provided a picture of the problem—a "snapshot" of case processing time in 21 courts, based on dispositions in 1976. It also presented an analysis of the problem that challenged many of the then-prevalent assumptions about court delay, its causes, and possible remedies. The *Justice Delayed* analysis focused attention on a set of factors not previously given much attention: the informal norms, expectations, and practices of the judges, lawyers, and court personnel in every local trial court:

> "As a general rule, the fastest courts tend to be the courts in which the attitudes and concerns of the legal community support a speedy pace of litigation. . . . Many of the slower courts visited in the project simply do not regard the existing pace of litigation to be a significant problem; if they address it at all, the response is typically a short-term burst of energy followed by a return to business as usual."[1]

The principal policy recommendation of the *Justice Delayed* study flowed directly from the authors' conclusions about the importance of norms, expectations, and practices: courts should institute case management systems that would enable them to monitor and control the progress of individual cases from filing to disposition and—

through sound continuance and trial setting policies—create an expectation that trial would commence on the date scheduled unless there were exceptional circumstances requiring a continuance.[2] For such systems to work, they emphasized, concern and commitment on the part of the judges would be essential.[3]

In the nine years that have passed since publication of *Justice Delayed*, significant efforts to reduce delay—many of them drawing heavily upon the insights and recommendations of that book—have been mounted at the national, state, and local levels. The efforts have included national conferences and workshops; provision of technical assistance by national organizations to local courts concerned about delay; several major nationally-funded experimental delay reduction programs in local trial courts; establishment by the American Bar Association of an on-going national task force to address problems of delay; development and endorsement of case processing time standards by major national organizations including the Conference of Chief Justices and the ABA; adoption of such standards by more than 20 states; and, at both the state and local levels, the initiation of a large number of programs aimed at reducing or preventing delays.[4] As we have seen in Chapter 4, there are now a number of courts that are using the type of case management procedures recommended by the authors of *Justice Delayed*.

Viewed in retrospect, the period since publication of *Justice Delayed* has been one of tremendous ferment and change in many American trial courts and, indeed, in some entire state court systems. In other courts, however, there seems to have been little change. Concepts such as time standards and caseflow management have made little, if any, impact in these places.

One of the central objectives of this research is to develop knowledge about the dynamics of the change process in courts—the extent to which practices, attitudes, and case processing times have changed in the past decade, and the reasons for the changes or lack of change. Our starting point for this inquiry is the quantitative data collected from court records.

B. Changes in Case Processing Times, 1976–1985

Because we have data on case processing times in prior years in the 18 courts participating in the project, it is possible to track the direction and extent of changes in disposition times that have taken place in these courts. Once we have a sense of the extent of the changes on a court-by-court basis, we can then explore reasons why some courts have become faster or slower, or have maintained a relatively constant pace over time.

The methodological difficulties of this undertaking are substantial. Four different sets of data on case processing times are involved:

- For 13 of the courts, our baseline data set consists of the samples of civil and criminal cases disposed of in 1976, collected by the research staff of the National Center's *Justice Delayed* project.

- For three courts—Providence, Dayton, and Detroit Recorder's Court—baseline data on criminal case processing times is available from a comprehensive study of delay reduction programs undertaken in those jurisdictions during the late 1970s, conducted by the American Judicature Society. The AJS study methodology was, however, different from the approach followed in *Justice Delayed* and in this study, thus making comparisons somewhat tricky. Additionally, since the AJS study focused only on criminal case processing, there is no baseline data set for civil cases in the Providence and Dayton courts. For Detroit Recorder's Court, we also have data collected on samples of 500 dispositions in 1975, 1976, and 1977, using the same methodology as the *Justice Delayed* study. These data were collected by NCSC staff in 1979.

- For the two courts in which there had been no prior research on case processing times—Jersey City and Wichita—we collected our baseline data from samples of approximately 500 civil and 500 criminal cases disposed of in 1979, the year just prior to the initiation of statewide delay reduction programs in New Jersey and Kansas. The sampling and data collection methodology was similar to that used in the *Justice Delayed* study.

- For all 18 courts, we collected data on samples of civil and criminal cases disposed of in the years 1983, 1984, and 1985. The sampling techniques and data collection procedures used in each court for this data set are virtually identical to those employed in these courts in the *Justice Delayed* study. Nevertheless, in some courts there have been changes in operational procedures and in the ways in which information is collected and stored which may affect the comparability of the samples.

Even with data collected using a similar methodology, there are problems of comparability across time. It is possible that sampling techniques applied uniformly in two different years could still result in the inclusion of different categories of cases in each year. For example, as footnote c in Table 5A indicates, the 1976 San Diego

Table 5A
CHANGES IN CIVIL CASE PROCESSING TIMES, 1976–1985

	Median Tort Disposition Time (in days)				Median Trial List Disposition Time (in days)			
	Base Year[a]	1983	1985	Change	Base Year	1983	1985	Change
Bronx, NY	*	*	*	*	980	718	772	−208
Jersey City, NJ	584[b]	425	394	−190	*	*	*	*
Wayne County, MI	788	721	648	−140	*	*	*	*
Minneapolis, MN	*	*	*	*	710	818	603	−107
Dayton, OH	*	345	279	*	*	*	*	*
Cleveland, OH	384	318	343	− 41	*	*	*	*
Newark, NJ	654	544	624	− 30	*	*	*	*
Boston, MA	811	701	782	− 29	*	*	*	*
Phoenix, AZ	308	317	292	− 16	416	561	505	+ 89
Miami, FL	331	408	325	− 6	*	*	*	*
Pittsburgh, PA	583	657	651	+ 68	727	601	694	− 33
Portland, OR	310	393	389	+ 79	*	*	*	*
New Orleans, LA	288	401	403	+115	357	494	560	+203
Wichita, KS	290[b]	492	411	+121	*	*	*	*
San Diego, CA	574[c]	*	719[c]	+145[c]	608	784	696	+ 88
Providence, RI	*	516	697	*	*	886	1,304	*
Oakland, CA	421	528	637	+216	569	697	838	+269

*Data unavailable or inapplicable
[a]Unless otherwise indicated, the base year is 1976. The data for 1976 are derived from Table 2.1 in *Justice Delayed* (pp. 10–11).
[b]Source: Sample of cases terminated in 1979.
[c]In the base year (1976), the median tort disposition time in San Diego included cases disposed of prior to the filing of an at-issue memorandum. In 1983–85, it included only cases in which an at-issue memo had been filed.

civil case sample included cases terminated prior to the filing of an at-issue memorandum, but the 1983–85 samples do not. Inclusion of cases terminated at an early stage (which was not possible in 1983–85 because of changes in the San Diego court's record-keeping system) will tend to produce a shorter median tort disposition time. Further, having only two or three years for comparison makes it difficult to separate true trends from non-recurring observations. One year may be a "fluke" year, when disposition patterns were influenced by factors unlikely to occur again.

Still, the data base derived from these four sets of case records allows us to make a start on longitudinal analysis of case processing times and efforts to reduce delay in the participating courts. This section provides a brief overview of changes that have taken place in the pace of civil and criminal litigation between our baseline year (1976 in most of the courts) and 1985.

On the civil side, Table 5A shows that seven of the courts reduced their median tort disposition times by periods ranging from a few days to more than six months. Additionally, both of the courts in which measurement of tort disposition time is not feasible—Bronx County and Minneapolis—recorded very substantial decreases in their trial list disposition times. In six courts, however, the trend was in the opposite direction, with increases in median tort disposition time of two to seven months.

As Tables 5B and 5C illustrate, the trends with respect to criminal case processing time are also mixed. Of perhaps the greatest significance, three courts in which delays had been particularly egregious in the baseline years—Jersey City, the Bronx, and Providence—show very striking improvements in both total felony case disposition times and upper court case processing times. In all three courts, substantial reductions in case processing times had been made by 1983. At least through 1985, these courts were able to maintain (and improve upon) the faster pace; they did not immediately slide back into their old ways. Two other courts (Phoenix and Dayton) were already handling their felony cases relatively speedily in the baseline year, but were markedly faster in 1985.

At the other end of the spectrum, there are several courts in which felony case processing has become considerably slower. Boston, which in the *Justice Delayed* study was characterized (along with the Bronx) as "pathologically delayed," was even slower in 1985. At 332 days, its median upper court time is 51 days longer than in 1976, and is more than twice as long as the median time for any other court in the study. In Newark, greatly lengthened pre-

Table 5B
CHANGES IN TOTAL FELONY CASE DISPOSITION TIMES, 1976–1985

	Median Total Disposition Time (in days)				Percentage of Cases Over 180 Days			
	Base Year[a]	1983	1985	Change	Base Year	1983	1985	Change
Jersey City, NJ	510[b]	213	163	− 347	94%	53%	43%	− 51%
Bronx, NY	343	218	121	− 222	75%	56%	37%	− 38%
Phoenix, AZ	114	64	78	− 36	14%	11%	12%	− 2%
Oakland, CA	116	81	87	− 29	29%	29%	12%	− 17%
Portland, OR	67	62	55	− 12	3%	3%	9%	+ 6%
San Diego, CA	71	89	77	+ 6	6%	12%	14%	+ 8%
New Orleans, LA	67	73	83	+ 16	16%	16%	20%	+ 4%
Miami, FL	106	108	123	+ 17	22%	27%	35%	+ 13%
Cleveland, OH	103	123	121	+ 18	24%	29%	29%	+ 5%
Wichita, KS	88[b]	118	115	+ 27	*	17%	26%	*
Minneapolis, MN	60	84	88	+ 28	*	13%	22%	*
Pittsburgh, PA	103	135	149	+ 46	9%	27%	50%	+ 41%
Wayne County, MI	64	96	133	+ 69	10%	22%	39%	+ 29%
Newark, NJ	209	253	300	+ 91	57%	65%	74%	+ 17%

*Data unavailable or inapplicable.
[a]Unless otherwise indicated, the base year is 1976. The data for 1976 are derived from Tables 2.4 and 2.6 in *Justice Delayed* (pp. 14–18).
[b]Source: Sample of cases terminated in 1979.

Table 5C
CHANGES IN UPPER COURT FELONY CASE PROCESSING TIMES, 1976–1985

	Median Upper Court Disposition Time				Third Quartile Upper Court Disposition Time			
	Base Year[a]	1983	1985	Change	Base Year[a]	1983	1985	Change
Jersey City, NJ	376[b]	121	115	− 255	639[b]	371	234	− 405
Providence, RI	277[c]	*	63	− 214	573[c]	*	175	− 398
Bronx, NY	328	230	152	− 176	499	420	277	− 222
Phoenix, AZ	98	44	58	− 40	134	82	105	− 29
Dayton, OH	69[c]	64	47	− 22	104[c]	119	85	− 19
Detroit Rec Ct, MI	40[c]	43	31	− 9	170[c]	117	141	− 29
New Orleans, LA	50	49	48	− 2	115	98	105	− 10
Oakland, CA	58	96	57	− 1	116	244	144	+ 28
San Diego, CA	45	43	49	+ 6	64	61	72	+ 8
Portland, OR	51	52	56	+ 4	81	90	108	+ 27
Cleveland, OH	71	88	90	+ 19	150	168	185	+ 35
Newark, NJ	99	146	124	+ 25	179	356	294	+ 115
Miami, FL	81	93	108	+ 27	148	207	257	+ 109
Minneapolis, MN	60	84	88	+ 28	139	132	162	+ 23
Wayne County, MI	33	49	64	+ 31	70	92	158	+ 88
Wichita, KS	76[b]	108	115	+ 39	136[b]	140	156	+ 20
Boston, MA	281	307	332	+ 51	487	478	665	+ 178
Pittsburgh, PA	58	90	120	+ 62	91	161	165	+ 74

*Data unavailable or inapplicable.

[a]Unless otherwise indicated, the base year is 1976. The data for 1976 are derived from Tables 2.4 and 2.6 in *Justice Delayed* (pp. 14–18).

[b]Sample of cases terminated in 1979.

[c]Source: David W. Neubauer et al., *Managing the Pace of Justice* (Washington, D.C.: National Institute of Justice, 1981). For these three courts, the baseline data are derived from a sample of cases *filed* prior to the start of a delay reduction program. In Detroit Recorder's Court, the base period is April–October 1976; in Providence it is all of 1976; and in Dayton it is July 1977–October 1978.

indictment periods have resulted in increasing the median total felony case disposition time from 209 to 300 days.

What accounts for these changes? Why are some courts apparently able to reduce delays significantly, while others see their case processing times become markedly longer? How are some courts able to sustain a relatively swift pace of litigation over time and prevent delay from developing?

C. Assessing the Effects of Changes in Workloads and Judicial Resources

The quantitative data from court records provide indications of the duration and extent of change in case processing times in specific courts, but they tell us nothing about the reasons for the changes. It is possible that changes in case processing time are at least in part the result of changes in the workload and/or resources of a court. Following the logic of the "old" conventional wisdom, it might be hypothesized, for example, that an increase in caseloads, if not accompanied by a proportionate increase in judges, would lead to slower case processing times. This same logic would suggest that, if judge-power increased and caseloads remained constant, delays would be reduced.

Assessing the extent to which caseloads and judicial resources have changed over time is a hazardous undertaking, one that in practice is even more difficult than measuring changes in case processing times.[5] At least with respect to criminal case processing, however, we have some data that we believe are sufficiently reliable to enable us to make comparisons of workloads and judicial resources, as well as of case processing times, over time and across the courts that have been involved in both the *Justice Delayed* study and this research.[6]

As Table 5D shows, felony filings increased from 1976 to 1985 in all but two of the 11 courts for which we have data from both years. However, because the number of judges assigned to handle criminal cases also increased in virtually every court, the number of filings per judge was higher in only five of these courts. Contrary to what might be expected, three of the five felony courts in which per-judge case volume increased actually recorded *faster* case processing times in 1985 than in 1976. In two of these courts, the changes are especially dramatic. In the Bronx, for example, filings per judge were 54% higher in 1985 than in 1976, but median upper court time was down to 152 days compared to 328 days in 1976. In

Table 5D
CHANGES IN FELONY FILINGS AND CASE PROCESSING TIMES, 1976–1985

Court	Total Felony Filings			Felony Filings per Judge			Median Upper Court Time (in Days)		
	1976[a]	1985	Change	1976[a]	1985	Change	1976[a]	1985	Change
Bronx, NY	3,518	6,700	+90%	121	186	+54%	328	152	−176
Phoenix, AZ	5,218	9,792	+88%	522	725	+39%	98	58	− 40
San Diego, CA	4,254	7,422	+74%	473	619	+31%	45	49	+ 4
Oakland, CA	2,648	4,475	+69%	265	373	+41%	58	57	− 1
New Orleans, LA	2,746	4,385	+60%	275	274	-0-	50	48	− 2
Portland, OR	3,213	4,392	+37%	*	*	*	51	56	+ 5
Cleveland, OH	6,632	9,009	+36%	*	*	*	71	90	+ 19
Minneapolis, MN	2,305	3,004	+30%	384	376	− 2%	60	88	+ 28
Wayne Co., MI	4,028	4,165	+ 3%	575	521	− 9%	33	64	+ 31
Newark, NJ	7,083	6,968	− 2%	443	367	−17%	99	124	+ 25
Boston, MA	1,965	1,211	−38%	218	151	−31%	281	332	+ 51

[a]Source: Derived from data in *Justice Delayed*, Appendix C, pp. 98–101.

Phoenix, felony filings per judge were up by 39%, but median upper court time was less than half of what it had been a decade earlier. At the other end of the scale, the court that had the most significant reduction in the volume of new filings, Boston, showed even slower case processing times in 1985 than in 1976. Indeed, all of the courts in which the volume of filings decreased showed slower median times in 1985 than in 1976.

Of course, raw filings present only a partial picture of workload. When cases pending at the start of the year are added to the year's filings, it is possible to get a somewhat more complete sense of the overall workload of a court. Table 5E, which presents data on per-judge workloads in 1976 and 1985, for the five courts for which it is possible to do this, shows that in one of them (Oakland), upper court time was reduced slightly despite a large increase in workload. In another (Bronx County), there was a 9% increase in workload but a very significant drop in case processing times. By contrast, in the one court where the workload was much less in 1985 than it had been in 1976 (Boston), case processing times were even longer.

The data in Tables 5D and 5E, although very rough, provide further evidence that problems of trial court delay cannot be cured simply by adding more judges. Clearly, lower per-judge workloads do not automatically result in speedier dispositions, nor does an increase in workload necessarily lead to slower disposition times. The relationship between workloads and case processing times appears, rather, to be a very complex one in which a number of other factors—including changes in the court's approach to managing its caseload—are involved.

An analysis of changes in case processing time that is based essentially on two "snapshots," taken nine years apart, cannot take account of short term changes in workloads and resources that may affect the case processing times for either of the two years for which data are available. Equally important, an analysis based solely upon limited quantitative data cannot take account of specific policies, procedures, or personalities that may affect case processing times in a court. In any single situation, there are a number of possible explanations for why case processing times have become longer, or shorter, or have remained relatively unchanged. In seeking to develop a more complete understanding of the dynamics underlying changes in case processing over time in different courts, it is helpful to take a first hand look at how the courts actually function and how (if at all) they have addressed problems of delay.

Table 5E
CHANGES IN FELONY CASE WORKLOADS AND CASE PROCESSING TIMES
1976–1985

Court	Felony Case Workloads per Judge			Median Upper Court Time (in Days)		
	1976[a]	1985	Change	1976[a]	1985	(Change)
Oakland, CA	313	435	+39%	58	57	− 1
Bronx, NY	223	243	+ 9%	328	152	−176
Minneapolis, MN	437	476	+ 9%	60	88	+ 28
Newark, NJ	710	738	+ 4%	99	124	+ 25
Boston, MA	733	345	−53%	281	332	+ 51

[a]Source: Derived from data in *Justice Delayed*, Appendix C, pp. 98–101

D. The Case Studies: An Overview

The courts included in the study fall across a wide spectrum with respect to the scope and intensity of efforts to reduce or prevent delay. At one end of the spectrum are courts that have undertaken comprehensive caseflow management programs, aimed at achieving specific case processing time goals. At the other end, there are courts that have not addressed the problem at all. In between, there are a number of courts that made some efforts to improve case processing but (at least during the 1978–85 period) did not really commit themselves to a high priority program aimed at achieving concrete measurable goals.

As a practical matter, it has simply not been possible to obtain the level of detailed first hand knowledge about programmatic initiatives and day-to-day operation that would enable us to explain all of the changes in all of the courts. We have, however, made site visits to half of the courts participating in the study, to observe court proceedings and administrative procedures and to interview judges, attorneys, and members of the court staff. The number and duration of the visits varied, as did the topics covered in the interviews.[7] In six of the jurisdictions, we concentrated particularly on learning about delay reduction (or delay prevention) programs that have been undertaken in recent years.

These programs have varied considerably in scope and in the degree of success they have achieved. Most of them have also been the subject of some prior examination, which provides a basis for starting our own analysis. In the next three chapters, we draw on information acquired through the site visits to describe approaches that have been tried in specific jurisdictions, focusing on the impetus and sources of the initiatives, the principal techniques that have been employed, and the results to date. We begin in Chapter 6 by examining innovative caseflow management programs undertaken in Phoenix (Civil Division) and Dayton, where delay was not a serious problem but where court leaders nevertheless felt a need to improve the court's management capabilities in order to prevent delays from developing. Chapter 7 describes the program initiatives in four trial courts—Phoenix (Criminal Division), Detroit Recorder's Court, Jersey City, and Wayne County—where delays clearly were a problem. Chapter 8 looks at state-level delay reduction programs in Ohio, Kansas, and New Jersey, focusing particularly on the linkages between state initiatives and local level implementation in courts in Dayton, Wichita, Jersey City, and Newark.

ENDNOTES–Chapter 5

1. *Justice Delayed*, p. 83.

2. *Ibid.*, pp. 65–72, 83–84.

3. *Ibid.*, pp. 72, 84.

4. For a detailed review of most of these efforts, see Larry L. Sipes, "Reducing Delay in State Courts—A March Against Folly," *Rutgers Law Review*, Vol. 37 (Winter 1985), pp. 299, 300–11.

5. In any single court, it is possible that over a period of several years there will be changes in court procedures and in the way that statistics are collected and reported. For example, only 12 of the 21 courts involved in the *Justice Delayed* study could provide data on pending felony caseloads as of January 1, 1976. In our current study, 15 of the 18 courts were able to provide such data for January 1, 1985. Even if there are no such changes in a court's statistical procedures, it is likely that even similarly worded questions (about workloads and resources, for example) will be interpreted and answered differently at different times. Sources available to a researcher in one year are often unavailable for an earlier or later year. The problems are compounded, of course, when 18 different courts are involved.

6. Although data on civil filings and the number of judges handling civil cases exist for most of the courts for both 1976 and 1985, it is much more difficult to construct a meaningful table showing comparisons over time and across courts for civil litigation than for felony case processing. Our own examination of the data from these years makes it clear that, even within the same courts, data on civil filings are often non-comparable because of changes in the court's civil case jurisdiction or because of changes in how cases are counted. Across courts, the definitions of what constitutes a civil case and what constitutes a "filing" vary widely (see Chapter 2, supra). Some courts count every type of action filed with the court as a civil filing, while others focus only on cases that reach a trial readiness stage and count only certificates of readiness or at-issue memos. It is clearly possible to develop procedures for making meaningful comparisons, but to do so will require a more extensive data base than is available from this study.

7. In six of the trial courts, interviews and observations during the site visits dealt with both civil and criminal case processing, which in five of the six were handled by separate divisions of the general jurisdiction trial courts. The one "mixed calendar" court was the Montgomery County Court of Common Pleas in Dayton, Ohio. The five courts with separate civil and criminal divisions were Maricopa County Superior Court (Phoenix, Arizona), Alameda County Superior Court (Oakland, California), Wayne County Circuit Court (Detroit, Michigan), Hudson County Superior Court (Jersey City, New Jersey), and the Sedgwick County (18th Judicial District) District Court (Wichita, Kansas). In the Essex County Superior Court (Newark, New Jersey), which also has separate civil and criminal divisions, our focus

was exclusively on criminal case processing. The eighth court, Detroit Recorder's Court (Detroit, Michigan) handles only criminal cases. For information on the ninth "case study" court—Bronx County Supreme Court (Bronx, New York)—we have relied on information obtained in contemporaneous studies of felony case processing in New York City during 1983–85. See Sally T. Hillsman et al., *The New York City Speedy Disposition Program* (New York: Vera Institute of Justice, 1986); Thomas W. Church and Milton Heumann, *Monetary Incentives and Policy Reform in the Criminal Courts* (Final Report submitted to the National Institute of Justice; draft, 1987). Interviews were also conducted with present or former state-level judicial leaders in the states of Ohio, Kansas, New Jersey, and New York.

Chapter 6
PREVENTING DELAYS: CASEFLOW MANAGEMENT IN CONSISTENTLY FAST COURTS

General jurisdiction trial courts in the American states are for the most part local, county-based institutions. They function in a structural framework established by state constitutions and statutes, but the focus of their activity is the county courthouse and most of the participants in the court process are also based in the county.[1] In their day-to-day operations they are remarkably autonomous, even in states where all or most of their funding comes from the state level. Within the same state, it is common to have courts with similar caseloads pursuing very different approaches to issues of caseflow management and having widely varying paces of litigation.

The great diversity in American courts provides a fertile ground for innovation, and much of our current knowledge about ways to address problems of delay has emerged from initiatives undertaken in local trial courts. This chapter examines the experiences of two well-functioning urban trial courts—one located in Dayton, Ohio, the other in Phoenix, Arizona—that decided to undertake experimental caseflow management programs because they felt that such programs could produce a better quality of justice. Trial court delay was simply not a problem in Dayton when that court began the experiments described in this chapter; both its civil and criminal case processing times were already very expeditious compared to most urban courts. In Phoenix, civil case processing times were relatively speedy by comparison to other courts in the *Justice Delayed* study, but the court's leaders (and some bar leaders too) were concerned about indications of problems on the horizon.

The Dayton court is one of three in this study (Cleveland and Portland are the others) in which judges handle "mixed" dockets—

both criminal and civil cases. Its experience is particularly relevant for courts of all sizes that follow this approach. The Phoenix court, which is much larger, has separate civil and criminal divisions. On the civil side, which is the focus of attention in this chapter, its procedures prior to the start of its experimental program in 1979 were similar to those in many other courts. It operated with a certificate of readiness system under which the court had historically not become involved in the litigation process until the certificate of readiness was filed.

In the course of planning and implementing the programs described in this chapter, judges and staff of both courts became substantially more involved in caseflow management than they had been previously. As we shall see, the results have been positive. Both the processes of program implementation and the actual programs now in place in these courts provide models for courts interested in strengthening their caseflow management.

A. Dayton: Criminal and Civil Case Management Programs

The Montgomery County Court of Common Pleas, in Dayton, Ohio, is one of the smaller courts participating in this study. It has thirteen judges in all, nine of whom sit in the court's General Division where each is responsible for a docket that includes both civil cases and felony-charge criminal cases.[2]

Montgomery County, with a population of 571,000, has a mix of urban and suburban communities. Dayton, the county seat and the largest municipality in the county, has a reputation as a model good government city. The Common Pleas Court fits this image—it is efficient, well-run, and open to innovation. In initiating a criminal case delay reduction program in November 1978, the court was not responding to a perceived problem of delay nearly so much as it was experimenting with a new and promising management approach that held the prospect of improving productivity and preventing the development of delays.

Like other trial courts in Ohio, the court in Dayton functions within a legal framework that changed dramatically in the late 1960s and early 1970s. The basic structure of the present Ohio court system was established in 1968 when voters approved the Modern Courts Amendment, a major revision of Article VI (the Judicial Article) of the Constitution. The Amendment gave the Ohio Supreme Court general superintending authority over all courts in the state and vested it with broad rule-making authority. In 1971, the Supreme Court exercised that authority by promulgating the Ohio Rules of Superintendence, which created a new administrative system designed to address problems of backlogs, delays, and judicial inefficiency. The Rules created an infrastructure of presiding and administrative judges in multijudge common pleas courts, required all common pleas courts to use the individual assignment (individual calendar) system, and set up a monthly reporting system that forced each trial judge to focus on the number and age of his pending cases. The Rules also placed a six month limit on the time from arraignment to trial in criminal cases and established guidelines, reinforced by reporting requirements, designed to limit the granting of continuances.[3]

The Rules of Superintendence, particularly the reporting requirements, were unpopular among some Ohio judges from the outset, but they had a relatively modest impact in Dayton. The Montgomery County Court of Common Pleas had adopted the individual calendar system in 1968 (and thus did not have to go through a difficult change-over of calendaring systems); the dockets of the individual judges were already in pretty good shape; and there was a well-established tradition of concern about effective management of the court's business. The enactment of a criminal Speedy Trial Act by the Ohio Legislature, in 1973, may have had a greater impact. Under the Speedy Trial Act, which is designed to protect the defendant's constitutional right to a speedy trial, defendants have a right to be brought to trial within 90 days after arrest or service of a summons if they are in custody or within 270 days if they are on bail.

Although the time limits in the Ohio Speedy Trial Act are subject to numerous exceptions, the statute provides strong incentives to handle criminal cases expeditiously. Both prosecutors and judges would be embarassed by the dismissal of charges which could not be re-filed because a case had "slipped through the cracks" and a defendant invoked the statute. While the time frames in the Speedy Trial Act are different from those in the Rules of Superintendence, the practical effects were complementary. The Act compelled the prosecutors as well as the judges to become conscious of the status of the docket and the passage of time in criminal cases.

The Criminal Case Management Plan

In Montgomery County, the Speedy Trial Act was felt by the judges to have created strong pressures for the rapid handling of felony cases, especially cases involving jailed defendants. After it became effective in 1974, there was some feeling among the judges in the court's General Division that they were having to place too much emphasis on their criminal dockets, to the detriment of their civil cases. One impetus for the court's decision to undertake a criminal case delay reduction program in 1978 was a sense that improved management of the criminal caseload would also allow judges to devote more time and attention to their civil caseloads. Another factor was a concern about the economic situation in Montgomery County. Presiding Judge Carl Kessler felt that an economic pinch in Montgomery County could lead to budget problems for the court, and was interested in management innovations that could produce cost savings.

In late 1977, the Dayton court was approached by the Whittier Justice Institute with an invitation to participate in a multijurisdictional project involving felony case processing. The Whittier team, led by Dean Ernest Friesen, had received funding from the federal Law Enforcement Assistance Administration (LEAA) for the first phase of a national study experimenting with innovative case management and delay reduction techniques. The prospect of being involved in such a project was intriguing enough that the court agreed to participate, even though most of the judges felt that delay was not a significant problem in Montgomery County.

Phase I of the project (1977–78) involved documenting the structure and process for dealing with felony cases in Dayton and three other metropolitan areas (Providence, Miami, and Houston) and comparing them with the system operating in Multnomah County (Portland), Oregon, which had attained national recognition for its efficient handling of criminal cases. Using an interactive process in which issues that were identified in the four comparison sites were explored through further study in Multnomah County, the Whittier team sought to develop a model of felony case processing that could be applied to help reduce delay in a broad range of courts handling criminal cases. Phase II of the project would involve actual implementation of the model.

The Whittier model, as it evolved in 1977 and 1978, included an emphasis on communications and problem-solving by key criminal justice policymakers, strong leadership within the court, use of critical events in the arrest-to-disposition process as control points, establishment of time frames and specific procedures for completion of each stage of the process, and—of particular importance—collection and use of management information.[4] Initial planning for the

Dayton program took place early in 1978, as members of the Whittier team worked with judges and court staff to collect data on the felony case processing system in Montgomery County. They identified the events in the process from arrest to disposition, measured the time intervals, tracked the paperflow, and examined the existing process in light of the Whittier model. The information and analysis were presented both to the judges of the court and to a newly formed Criminal Justice Coordinating Committee that Presiding Judge Kessler organized and chaired.

After several months of consideration, and apparently despite the fact that many practitioners saw no real need for a highly structured felony case management program, a plan based on the Whittier model was approved both by the coordinating committee and the judges of the common pleas court. As implemented beginning November 1, 1978, the plan called for a maximum period of ten weeks from arrest to disposition, including no more than six weeks from indictment to disposition. Specific features included rapid case screening by the prosecutor's office, mandatory (and reciprocal) early discovery, centralized arraignments in the common pleas court, and structured plea negotiations between prosecutors and defense lawyers. The plan also provided for establishment of a plea cut-off date at a scheduling conference held before the judge to whom the case was assigned, an overall tightening up of the time intervals between events in the process, and a strong emphasis on making the trial date (set at the scheduling conference) a firm one.[5]

Implementation of the plan required development of new scheduling procedures (with substantially increased duties for the assignment commissioner's office), design of new forms to exchange information between the central staff and the judges' chambers, collection of statistical data for monitoring purposes, and considerable time for staff training. The open communications system already in place, including regular meetings of the judges as a group and periodic meetings of the Criminal Justice Coordinating Committee, continued to operate and provided opportunities to discuss problems and consider modifications in the plan.

By and large, the implementation process proceeded smoothly. In their evaluation of the program, which included interviews with practitioners in Dayton during an 18-month period following its start-up, American Judicature Society researchers found general agreement that the plan was beneficial to the court, although there were some problems and criticisms. The problems centered around the arrangements for early disclosure, plea negotiations, and trial scheduling. They are worth some attention because they are ones that can be anticipated in any felony court that might consider adopting an approach like Dayton's.

First, some of the assistant prosecutors initially resisted the innovations regarding discovery. And, even where assistant prosecutors sought to comply in good faith with requirements for disclosure, there were some cases in which supplemental reports—lab tests or additional witness statements—could not be made available until the pretrial conference. The prosecutors, for their part, complained that defense attorneys were not providing reciprocal discovery. There was general agreement, however, that the arrangements for early discovery had reduced the number of preliminary hearings (which had often been used as a mechanism to obtain discovery), had reduced the number of motions for discovery, and had provided attorneys with essential information at an earlier stage in the process. The resistance to disclosure by a few of the prosecutors ultimately became a subject of discussion at a meeting of the Criminal Justice Coordinating Committee. With the chips down, the prosecutor strongly backed the open disclosure policy, both at the CJCC meeting and within his office.

A second problem area was the pretrial conference, which was criticized for failing to produce meaningful negotiations in many cases. This criticism seemed to have two main roots: (1) delays in the disclosure process which, when they occurred, meant that neither the prosecutor nor the defense attorney had an opportunity to fully evaluate the case prior to the time of the pretrial conference and thus could not engage in realistic negotiations at the conference; and (2) inexperienced defense attorneys who, even though they might have received full disclosure, did not fully understand the significance of the information they had or were simply not able to negotiate effectively. Related to this, there were indications that the scheduling conference, which was supposed to serve as a plea cut-off point, was manipulated in a variety of ways. For example, judges would commonly continue the conference for one or two weeks to allow further negotiations. Sometimes judges would allow two or three continuances, and some of them also became involved (as they had before the implementation of the plan) in discussions about possible pleas. Perhaps more seriously from the standpoint of the management plan, some judges would accept a plea to a reduced charge after the scheduling conference, even on the date set for trial. Nevertheless, the court's statistics indicated that pleas on the day of trial had been reduced sharply under the new system.

Third, most practitioners felt that the time frame contemplated by the plan was adequate for most cases, but was too fast for the 25–30% of felony cases that involved very serious charges, multiple witnesses, or other complicating factors. Finally, from the court's own staff, there was a sense that planning and decisionmaking regarding the plan was confined to the top-level administrators, without sufficient input from the clerks, bailiffs, and other staff personnel whose day-to-day work was essential to (and would be significantly affected by) the program.

Despite the problems and criticisms, the program was basically well received by practitioners in Montgomery County. Quantitative data from the AJS evaluation indicated that it had led to significant decreases in case processing times on all key measures (Table 6A). The AJS researchers summarized the impact of the criminal case management program, over its first 18 months, as follows:

> "The Common Pleas Court was getting cases sooner, prosecution and defense were being forced to deal with individual cases sooner and had relevant case materials sooner, the court was being managed more efficiently, judges had more time for their civil cases, and cases were being resolved sooner. Some judges have deviated somewhat from the plan by participating in pretrials or by accepting late pleas to reduced charges, but virtually all of them noted improvements in setting a real trial docket and in knowing more about the size and nature of their caseloads."[6]

During the 1980s, the court has continued to follow the same basic approach to managing its criminal caseload. In doing so, however, it has worked in cooperation with the prosecutor and defense

Table 6A
CRIMINAL CASE PROCESSING TIME IN DAYTON, 1977–1979

	Pre-Innovation*	Post-Innovation*
Median	69 days	43 days
75th Percentile	104 days	87 days
90th Percentile	167 days	153 days

*Pre-innovation cases are those filed between July 1977 and October 1978. Post-innovation cases are those filed between November 1978 and June 1979. The times shown are from the date of the filing of an indictment or information to the date of disposition by plea, verdict, or dismissal. Source: David W. Neubauer et al., *Managing the Pace of Justice: An Evaluation of LEAA's Court Delay-Reduction Programs* (Washington, D.C.: National Institute of Justice, 1981), p. 225.

bar to modify the system, taking account of the early criticisms. The interrelated problems of providing for early discovery and structuring a meaningful process aimed at expeditious resolution of cases have been addressed in several ways. First, the prosecutor, recognizing the importance of early case preparation for effective prosecution, has reorganized his staff so that assistant prosecutors are assigned to cases prior to the preliminary hearing and in most instances are responsible for all subsequent proceedings. The assistant prosecutors therefore have an incentive to pull their cases together quickly, and defense lawyers know who they will be dealing with throughout the duration of the case.

Second, the court has worked with the Montgomery County Bar Association and the University of Dayton Law School to present seminars on the practice of criminal law that include discussion of the operation of the case management system. Young lawyers going to work with the prosecutor or the public defender, or into practice on their own, thus became familiar at an early point in their careers with a system in which early reciprocal discovery and speedy case processing are the norm.

Third, for the more complicated cases and others in which there has been a foul-up in the discovery process or a lack of meaningful discussion between prosecution and defense, the judges have been flexible in handling the scheduling conferences. The scheduling conference is held at an early enough point—two weeks after arraignment on the indictment—that the judge can use it as an opportunity to resolve discovery problems that have arisen, set hearings on motions that may affect the course of plea discussions (e.g., motions to suppress key items of evidence), and allow a short continuance (a week or two is common) to enable further discussions about dispositions.

There is broad agreement that the more complicated cases often require additional time, but even in these cases the pace is brisk. Motions are expected to be filed prior to the scheduling conference, and hearings on motions are typically held within three weeks following that conference. The judge's decision on a motion is often made on the date of the motion hearing and is rarely reserved for more than a week following the hearing. Once motions are decided, the case is generally set for a status conference at which, if no plea agreement is reached by then, a date will be set for trial.

Continuances on the date of trial still happen but are relatively rare, perhaps in part because the court has implemented an ongoing system of monitoring continuances requested by each lawyer and granted by each judge. The data on continuances are collected each month by the assignment commissioner's office and distributed to the judges along with the caseload statistics required by the Ohio Rules of Superintendence.

Guiding the institutionalization process have been two strong leaders, Presiding Judge Carl Kessler and Trial Court Administrator Judith Cramer. Ms. Cramer, who assumed her position in February 1980, was especially responsive to the criticism that the original plan had been too much a product of decisions by top-level policymakers, without sufficient participation by the court staff. Beginning early in 1980 she took a series of steps designed to involve the administrative staff more completely in the work of the court. In May 1980, for example, she organized committees of the clerks and bailiffs to review the plan's operation and help design new forms. The process of staff involvement has continued with twice-monthly meetings of work groups and regular training sessions including an annual two-day conference for the judges and the entire staff of the court.

The Civil Case Management Program

In 1983, after more than four years of experience with the criminal case management program, the judges in the Dayton court decided to take a similar management approach to handling civil cases. Presiding Judge Kessler appointed a three-judge committee to look into the development of a court-wide civil case management plan.

There seems to have been two main spurs to the appointment of the committee and development of the plan. First, the experience under the criminal case management plan had been a positive one. The judges clearly felt more in control of their caseloads. Although each judge has some distinctive ways of dealing with his calendar from the scheduling conference forward, all recognized the value of having a process that was essentially the same (including reliance on centralized scheduling for the early stages of cases and extensive use of standardized orders and other forms) for all of the general division judges. A good many problems of communication and coordination had been resolved in the course of implementing the criminal system, and lessons from that experience could be applied in developing a program for the civil cases. Second, with all of the general division judges having developed their own distinctive systems for managing their civil dockets, there were pressures from the bar for greater uniformity in judges' civil case management practices. There was also some pressure for greater uniformity from within the court itself, which was in the process of developing a new automated management information system. Both the staff and the judges involved in the automation effort recognized that greater commonality in practice would both simplify the development of the new information system and enable it to be more useful to all of the judges.

At the time the civil case management program was being developed, no one in the court felt that there were serious and pervasive problems of delay. It was recognized, however, that there were some civil cases that took longer than they should, and one objective of the program was to reduce unnecessary mechanical and procedural delays. In developing the program, the judges consulted with the Montgomery County Bar Association, but the program that emerged was one designed primarily by the judges.

The notion of "tolerable delays"—i.e. the period of time reasonably necessary to deal with a particular case—played an important role in the development of the program.[7] The judges' committee reviewed the court's experience in dealing with different types of civil cases, and came up with a recommended set of maximum time frames, as follows:

Habeas corpus	60 days
Mortgage foreclosure	120 days
Administrative appeals	120 days
Worker's compensation	180 days
Appropriation	180 days
Injunction	150 days
Personal injury	270 days
Medical malpractice	360 days
All others	150 days

The differentiation in time frames reflected the judges' views of the complexity of the litigation process in each type of case. In personal injury and medical malpractice cases, for example, discovery must be completed after the case has been filed, and the medical malpractice cases have the added feature of mandatory arbitration after completion of discovery. In the other types of cases, discovery was rarely an issue; both sides already had whatever evidence they would use if the case went to trial and the issues were generally pretty clear-cut. The report of the judges' committee recognized that "there may be exceptions due to the peculiarities of a given case," but took the position that the recommended limits were reasonable for the period from filing to termination. All of the time limits were considerably shorter than the times contemplated by the Ohio Rules of Superintendence.

The guiding principles for the civil case management plan are the same as for the criminal plan: early and continuous control by the court. Once a complaint is filed and a case thus commenced, the court assumes responsibility for ensuring that it—along with all the other cases before the court—is brought to a conclusion in an efficient fashion. The system is one that has been designed to take advantage of the capabilities for information retrieval and case monitoring provided by modern technology. Although the specific techniques used by the judges vary somewhat, all of the judges routinely look at every civil case file at some point between 45 and 75 days after the complaint is filed, and they all hold a scheduling conference with the lawyers (either at the courthouse or via telephone) to arrange schedules for completion of discovery and set a tentative trial date. The judges utilize their staff (bailiff, secretary, and part-time student law clerk) to help monitor caseload status, using the court's automated civil case information system. These staff members will also maintain contact with the lawyers as a scheduled trial date approaches.

The court as a whole uses several techniques to help manage its caseload. First, it makes provision for non-binding arbitration in two types of cases. One category is fairly broad—any case in which the amount of controversy is less than $15,000 ($25,000 as of 1987) can be referred by the judge to a panel of three volunteer attorneys. The referral will ordinarily take place at the time of the pretrial scheduling conference (two to three months after initial filing), and usually leads to a resolution of uncomplicated cases within about two months. The second category consists of medical malpractice cases, all of which go to arbitration before a three-member panel consisting of one salaried arbitrator employed by the court plus two other persons, one designated by each party. Both programs help ease the caseload pressure on the court, although there is a sense that many of the medical malpractice cases end up back in the court because one party is dissatisfied with the arbitration ruling.

A second device employed by the court to help handle its caseload expeditiously is the use of visiting judges, drawn from a pool of retired judges and judges from low volume courts in less populous nearby counties. The visiting judges are available "in the bullpen," to help with last-minute calendar adjustments on a day-to-day basis. Many courts have some sort of "reserve judges" system, but the unique feature of the Dayton system is the way that access to the visiting judge's assistance is rotated among the general division judges. Each week, a different judge has priority for the visiting judge's services. The court's administrative staff makes arrangements for the visiting judge well in advance, and each of the nine regularly sitting judges knows that he will have a "priority week" every nine weeks. The judge's trial calendar can be overset more than usual for that week, since the visiting judge will be available to handle a trial or two if more than one case scheduled for trial does not result in a settlement. The scheme helps to ensure that the court's promise of a firm trial date can be kept and provides something of a safety-valve for caseload pressure.

Third, to help ensure that the court can meet its commitment to provide a firm trial date, the judges themselves serve as "back-ups" to each other. If one judge has two cases in which the lawyers are ready to go to trial, it is almost always possible to find another sitting judge to take one of the trials if a visiting judge cannot do so. The court makes it clear that it has the capacity to hold trials when they are scheduled and that continuances will not be granted lightly. By doing so, it encourages the lawyers to prepare their cases in a timely fashion—a process that often leads to settlement as the lawyers contemplate the alternative of an "all-or-nothing" trial.

Fourth, the court regularly collects data on key indicators of case processing effectiveness: size and age of pending caseloads, age of cases at disposition, and continuances requested and granted. The pending caseload information is regarded as especially important; as a rule of thumb, the court administrator and presiding judge regard a caseload of over 450 for a judge as an indication of developing problems. The informaton is *used*. It is discussed by the court administrator and presiding judge, is distributed to all the judges, is a topic of discussion at their regular meetings, and provides a starting point for inquiry into problems as they appear on the horizon.

Quantitative data in Table 6B indicate that the court's caseflow management programs have been highly effective. Interestingly, implementation of the civil case management plan in 1984 and 1985 seems to have helped the court in dealing with its criminal docket. Felony case processing times, which had slipped back in the 1978–83 period, are as speedy in 1985 as the American Judicature Society found them to be in the "post-innovation" period in 1978, and the Dayton court is at or very near the top of our rankings of 18 felony courts on every dimension. On the civil side, too, it is clearly one of the speediest courts in our study. A comparison of data on 1983 and 1985 dispositions indicates that adoption of the civil case management plan in the fall of 1983 has made a difference. The court is even faster in 1985 than it was in 1983, particularly in handling its tort cases.

Table 6B
CASE PROCESSING TIMES IN DAYTON, 1978–1985

Felony Cases

| | Pre-Innovation | Post-Innovation | | |
	1977–'78	1978	1983	1985
Total time, arrest to disposition (in days)				
Median	—	—	88	61
75th Percentile	—	—	151	99
90th Percentile	—	—	226	190
Upper Court Disposition Time (in days)				
Median	69	43	64	47
75th Percentile	104	87	169	87
90th Percentile	167	153	206	177

Civil Cases

	Pre-Innovation 1983	Post-Innovation 1985
Tort Disposition Times		
Median	345	279
75th Percentile	504	445
90th Percentile	795	744
General Civil Docket Disposition Times		
Median	178	178
75th Percentile	382	357
90th Percentile	636	628

At least equally important, there is a sense in the court—among the judges and staff—that this is a good court, one that functions efficiently and does an effective job of providing justice to litigants. Our interviews with practitioners indicate that they, too, have a favorable view of the court and its management programs.

As in the case of several of the other courts that operate effectively, it is not possible to explain the success of the Dayton court and its programs in terms of any one or two things. The court operates in a socio-political environment that is conducive to good management of public institutions, has had strong leaders who have been interested in innovation and willing to try new approaches, has employed a wide range of managerial techniques to help achieve goals it has set for itself, and has encouraged open communications with practitioners and policymakers about issues of broad concern. Perhaps most important, it has taken the position that court business is public business, and that if it is to be handled efficiently and effectively, the court must take responsibility for doing so.

B. Phoenix: The Civil "Fast-Track" Program

The Maricopa County Superior Court, in Phoenix, Arizona, was one of the 21 courts that participated in the National Center's *Justice Delayed* study. By comparison to most of the other courts in that study, its 1976 civil case processing times were relatively speedy; the data indicated a median tort disposition time of 308 days, which ranked it ahead of all but two of the courts on that measure. However, the median time to jury trial (607 days) seemed longer than necessary and last-minute continuances were common. With a 1980 population of 1,509,000 and with forecasts calling for continuation of the population influx that made Maricopa County one of the most rapidly growing urban areas in the nation during the 1970s, some action seemed necessary to avoid the development of serious backlogs and delays.

The court's presiding judge, Robert Broomfield, took the lead in developing a program aimed at improved civil case management. During the fall of 1978 he arranged for National Center staff to collect additional data and interview judges handling civil cases, in order to develop a picture of the overall operation of the civil litigation process in the court. He also convened a special bench-bar committee that included leaders of the county bar association and the trial lawyers associations. This group, called the Civil Study Committee, was asked to examine several court problems and to help in the planning and implementation of an experimental civil case management program. For the bar leaders on the committee, one goal of any such program was especially important: the establishment of a system in which trial dates were really "firm," thus enabling trial lawyers to organize their schedules and arrange for witnesses to be available with confidence that a trial would actually take place on the scheduled date.

Prior to this time, civil case processing in Phoenix had been a lawyer-dominated system. The court operated on an individual calendar system, with cases randomly assigned to the judges handling civil cases at the time of filing, but nothing was done about monitoring case progress or managing the caseload until one party (usually the plaintiff) filed a Certificate of Readiness.[8] The filing of the certificate signified that the parties desired a trial date and that discovery had been completed or would be completed prior to the trial date. At that point, the judge's secretary would set the case for trial, usually three to six months in the future. While continuance practices varied from judge to judge, the general practice was to allow two or three continuances of a scheduled trial by stipulation of the lawyers. Continuances of civil trials also occurred with some frequency because of "last day" criminal trials—i.e., criminal cases in which the charges would have to be dismissed under the Arizona criminal speedy-trial rule unless a trial could be held. These cases would sometimes be assigned to a judge with a civil trial about to start (or even in progress), and would "bump" the civil trial.

The experimental program developed by the court in consultation with the Civil Study Committee did not entirely abandon the pre-existing system, but it made four important modifications. First, while retaining the Certificate of Readiness procedure, it sought to make that procedure a meaningful one, operating within a defined period. On the theory that discovery could and should be completed within nine months after the initiation of a lawsuit in most cases, the court established a requirement that, for cases assigned to judges participating in the experimental program, the Certificate of Readiness would be filed within 270 days after the filing of the complaint. If not, the case would (with notice to the plaintiff's lawyer) be placed on the inactive calendar and automatically dismissed 60 days later unless a Certificate of Readiness and Motion to Set for Trial was filed within that period. Second, the court committed itself to scheduling trials promptly in cases in the experimental program (trials would be set for 30 to 90 days after the filing of the certificate), and to ensuring that it would be able to hold the trial in these cases on the scheduled date. Third, a manual information system and a set of internal coordinating mechanisms were put in place, to enable the court to monitor compliance with the Certificate of Readiness procedure and to make good on its promise to provide trials on the scheduled date. Fourth, with the approval of the Arizona Supreme Court, the court developed a pool of pro tempore judges—practicing attorneys in Maricopa County—who could be used to augment the court's permanently appointed judges when necessary.[9]

Implementation of a pilot program involving four of the court's 17 civil judges began in January 1979, and during its first year of

Table 6C
CASELOAD CHANGES IN MARICOPA COUNTY
SUPERIOR COURT CIVIL DELAY REDUCTION PILOT
PROJECT, JANUARY-NOVEMBER 1979*

	4 Pilot Project Judges	13 Non-Project Judges
Pending Caseloads	−36.1%	− 4.7%
Total Dispositions	35.9 per mo. per judge	25.8 per mo. per judge
Trial Rate	5.5 per mo. per judge	3.8 per mo. per judge
Settlements	20.9 per mo. per judge	16.0 per mo. per judge

*Source: Larry L. Sipes et al., *Managing to Reduce Delay*, Table A-1, p. 51.

operation the program was the subject of close scrutiny by the court
and by staff of the National Center for State Courts. The first year's
results, summarized in Table 6C, were striking. By comparison with
the other 13 civil judges, the four judges involved in the pilot project
had markedly greater reductions in the size of their pending caseloads. They also had a greater number of dispositions per judge per
month, a higher trial rate, and a larger number of settlements per
month. The judges participating in the project were enthusiastic
about it and so were the attorneys, who especially liked the fact that
they only had to prepare a case for trial once. The lawyers coined
the term "fast-track" to describe the pilot system, a term that has
continued in use.

In succeeding years, the "fast-track" program was expanded to
include other judges, a few at a time. By 1983 all of the judges in
the court's civil division were operating under the new system. The
current operation of the Phoenix court's civil case management system is basically the same as the design of the original pilot project,
although there have been a number of refinements over the past
eight years.[10] Of particular note, the court's presiding judge has
continued to play an important role in caseflow management. Both
Judge Broomfield and his successor, Judge Michael Dann, have continued to emphasize the importance of adhering to the case management policies that have been developed by the court, both in
meetings with judges and in public statements. Both have also used
their office as a resource center for the court, to help ensure that
the court's commitment to providing firm trial dates can be met.
For example, if a judge has two cases scheduled for trial on the same

date and no settlement has been reached in either case, the judge contacts the case transfer coordinator, who works in the presiding judge's office. It is her responsibility to obtain a second judge, a courtroom, a court reporter, and a bailiff, so that both cases can be tried as scheduled.

The court has set goals for itself with respect to the time required to deal with civil cases (basically the same as the ABA Standards) and with respect to ensuring that the commitment to a firm trial date is met. Information about the extent to which the court is meeting (or falling short of) its goals is collected manually, and is the subject of discussion at regularly scheduled meetings of the Civil Division judges. The Civil Study Committee is still in existence and meets monthly to discuss issues that arise in the operation of the programs, the most sensitive of which has been the handling of cases where the statute of limitations will come into play if a case is dismissed for failure to file a readiness certificate.

Upon initial examination, the impact of the Phoenix case management system on the court's civil case processing time seems relatively slight. The median tort disposition time decreased from 308 days in 1976 to 292 days in 1985, but the median time to jury trial increased slightly from 607 to 634 days. However, when we look at the changes that have taken place in the court's workload and in the makeup of its active pending caseload (Table 6D), we find strong evidence that the new system has enabled the court to maintain and even improve upon an expeditious pace of litigation in the face of sharply escalating pressures of case volume. Between 1976 and 1985, civil filings in Phoenix increased by 76%. The number of judges in the Civil Division increased from 17 to 20 (18%), but filings per judge have increased by 58%, from 1,104 in 1976 to 1,578 in 1985. At the same time, pending caseloads have decreased substantially. When data on time to disposition (Table 6E) are examined, improvement is apparent in almost every category except trial list disposition time and time to jury trial.[11]

Despite the positive evidence of success in Phoenix, there also is ample evidence of the difficulty of sustaining an effective caseflow management program. Ironically, much of the pressure to relax the policies that have proven effective has come from practicing lawyers who are quick to emphasize their support for the general objectives of the fast-track program, especially the reality of firm trial dates. While continuances can still be obtained (though usually only if sought early and for a good reason), lawyers want even greater flexibility in setting and changing their own schedules. There is

Table 6D
DATA ON CIVIL CASE FILINGS AND PENDING CASELOADS IN PHOENIX, 1976–85

| | Number of Cases Filed and Pending | | | % Change | Pending Cases per Judge | | |
	1976	1983	1985	'76–'85	1976	1983	1985
Civil Cases							
All Cases Filed	18,776	26,101	33,146	+76%	1,104	1,374	1,745
Pending	24,469	21,666	22,591	− 8%	1,439	1,140	1,189
Tort Cases Filed	4,230	6,209	7,461	+73%	254	327	393
Pending	5,696	7,376	7,339	+29%	335	388	386
"Active" Cases[a]							
Pending	5,766	4,555	1,763	−69%	339	240	93

Note: The Civil Division had 17 full-time civil judges in 1976, 19 in 1983, and 20 in 1985.
[a] "Active" cases are cases in which a Certificate of Readiness has been filed and a judgment or other dispositive order has not yet been entered.

Table 6E
CIVIL CASE PROCESSING TIMES IN PHOENIX, 1976–1985

	Median (in days) Filing to Disposition			75th Percentile (in days) Filing to Dispositions		
	1976	1983	1985	1976	1983	1985
Torts	308	317	292	471	478	420
All Civil Cases	196	164	131	—	405	400
Trial List Cases	416	565	505	612	710	733
Jury Verdict Cases	607	690	634	—	—	—

continual pressure on judges to grant additional time in specific cases and, from some quarters, a movement to give lawyers greater freedom to let cases remain on the inactive calendar.[12]

Responding to these pressures, the Phoenix civil judges worked with the Civil Study Committee to consider the criticisms and review a list of cases in which it was claimed that complaints had been unjustly dismissed, mainly in instances where the statute of limitations had run. The focus centered on varying interpretations of "good cause" for continuances by the 20 civil judges. Despite the difficulty of achieving accord, the judges affirmed the rules underlying the fast-track system and provided the bar with a new consensus statement of "good cause."[13]

The pressure to change the rule governing continuance of cases on the inactive calendar suggests less-than-univeral acceptance by the bar of the court's control of its docket. Different explanations were offered for the attack on the court's dismissal policies, but it is clear that at least some lawyers would like to have an unqualified right to stipulate to continuances on the inactive calendar—to again control the pace of civil litigation until they decide to file a Certificate of Readiness.

Part of the genesis of the bar's concern about court control is a factor seldom mentioned in writings on caseflow management: the economics of practice. Lawyers in Phoenix, as elsewhere in the U.S., feel that civil litigation is getting more complex. At least partially because of the expense of trials, it seems to involve more motions practice now than 10 or 20 years ago. Lawyers must carry fewer cases or extend the available time in order to handle the motions. The response of many lawyers is to stretch out the pretrial period— take more time—but in Phoenix the time frame is fixed by the court. Partners in several Phoenix law firms that handle a high volume of work for insurance carriers have said that "fast-track" has caused them to add associates so each lawyer could be responsible for fewer cases. Some of the plaintiffs' lawyers recognize that they too may have to add attorney resources in order to carry a large inventory of cases, but they have been much slower to respond. This economic reality helps explain why the "local legal culture" is hard to change over the long term and why an improved pace of litigation is hard to sustain.

Another factor that constantly threatens an improved pace of litigation in an individual calendar court is each judge's discretion over how his or her calendar is managed. Senior judges are sometimes reluctant or unwilling to change their old ways and adopt new techniques. New judges may join the bench long after a program is initiated and thus not be fully aware of the rationales for all the procedures. In Phoenix these problems are addressed in several ways, including monthly meetings and a judges' manual.

The Civil Study Committee of bench and bar meets monthly. So do the civil judges. Data are shared, problems identified and discussed, and options explored at these meetings. There is no effort made to require a group consensus among the judges, but the discussions tend to reinforce the generally accepted calendar management policies and procedures and thus to narrow differences.

The problem of the new judges is addressed by the judges' manual. The manual covers many topics, and includes both the local rules in the court and a chapter that explains the court's calendar management philosophy and practice. From the outset each new judge is told, "This is the way we do it and why we do it this way. We expect you to manage your calendar consistent with these policies and procedures." Room remains for individual discretion in particular cases, but choices are made within a uniform, consistent framework that thereafter is reinforced in the monthly meetings. Various views regarding calendar management among the judges are apparent during discussions with them, but there is no doubt that the Phoenix judges, like their counterparts in Dayton, are very much aware of the principles set forth in the modern texts on caseflow management.

The importance of the judges was remarked upon by several Phoenix lawyers, who say that the success of the programs is due to the generally high quality of the bench appointed by former Governor Bruce Babbitt. As of 1985, there were 33 of these judges on the bench, with an average age of only slightly over 40 years. These observers believe the younger judges have helped make the court more receptive to the new ideas and procedures.

The bar itself has continued to play a very important role in the Phoenix program, both through its participation in the Civil Study Committee and through its continuing involvement in the pro tem judge program. As part of the initial pilot program, the court developed a cadre of experienced lawyers who were willing to serve as pro tempore judges on short notice, as a third-level way to assure trials would start on the assigned day. The first level of backup is other civil judges. If no other civil judge is available, the court's "special assignment" judges (who do not have dockets of their own) serve as a second-level backup. Only when no regular judge is available does the court turn to its pro tem judges.

In the first year of the program, 1979, the four pilot-project judges rarely used special assignment or pro tem judges; when backup was needed they usually took each other's cases. As the number of judges using "fast-track" methods increased, so did the use of pro tem judges. In the second quarter of 1986, for example, civil division judges took 84 cases from their colleagues, the special assignment judges took 41 cases, and 90 cases (36%) were handled by pro tem or visiting judges. The fairly high use of the pro tem judges may be one reason why the court has been able to keep up with the rising tide of filings. It appears, however, that a measure originally viewed as a temporary, stop-gap measure—the use of pro tem judges—may now be becoming institutionalized.

There is one final factor in Phoenix that should be noted. The court had the same presiding judge, Robert Broomfield, for over 10 years, and he was a key actor in initiating both the civil case management program and the criminal case delay reduction program discussed in the next chapter. Without exception, he is regarded by bench and bar as a key factor in Phoenix's success. Because of Judge Broomfield's pivotal role, there was some concern that the court's gains would be lost when he was appointed to the United States District Court in 1985. Some expected the program to crumble upon or shortly after his departure, but this has not happened. The court's commitment to its programs has not changed with the change in presiding judge and the bar has not renounced its general support for the court-controlled civil case management program.

Indeed, one measure of Judge Broomfield's effectiveness as a leader is his apparent success in implementing changes that survive his departure. While some lawyers still begrudge the change from a lawyer-dominated system to one in which the court is in control of its calendar, almost all of them now accept it and acknowledge that the court now functions more efficiently. In interviews with over 30 Phoenix lawyers, we found a number of criticisms of specific aspects of the program but no one who would say they wanted to return to the days of attorney control of the calendar. All judges and most lawyers would echo the thought of one lawyer, who said, "I'm proud of what the court has been able to do." One judge summed it up: "Fast track is a good idea and it is working. I'd hate to lose it."

ENDNOTES–Chapter 6

1. See, e.g., Geoff Gallas, "The Conventional Wisdom of State Court Administration: A Critical Assessment and an Alternative Approach," *Justice System Journal*, Vol. 2, No. 1 (Spring 1976), pp. 38–39. As Gallas notes, most of the key non-judicial actors in the trial court process—law enforcement personnel, prosecutorial staff, public defenders, probation officers, and clerks of court—operate within county boundaries. So do most private attorneys, although some have practices that take them to more than one county.

2. The other four judges in Dayton handle probate, domestic relations, and juvenile cases.

3. For more detailed discussion of the Ohio Rules of Superintendence, see Chapter 8.

4. See generally Ernest C. Friesen et al., *Arrest to Trial in Forty-Five Days* (Los Angeles: Whittier College School of Law, 1978).

5. This discussion of the criminal case management program planning and implementation process in Dayton is drawn principally from the American Judicature Society's study of delay reduction programs in Dayton and three other cities. David W. Neubauer et al., *Managing the Pace of Justice: An Evaluation of LEAA's Court Delay-Reduction Programs* (Washington, D.C.: National Institute of Justice, 1981), esp. Chapters 7 and 8, pp. 199–247.

6. *Ibid.*, p. 218.

7. See Ernest C. Friesen et al., *Justice in Felony Courts: A Prescription to Control Delay* (Los Angeles, Whittier College School of Law, 1979), p. 74. The concept of time standards, reflecting what local practitoners regarded as acceptable maximum times, was an integral part of the prescription developed by the Whittier team led by Dean Friesen. When the Dayton judges were developing their civil case management plan, it was natural to utilize this concept, which was an important element of the successful criminal case management plan.

8. See *Justice Delayed*, p. 40; also Larry L. Sipes et al., *Managing to Reduce Delay* (Williamsburg: National Center for State Courts, 1980), pp. 42–43.

9. This discussion of the Phoenix experiment draws heavily on the description of the program in Sipes, *Managing to Reduce Delay*, esp. pp. 6–12, 41–61.

10. There are a number of articles discussing the Phoenix program and its evaluation. See, e.g., Robert C. Broomfield (with Howard Schwartz), "Delay: How Kansas and Phoenix are Making it Disappear," *Judges' Journal*, Vol. 23, No. 1 (Winter 1984), p. 23; Bonnie Dicus, "Phoenix Revisited," *State Court Journal*, Vol. 10, No. 1 (Winter 1986), p. 24; Noel Fidel, "Why the Court Measures Delay from Commencement," *State Court Journal*, Vol. 10, No. 3 (Summer 1986).

11. Even the slight increases in trial list time and time to jury trial cases may be misleading. In trial list cases, there has been a significant change in practice. Before the "fast-track" program began, Certificates of Readiness were routinely filed well before completion of discovery, simply to "get in line" for a possible future trial. Some of those cases would settle at a relatively early point. Today, the Certificate of Readiness is to be a "true" Certificate of Readiness. As a result, it is likely to be filed later and perhaps more likely to be filed only in cases where there is a real possibility of trial. With respect to jury trial cases, the measurement in 1976 was to the start of trial; for 1983 and 1985 it is to verdict, which will be a slightly longer period.

12. Some lawyers have complained that the discovery limitations are "a trap for the unwary." A few plaintiffs' lawyers have found their case dismissed for failure to comply with the 270-day discovery rule, with the statute of limitations having expired in the meantime. Others have argued that the times for discovery should begin at the point an answer is filed, instead of from filing. For contrasting views, see James Jasper, "Practicing in the Fast Track: Trap for the Unwary," *Maricopa Lawyer* (January 1986), p. 1; and Fidel, "Why the Court Measures Delay from Commencement," *supra* note 10.

13. The court's statement of what constitutes good cause for continuance of a case on the inactive calendar (thus forestalling dismissal for noncompliance with the time limits for completing discovery) reflects careful consideration of concerns voiced by both bar leaders and judges. The statement reads as follows:

IV. "Good cause" within the meaning of Rule V(e)(2):

The phrase "good cause" as used in Rule V does not lend itself to precise definition. Whether facts add up to "good cause" is a question for the sound discretion of each trial judge. *Walker v. Kendig*, 107 Ariz. 510, 489 P.2d 849 (1971). From a quantitative viewpoint, the "good cause" required for a continuance on the IAC is less than that required to continue a trial because the impact on the court's calendar is less. It does require far more cause than that needed to extend the time for the filing of a response to a motion. The party seeking the continuance is required to show some substantial basis for continuance and the court's focus is primarily upon whether there are unusal discovery or procedural problems which have prevented a case from proceeding at the presumptive pace.

From a qualitative viewpoint the following elements, although not exclusive, will be considered by the court in determining whether "good cause" exists:

A. Whether the underlying circumstances were unforseeable;

B. Whether the underlying circumstances were not due to lack of preparation;

C. Whether the grounds are relevant;

D. Whether the matter was brought to the court's attention in a timely manner; and

E. Whether the adversary is prejudiced.

See: ABA Commission on Standards of Judical Administration, *Standards Relating to Trial Courts*, Commentary to 2.55 (Revised 1984).

Some examples of what does not amount to good cause are:

A. Stipulations to extend on the IAC which are not supported by a factual basis;

B. Motions grounded on the fact that settlement negotiations are pending;

C. Motions grounded upon failure to serve the defendant when due diligence to serve has not been shown.

Note: The running of the statute of limitation is a factor which may be considered in extending a case on the IAC. However, Rule V does not provide that the running of the statute of limitation alone is grounds for a continance and dismissal under such circumstances may not be an abuse of discretion.

Chapter 7
REDUCING DELAYS:
EXPERIMENTATION AND CHANGE IN
LOCAL TRIAL COURTS

The caseflow management and delay prevention programs described in Chapter 6 were built upon solid foundations. The Dayton and Phoenix courts had strong and able leaders, and in both courts there was a cadre of judges willing to commit themselves to implementing case management programs and techniques. And, importantly, the courts were not facing a crisis of lengthy delays and heavy backlogs.

What happens when a court has serious delay problems and tries to remedy them? The results of delay reduction programs undertaken by the courts in this study are somewhat mixed, but they hold considerable cause for optimism. It is clear that there have been some major successes, and even where the results have been less positive there are some valuable lessons to be learned. This chapter examines the experiences of four jurisdictions in attacking problems of delay. Two of these courts (Detroit Recorder's Court and Phoenix) focused on criminal case delay reduction; one (Jersey City) on both civil and criminal case processing; and one (Wayne County Circuit Court) solely on delays in civil cases.

A. Detroit Recorder's Court: "Crashing" the Backlog and Institutionalizing a New System

In 1976, the Recorder's Court of the City of Detroit—the court that, at that time, handled all stages of all criminal proceedings instituted against persons charged with crimes committed in the nation's fifth largest city—was in serious trouble. As Table 7A shows, felony caseloads had been rising steadily for over three years, total

Table 7A

JUDGESHIPS, CASELOAD DATA, AND JAIL POPULATION IN DETROIT RECORDER'S COURT, 1970–1976

Year	Judgeships	Warrants Issued	Dispositions	Cases Pending 12/81	Jail Population
1970	13	10,988	11,098	3,418	1,007
1971	13	14,295	12,505	4,539	664
1972	13	12,213	13,224	2,059	389
1973	20	11,910	11,555	1,559	443
1974	20	12,296	10,977	1,805	622
1975	20	12,421	11,021	4,592	688
1976	20	13,005	10,959	6,331	1,073

Source: David W. Neubauer et al., *Managing the Pace of Justice: An Evaluation of LEAA's Court Delay-Reduction Programs* (Washington, D.C.: National Institute of Justice, 1981), Table 11-2, p. 334.

dispositions were decreasing (despite a 1973 increase from 13 to 20 in the number of judges on the court), and the number of Recorder's Court defendants held in the city jail had more than doubled in three years. The court had switched from an individual calendar system to a central docket (master calendar) system in 1975, apparently in an attempt to halt the growth in the size of the backlog, but during the year that followed the situation deteriorated markedly. By December 31, 1976, there were over 6,331 active pending cases, a fourfold increase over the same figure for the end of 1973. Within the court, there were deep divisions among the judges about the extent of the problem and about what should be done, as reflected in the subsequent remarks of one of them:

> We were at the point where we had something like 6,000 cases backlogged, and the top was about to blow off the building. The chief judge at that time ... was walking around telling everybody how wonderful everything was and how beautifully everything was working. ... In reality, the situation was such that it was going to end up in a conflagration in this court if not in the city of Detroit.[1]

As the crisis worsened during the summer and fall of 1976, the Michigan Supreme Court decided to intervene by, in effect, placing Recorder's Court in receivership. The supreme court appointed a Special Judicial Administrator, T. John Lesinski, to oversee a crash backlog and delay reduction program in Recorder's Court. At the same time it designated Samuel Gardner, one of the Recorder's Court judges, as Chief Judge of the court, vested with broad administrative authority. Through the state's Administrative Office of Courts, the supreme court also arranged for an infusion of state and federal funds—an estimated $8 million in all—to support the cost of temporary additional judges, prosecuting attorneys, administrative and clerical staff, and security personnel needed for the crash program.

The delay reduction program in Recorder's Court began in January 1977. Its initial goals were to reduce the Recorder's Court's share of jail inmates from slightly over 1,000 to a maximum of 550 within six months and to achieve a "normal" case processing time of 90 days from arraignment to trial. The initial focus was to be on case processing time in jail cases. From the outset, however, the program was conceived of as something more than "just another crash program." Heavy emphasis was placed on developing mechanisms for accountability in the management of caseloads, developing strong leadership in the court, and developing the court's capacity to maintain an expeditious pace of litigation long after the crash program ended.

The operation of the Recorder's Court delay reduction program, over its first 18 months, has been described in detail by American Judicature Society researchers who conducted an evaluation of it. The program involved a change from the master calendar system to a modified individual calendar system (with key administrative roles for five "executive judges" overseeing the cluster of courtrooms on each floor of the courthouse), establishment of new procedures to enable rapid screening and early control over incoming cases by the court, and implementation of a plea cut-off date policy coupled with an emphasis on providing firm trial dates. Other elements included improvement of the court's management information system, development of a "docket control center" responsible for monitoring the age and status of cases and for producing a variety of management information reports, and, at the outset, extensive use of visiting judges to help pare down the backlog of old cases.

The results indicate that the program was strikingly successful. Seventeen months after the program got started, the active pending caseload was down to 1,204 (from 6,311); the number of Recorder's Court jail cases was down to 580 (from 1,073); and the number of cases pending over six months had decreased from 418 to 237.[2] Case processing times became markedly shorter in newly filed cases, especially the tougher ones. The median time from bindover to disposition in these cases droppped from 40 days in mid-1976 to 19 days in late 1977 and early 1978. More significantly, the time for the 75th percentile case dropped from 170 to 60 days.[3] Remarkably, the results seem to have been achieved without lingering resentment, despite the fact that the judges, prosecutors, and other practitioners all had to work under considerable pressure for much of this period. AJS researchers, commenting on the lack of continued opposition, observed that the program may have contributed to judges' sense of satisfaction with their jobs.[4]

Among the tests of any innovative program are whether gains initially made can be sustained over time and whether the basic operational procedures established by the program remain in place after the proponents of the innovation have moved on to other arenas. These issues were of major concern to the leaders of the 1976–78 delay reduction initiative, who consciously sought to develop an organizational structure, an ethos, and a caseflow management system that would prove effective over time.

The state-appointed special judicial administrator left the court in 1979. At that point, the backlog had been reduced to what seemed like a manageable level, the redesigned caseflow management system was in place, and the situation was relatively stable. The chal-

Table 7B
FELONY CASE PROCESSING TIMES IN DETROIT RECORDER'S COURT, 1975–1985

	1975	1976	1977	1978	1983	1985
Total Time Arrest to Disposition						
Median	43	58	87	54	69	58
75th Percentile	143	170	231	125	143	109
Times from Arraignment to Disposition						
Median	31	49	62	19	43	31
75th Percentile	111	153	188	60	117	80

lenge for the court was whether the gains made in the crash program could be sustained in the face of continued caseload pressures. It appears that the challenge has been successfully met, despite two major system changes—a Michigan Supreme Court opinion barring judges from involvement in negotiations about sentences and the introduction of sentencing guidelines—that decreased judges' discretion and seemed to provide greater incentives for defendants to take cases to trial.[5]

As Table 7B shows, the median and 75th percentile case disposition times are about the same in 1983–85 as they were in the period immediately following the crash program. They are substantially less than they were in the period preceding the start of the program or during the program's initial stages.[6] The active pending caseload has increased somewhat from mid-1978 (it stood at 1,849 as of December 31, 1984), but is still relatively low in relation to filings. With a 1985 median time from bindover to disposition of only 31 days, and with only 10% of its cases taking over 180 days from arrest to disposition, Detroit Recorder's Court is clearly one of the outstanding urban courts in the United States in terms of the promptness with which it handles its cases.

What explains the court's success in maintaining an effective system over the period from 1978 through 1985? Part of the answer lies in the concern of the program's leaders during the 1976–78 crisis period to do more than simply "crash" the backlog. They took advantage of the crisis to design and put in place a comprehensive caseflow management system—one that had ambitious but achievable goals, clear allocation of management responsibility, an on-going flow of information relevant to key management objectives, and open communications among practitioners.

Dynamic and able leadership is an important part of the story, but it is not the only part. There has also been an increase in judicial resources, achieved by adding judges and dropping a portion of the court's former workload. As of 1985 there were 29 judges (up from 20 in 1976), and a limited jurisdiction court had been created with responsibility for handling misdemeanor cases and initial post-arrest proceedings (up to bindover) in felony cases in the city of Detroit. Despite the increased resources, however, the court is not "over-judged" in comparison with other urban courts in this study. The fact that it has been able to maintain an expeditious pace in handling its felony caseload is due in large part to the refinements it has made in the caseflow management system that was originally set up during the crash program.

Under the system operating in 1985, the 29 Recorder's Court judges are organized into five teams according to the floor on which their chambers and courtrooms are located. Each team is headed by a "Floor Executive Judge" who handles initial arraignments, at which there are usually discussions about the possible disposition of the case. Decisions about disposition at this early point are pos-sible in a high proportion of cases because, as in Dayton, the case file has already been reviewed by an experienced prosecutor and the defense has received copies of relevant police reports and witness statements. Only if an agreement is not reached on disposition at that time does a case go (by blind draw) to one of the other judges to handle all subsequent proceedings.

Although the post-arraignment procedures followed by the judges are not completely uniform, a calendar conference is usually held a week after the arraignment. At this calendar conference, a schedule is established for filing and hearing motions, and a pretrial confer-ence date and tentative trial date (not more than 90 days from arraignment) are set. All pretrial motions, including motions re-quiring an evidentiary hearing, will be heard and decided at or before the final pretrial conference, which is usually scheduled for about four weeks after the calendar conference. The final pretrial conference is also the plea cut-off date. In any case in which a dis-position has not been reached at the conclusion of this conference, a firm trial date is set. Continuances of that trial date may be granted only by the Chief Judge.

The management information system, initially developed during the crash program, has been gradually expanded and enhanced. In the process, a great deal of attention has been paid to training clerical staff in the courtrooms to make sure that they know how the system operates and how they should use it to do their jobs effectively. The court's computer system now has terminals in every courtroom, which are used to provide judges and staff with information on case status and attorney schedules. Data entry is done mainly by the courtroom clerks, and is monitored regularly by the court's central staff.

The Docket Control Center, still in existence, provides a central point for collection, analysis and dissemination of management information. The Docket Control Center produces a variety of reports, most now generated by computer, and the Docket Control Manager works closely with the Chief Judge and Court Administrator in identifying problems and developing solutions. A set of docket directives issued by the Chief Judge, setting forth the court's procedures and the related data collection forms and management information reports, is provided to all judges and to members of the court's staff, and is updated regularly.

The system is still evolving. During 1985 for example, the Chief Judge and Court Administrator undertook a major effort to see that no cases remained pending more than 180 days from arrest. The number of cases in this category was brought down to a low of 12 during 1986. As part of this program, the court developed procedures that included stamping CASE AGE ALERT in large blue letters and indicating the speedy trial deadline data on the front of the file for any case that reached 120 days in age from arrest. The few cases that reach the 180 day mark receive a large red SPEEDY TRIAL ALERT stamp, with an indication of the precise age of the case.

At the end of 1986, the Recorder's Court found itself facing new challenges. Its Chief Judge for more than ten years, Samuel C. Gardner, would be retiring in 1987 and, as part of a long-planned merger of Recorder's Court with the Wayne County Circuit Court, Recorder's Court would begin handling all of the felony cases in Wayne County. Wayne County has 42 municipalities outside the city of Detroit, and the impact on the court's caseload will be substantial. Initial estimates forecast 4,000 cases (about 40% over the 1985 and 1986 levels) with five circuit court judges being added to the court's existing complement of 29 judges. The court will undoubtedly be under stress during this period, and the extent to which it is able to cope effectively with the changes will be a further test of the system developed over the past decade.

B. Phoenix: The Criminal Delay Reduction Program

Success begets success. In Phoenix, the early success of the court's experimental civil case management program was a major factor contributing to the decision to undertake a criminal case delay reduction program.

Data from the National Center's *Justice Delayed* study indicated that, by comparison with other courts, Phoenix was not handling its criminal caseload as well as it was handling its civil caseload, or as well as most other urban courts were handling their felony caseloads. Its 1976 median upper court disposition time of 98 days ranked Phoenix 14th among the 21 courts in the *Justice Delayed* study. It ranked only slightly higher in terms of arrest-to-disposition time, where its median was 113 days. As on the civil side, the court's criminal division operated on an individual calendar basis, but there was little active involvement by the judges in managing cases. The first trial date was set by the court administrator's staff, but cases rarely went to trial or reached any other disposition on that date. Even with a speedy trial statute that provided for a maximum 180-day period from arrest to disposition or start of trial, there was little sense of urgency in dealing with criminal cases. Judges would routinely grant continuances and, with the concurrence of defense attorneys, the time would be excluded from the calculation of time under the speedy trial statute.

In December 1980, in response to an invitation from the Institute for Court Management and the National Judicial College, Presiding Judge Robert Broomfield arranged for a group of key criminal justice policymakers and practitioners in Maricopa County to attend a workshop on reducing trial court delays. The format of the ICM-NJC workshop, which brought together teams from eight urban courts in the western United States, provided an opportunity for the Phoenix group to focus on the operation of their system, set tentative goals, identify key problem areas, and develop the outlines of an action plan for reducing delays.

Back in Phoenix after the three-day workshop ended, they formed a more broadly representative Criminal Study Committee, chaired by Presiding Judge Broomfield. The committee had as its primary task the development of a plan for improving the Maricopa County criminal justice system, with particular emphasis on reducing case processing times.

The Criminal Study Committee brought together representatives of all of the agencies involved in criminal case processing in Maricopa County. In addition to Judge Broomfield, it included the court administrator, the county clerk, judges of the superior court (including the criminal presiding judge) and of the justice of the peace courts, the prosecuting attorney, public defender, chief probation officer, sheriff, two chiefs of police, and representatives from the state supreme court, the attorney general's office, the private defense bar, and the lay public. All had the opportunity to make suggestions and respond to proposals made by others during this planning phase.

By spring of 1981, most of the planning had been completed for what came to be known as the Criminal Delay Reduction Project, and the project was announced in a press release on Law Day, May 1, 1981. Its original goals were to terminate half of the court's criminal cases within 95 days of the defendant's initial court appearance and 90% within 120 days.[7]

Operationally, the program laid out a set of time frames to be met and procedures to be used in handling all felony charge cases in Maricopa County. The program called for rapid preparation of police reports and screening by prosecutors, early disclosure of the prosecution case to the defense, and structured plea negotiations. Under the court's then-existing rules, pretrial conferences were supposed to have been mandatory, but in fact they had rarely been held unless there was a special request. The new program made the pretrial conference the focal point of the pretrial process.

Under the plan, prosecutors would make their plea offers known to the defense prior to the pretrial conference, the date for which would be set for not more than 30 days after the arraignment of the defendant in superior court. With information about the prosecution case fully disclosed not later than the arraignment date, defendants and their lawyers would presumably have ample time to decide how to proceed prior to the pretrial conference. The pretrial conference was also to be a plea negotiation cut-off point; if the case was not resolved at or before the conference, it would be set for a trial within 21 days thereafter. To help make the trial date credible, the court pledged that four "special assignment" judges who did not have calenders of their own would be available to conduct trials if necessary.

In order to deal with cases already pending in the court, it was agreed that the judges would hold calendar calls and set them promptly for pretrial conferences and trials. The special assignment judges

Table 7C
FELONY CASE PROCESSING TIMES IN PHOENIX, 1976–1985

	Full Year 1976	Jan. 1982	June 1982	Full Year 1983	Full Year 1984	Full Year 1985
Total Time Arrest to Disposition						
Median	114	—	—	64	72	78
75th Percentile	152	—	—	112	128	125
Upper Court Disposition Time						
Median	98	54	33	44	51	58
75th Percentile	134	77	71	82	102	106
Lower Court Processing Time						
Median	14	—	—	16	16	15
75th Percentile	—	—	—	26	28	25

would provide a reserve pool of judges to be used for trying these cases, if necessary.

The initial impact of the Criminal Delay Reduction Program in Phoenix was dramatic. On June 30, 1981, there were 1,561 defendants awaiting trial in the criminal division. One year later that pending caseload had been reduced by 41%, to 916. Criminal case processing times also improved markedly. In June 1980, the median number of days from initial appearance in the lower court to termination (defined as date of sentence in cases where there was a guilty plea or verdict) was 126 days. By June 1982, this figure was down to 84 days. Median upper court disposition time (arraignment to disposition in superior court, not including time from disposition to sentence) dropped to as low as 33 days in June 1982.[8]

The court has not been able to sustain that pace, although its case processing times are still much faster than they were in the National Center's *Justice Delayed* study. As Table 7C shows, there has been a gradual increase in felony case processing times, by every measure, since 1983. The slippage has occurred in the superior court, not the justice court, and is recognized by judges and lawyers alike. There appears to be several interrelated contributing factors.

One factor is an increase in caseloads. Between 1976 and 1985 there was an increase from 10 to 13.5 (35%) in the number of judges in the Criminal Division, but a rise from 5,218 to 9,792 (88%) in the number of cases filed in superior court. On a per-judge basis, the number of filings increased from 522 in 1976 to 725 in 1985. The judges have not been the only ones to feel the caseload pressure; it has had an especially severe impact on the public defender's office. Following a 1984 Arizona Supreme Court decision that established caseload standards for public defenders in a case that arose outside of Maricopa County, public defenders in Phoenix began filing motions to withdraw from some cases on the grounds that their caseload exceeded time standards set by the supreme court. In most cases the judges denied the motions, but they also began to be more lenient in granting continuances.

The first deadline that came to be "flexed" was the pretrial conference, which under the delay reduction program plan was to be scheduled for not more than 30 days from arraignment in superior court. The court's rules called for trial counsel to be present at this conference and for the defense lawyer and deputy county attorney to have discussed possible pleas or other non-trial disposition prior to this conference. Increasingly, however, the court accepted a practice of lawyers other than the trial counsel appearing at the conference. The judges also began to lower their expectations that serious discussions about disposition would be held prior to this conference. The initial trial date, usually set for 21 days after the pretrial conference, then became the date for a "real" pretrial conference, with a new trial date set for a month later. The result was, of course, a lengthening of about 30 days in the time taken to bring the case to conclusion.

Second, there were inevitably some "glitches" in the system that led to delays in specific cases. One of the most common involved preparation of copies of police reports and other items needed for full disclosure. Particularly in cases where supplemental reports were completed after the preliminary hearing in justice court, these would not always be provided immediately to the defense attorney. Delays in exchanging discovery materials could also occur if the defendant changed attorneys.

A third factor affecting time to disposition was a significant change in personnel in the public defender's office. A number of experienced deputy public defenders who had participated in the development and initial implementation of the delay reduction program left the office during the 1982–85 period. They were replaced by less experienced attorneys, many of whom did not have the same positive feelings about the program as the departed attorneys had.

Fourth, within the prosecutor's office there was also some turn-over. New deputy county attorneys, not involved in the initial development of the program, were not as committed to the "fast track" concepts and procedures. Carrying heavy caseloads themselves, they would often acquiesce in continuance requests. Many of them were also willing to accept pleas to reduced charges as late as the scheduled trial date, thus undercutting the policy of a plea cut-off date linked to a firm trial date.

Fifth, there was also turnover among the judges in the court's criminal division, including the rotation of the former criminal presiding judge (who had been instrumental in getting the program started in 1981–82) into one of the court's other divisions. Although some of the judges sitting in the criminal division in 1985 were strongly committed to the principles of calendar management that were the foundation of this program, others were not. Observation and interviews indicated considerable variation in judges' practices regarding the number and length of continuances they would allow in a case.

Finally, in contrast to the court's civil division, where the judges have regular monthly meetings, by 1985 the criminal division judges were meeting less frequently as a group. And, while the court's Civil Study Committee continued to be an active group that provided a forum for ongoing exchange of ideas between judges and bar leaders, the Criminal Study Committee had become totally dormant.

Despite the loss of momentum and a clear slippage in case processing times from 1983 to 1985, it is clear that the Criminal Delay Reduction Program has had a significant impact in Phoenix. Time standards, similar to those adopted by the ABA, are in place; the court has an automated information system that provides reports on the extent to which the court is meeting those standards; and the court's felony case processing times are faster, on every measure, than they were prior to the inception of the program. While there is still room for improvement, much has been accomplished since 1980. The court, however, has become increasingly concerned about the slippage in case processing time. Late in 1987, it began making plans for a renewed criminal case reduction program aimed at bringing case processing times closer to what they had been in 1982.

C. Jersey City: Simultaneous Civil and Criminal Delay Reduction

Hudson County, New Jersey, might initially appear to be a rocky field upon which to cultivate court reform. Located across the river from New York City, the county has a population of about 550,000. It contains twelve municipalities, which are part of a string of aging industrial cities stretching along the Hudson River. The home territory of Boss Frank Hague in the 1930s and '40s, Hudson County has a checkered history of machine-dominated politics in which public employment has long been used as a reward for political support. The close linkage between politics and the courts in Hudson County was, in fact, one of the primary factors motivating the court reforms undertaken in New Jersey in the 1940s under the leadership of Chief Justice Arthur Vanderbilt.

One of Vanderbilt's most important reforms was establishment of a strong hierarchical administrative structure with the Chief Justice at the apex. At the local level, the key figure is the Assignment Judge—the chief judge for the county or for a multicounty vicinage. The Assignment Judge is appointed by the Chief Justice, and has administrative authority over all of the judges and all of the non-judicial staff personnel (e.g. court clerks, probation officers) working in trial courts in the vicinage. It is common for Assignment Judges to be appointed to this position without ever having served as a trial judge in the county.

Both the current Assignment Judge and his predecessor came to their position in Hudson County from service on trial benches elsewhere in the state, and both brought with them a strong orientation toward sound management as well as considerable leadership skills. Judge Thomas O'Brien, who became the Assignment Judge in Hudson County in 1975, found civil and criminal calendaring systems that were in considerable disarray, with virtually no management controls exercised by the court. Over the next seven years, Judge O'Brien and his court administrator, Gori Carfora, experimented with a variety of approaches to expedite case disposition and bring some coherence to the process. Their successors, Judge Burrell Ives Humphries and Trial Court Administrator John Clarke, have also been committed to strong management, and have consolidated the gains made under O'Brien and Carfora.

Civil Case Management. The changes undertaken on the civil side, where the problems were much less serious than on the criminal side, were relatively simple. Perhaps the most important change was Judge O'Brien's appointment of two well-respected and highly competent persons to key managerial positions. Judy Moran, who had previously worked as a clerk in the assignment office, was made the civil calendar clerk in 1978. Shortly thereafter, Judge John Geronimo was designated Presiding Judge of the Civil Division. He and Ms. Moran worked closely together in managing the court's master calendar system until the judge's retirement in 1986.

Under the system they established, the court takes cognizance of the case when the complaint is filed, and active monitoring begins when the answer is filed. All case files are sent to Ms. Moran's office on the date that the answer is due, and subsequent monitoring of all cases is centered in her office. Cases follow one of two main tracks. First, cases in which an answer has not been filed (and in which the plaintiff has not moved for a default judgment) are placed on a dismissal list approximately six months after the complaint is filed. They will be dismissed automatically unless the plaintiff files an affidavit setting forth facts and reasons why this should not be done. Second, in cases in which an answer has been filed, Ms. Moran's office will send two notices to the lawyers involved. The first notice, usually sent out three to four months before a case is expected to reach the top of the trial calendar, tells the attorneys to be prepared for the "Early Calendar Call," at which specific trial dates will be assigned. The second notice, sent about three weeks before the early calendar call, informs the lawyers of the specific date on which the calendar call will be held. On that date, the presiding judge conducts the calendar call, attempts to deal with pretrial problems that have arisen (e.g. resolution of discovery issues, addition of third parties, motion for assignment of a complex matter to a particular judge for on-going case management), and sets a date for the parties to return to court.

Cases are ordinarily assigned to trial dates within a two-week period beginning three weeks after the early calendar call. The number of cases set for a particular trial week has fluctuated, but during 1985 (when the court was operating with six civil judges) was usually about 70 per week—40 set for Monday and the balance for the remainder of the week. The court places considerable stress on making the trial date a firm one. On the scheduled date, attorneys are expected to be in the courthouse with their clients. If they are not present, they risk severe sanction: summary judgment for the plaintiff if a defendant fails to appear; dismissal of the complaint if the plaintiff fails to appear. Trial-ready cases are assigned to the judges of the court's civil division by Ms. Moran, operating under the supervison of the presiding judge. The judges are expected to initiate discussions about possible settlements when the lawyers arrive at their courtrooms, but if the discussions do not show rapid progress they move directly to jury selection. Most cases settle at this point if they have not already done so.

The system is not a complicated one, but it worked effectively in Hudson County while Judge Geronimo headed the civil division. In interviews conducted before Judge Geronimo's retirement, judges and trial lawyers attributed much of the civil program's success to him and to Ms. Moran. Both were regarded as having a good grasp of the calendar management issues and details and as being forceful personalities who exhibit low tolerance for frivolous requests for continuances. Indeed, Judge Geronimo's success in civil case management was widely attributed to his effectiveness in dealing with attorneys at the early calendar call. "He's tough, but he understands when you have problems," was a typical comment reflecting the attorneys' appreciation of Judge Geronimo's skill at managing the calendar and encouraging settlements. Both Judge Geronimo and Ms. Moran made clear their commitment to expeditious civil case processing. They were using an information system that was rudimentary and largely manual, but they regularly monitored the size and age of the pending caseload.

The effect of their efforts has been to accelerate the pace of civil litigation and to help reduce the backlog of civil cases. Median tort disposition time, which had been 584 days (about 19 months) in 1979, was down to 394 days (13 months) in 1985. In the same period, the number of pending civil cases dropped 18%, from 4,045 to 3,315. During 1985, when a new statutorily-mandated automobile tort claim arbitration program went into effect, a number of cases were removed from the pool of cases awaiting trial scheduling and diverted to arbitration. At this point, the backlog of cases was so low that trials were being scheduled as soon as three to four months after answers were filed. The bar complained that this was too fast, even for simple cases, and the court listened. After discussion involving judges and bar leaders, it was agreed that the time frame would be extended so that the early calender calls would routinely be set for about six months after the answer was filed.

With the retirement of Presiding Judge Geronimo in 1986, civil case management in Hudson County has entered a new phase. His successor as civil presiding judge is less oriented to personal involvement in resolving problems in individual cases, but recognizes the importance of sound overall caseflow management by the court. To help maintain an expeditious pace, the court is increasing its capacity to monitor case progress from filing and will make use of an automated information system now being developed. As in many developing organizations, the movement is from a highly personalistic model of organizational leadership to a more "managerial" style. The challenge in the years immediately ahead will be to consolidate and build upon the gains made in large part through the efforts of a forceful individual leader.

The Criminal Case Management Program. The criminal case delay reduction program in Hudson County bears little resemblance to the civil program in the same court. Where the civil program originated with the court itself, the criminal program was the product of several sources, including state-level judicial leaders, the county prosecutor, the sheriff, and other local officials. And where the civil program was primarily managerial, the criminal program involved procedural changes and structural reorganization in addition to new managerial techniques.

Criminal case delay reduction efforts in Hudson County developed initially from concerns about a severe problem of overcrowding in the county jail. An interagency planning group, formed in 1979 to help devise methods of dealing with the jail overcrowding problems, identified accelerated case processing as one potential source of relief. Faster case processing would mean earlier release from jail for pretrial detainees and speedier transfer to state facilities for convicted felons.

Planning for speedier criminal case processing in Hudson County was thus already underway when New Jersey's new Chief Justice, Robert Wilentz, announced in early 1980 that reducing trial court delay would be his number one priority. As the statewide criminal speedy trial program began to take shape during 1980, one important component would be the creation of local delay reduction planning teams. The teams were to be chaired by the assignment judge and were to include representatives from the various agencies involved in dealing with criminal cases from inception to disposition (e.g. prosecutor, public defender, county executive, chief probation officer, municipal court judge, county clerk, bar president).[9]

The interagency group already in existence in Hudson County became the county's delay reduction planning team. By the fall of 1980, it had developed a program to reduce delays in both the pre-indictment and the post-indictment stages of the process.

The prosecutor in Hudson County, Harold Ruvoldt, took the lead in devising an innovative plan to reduce pre-indictment delays. Part of the problem was that arrests and initial court appearances took place in the 12 municipalities in the county. The prosecutor's office could not efficiently handle newly filed charges in each of the 12 municipal courts, to determine which ones warranted prosecution in superior court as an indictable offense. Additionally, transfers of documents (police reports, results of lab tests, records of municipal court proceedings, etc.) from the municipality to the prosecutor's office and to the superior court would often take long periods of time. Ruvoldt proposed that all initial appearances in cases in which the defendant was charged by the police with an indictable offense be centralized in a single court in Jersey City. He would assign a senior prosecutor to the court, one who could make decisions about charges and pleas. To encourage cooperation by the public defender's office and enable rapid disposition of a significant percentage of cases, Ruvoldt also agreed to provide full discovery at the time of the initial hearing in the new centralized court.

The concept was approved by the Hudson County planning group, agreements were reached with county and city governments to provide the necessary funding, and the new court—called the Central Judicial Processing (CJP) court—went into operation on the first floor of the Hudson County courthouse in Jersey City in January 1981. It quickly became a keystone for reducing delays.

All defendants arrested for an indictable offense now make their first court appearance at CJP. This takes place on the first working day after arrest if the defendant is in jail, otherwise within five days. A municipal court judge experienced in handling criminal matters presides over the court, which also has an experienced assistant prosecutor, a senior attorney from the public defender's office, and interviewers from the court's bail and pretrial diversion programs. CJP operates as a central intake point, at which the agencies and individuals who need to obtain key items of information about a case can do so quickly. Rapid screening by veteran prosecutors is a key element; the assistant prosecutor at CJP is under instructions to review police reports immediately and make the decision on the spot to dismiss the case, reduce the charges, accept a plea, or forward the case for action by the grand jury and prosecution in superior court. The presence of the public defender, coupled with the prosecutor's commitment to provide open-file disclosure at CJP, means that it is possible to have informed discussion about possible dispositions while the case is still very fresh. If agreement is reached on a plea to a non-indictable offense, the plea can be entered immediately. If the prosecutor's review leads to a charge reduction but no plea agreement is reached, bail is fixed and the defendant is given a date to appear for trial in the municipal court. If the prosecutor decides that the case should go forward as an indictable offense, the CJP court can conduct a probable cause hearing or accept a waiver so that the case can go directly to the grand jury. Regardless of the outcome, the public defender (or private defense counsel, if one is involved) has full information about the case at an early point.[10]

Establishment of the CJP system has had a dramatic effect on pre-indictment delays. Processes that used to take weeks to complete are now accomplished in a matter of days and, in the opinion of the practitioners involved, with much sounder results. The effects are perhaps most noticeable in cases where the original charges are dismissed or downgraded to non-indictable offenses. Formerly, these cases would have remained in the system for many weeks; with CJP they are now frequently concluded within a day or two. Cases that are not downgraded still encounter some delays in going through the grand jury process after the initial screening at CJP, but overall pre-indictment case processing time has been significantly reduced. For cases in our 1985 sample of superior court dispositions, the median pre-indictment time was 50 days. By comparison, it was 125 days in the 1979 sample.

Even more dramatic reductions have been achieved in the post-indictment stage of the process in Hudson County, with both the prosecutor's office and the court playing key roles. The prosecutor's office conducted a complete inventory of all of the pending cases, to determine which ones should be actively prosecuted, and cooperated with the court in conducting an old case backlog reduction program. As part of the structural reorganizaton that produced CJP, the prosecutor's office also adopted a policy of "vertical" representation, under which the same assistant prosecutor would ordinarily be responsible for a case from the time it left CJP until it reached disposition.

In the superior court, Assignment Judge O'Brien instituted an individual calendar system, designated a presiding judge of the criminal division, and began a practice of closely monitoring judges' performance. The same basic system has been continued under O'Brien's successor, Assignment Judge Burrell Ives Humphreys. Although the information system has been gradually improved and is now being automated, management information actually used at the outset of the delay reduction program was rudimentary. It consisted mainly of simple statistical reports on each judge's caseload showing the number of cases assigned, number disposed, and number of trials conducted, distributed each month by the presiding judge with an accompanying memo. What seems most important is that it was *used*: everyone in the courthouse knew that the Assignment Judge was very concerned about delay, and they became more conscious of the passage of time in the cases for which they were responsible.

The organization of criminal case processing within the courthouse may also have played a role in reducing delays. Courtrooms have been organized on a "team" or "work group" concept, with the semi-permanent assignment of assistant prosecutors and public defenders, probation officers, clerks, and bailiffs to the same courtoom. The attorneys are periodically rotated among judges to avoid too close a working familiarity, but there is nonetheless a high degree of stability in the work groups. It is a system that tends to promote mutual trust, and willingness to negotiate. Not suprisingly, the trial rate in Hudson County is lower than the rate in most other courts in this study. There also appears to be a high degree of cooperation in seeking to achieve goals of expeditious case processing, which have consistently received the strong backing of the assignment judge and the prosecutor and at least the endorsement of the chief of the statewide public defender's office.

The concern about delays manifested by leaders in the courthouse has been reinforced by state-level leaders. The state's Administrative Office of Courts began collecting data and publishing reports on filings, dispositions, and pending cases, in all of the state's 21 counties, for discussion of the statewide speedy trial program at regular meetings of all of the assignment judges and trial court administrators. The Chief Justice continued to make court delay a priority issue, and it is usually the first item of business at the meeting of assignment judges at which he presides. As one Hudson County administrator said, "You become what you are thinking about, and here you are always thinking and talking about speedy trial."

State-level leaders were also instrumental in providing needed resources at a critical time. As the program gathered momentum in 1982, three additional judges were temporarily assigned from other parts of the state to help provide the capacity to hold pretrial conferences and trials. The pending caseload in the superior court, which had been over 1,800 in 1980, was pared down to less than 500 cases in January 1984.

As Table 7D shows, the results of the delay reduction effects in Hudson County have been spectacular. The data from our sample of 1979 dispositions shows that felony case processing times in the Jersey City court were far slower than the baseline year times recorded for any of the other 17 courts involved in the study. By 1983, the court had reduced its median overall time from 510 to 191 days

Table 7D
FELONY CASE PROCESSING TIMES IN JERSEY CITY,
1979–1985

	1979	1983	1984	1985
Total Time, Arrest to Disposition				
Median	510	191	190	163
75th Percentile	843	315	517	264
Percent Over 180 Days	94%	54%	53%	43%
Upper Court Disposition Time				
Median	376	120	120	115
75th Percentile	643	343	946	234
Percent Over 150 Days	84%	44%	44%	38%
Time from Arrest to Indictment				
Median	125	84	76	54
75th Percentile	176	120	127	75

and its median upper court time from 376 to 120 days. Progress continued, though at a slower rate, in 1984 and 1985.

The successes in Hudson County are dramatic evidence of what can happen when capable leaders decide to address problems of delay head-on. On the civil side, much of what was accomplished can be credited to initiatives taken by the local court, especially the assignment judge and the civil presiding judge, and to their continuing perseverance, attention to detail, and open communication with the bar. On the criminal side, more institutions and individuals were involved, but the leaders demonstrated a remarkable ability to work cooperatively and to share both the responsibility for making the problem work and the credit for its success. At the local level, the prosecutor, assignment judge, and trial court administrator were key figures, with important roles also played by the public defender and by municipal and county officials in setting up the CJP program.

State-level leaders, especially the Chief Justice and State Court Administrator, also had important roles in Hudson County. They made the issue of delay a central and continuing one for the entire state court system, gave impetus and encouragement to the efforts of county level leaders, helped provide temporary additional resources at a key juncture, and recognized (and publicized) the program's achievements as the success story began to emerge.

In assessing what happened in Hudson County, two additional factors seem especially worth noting. First, it is a good illustration of how structural impediments to efficient case processing can be overcome. The combination of the two-tier criminal court system plus a fragmented local government system that disperses responsibility for initial case processing among police departments and municipal courts in many different municipalities is one that is common not only in New Jersy but in many other American states. Speeding up the process is possible only if all the actors involved are willing to address the problem directly and to work cooperatively on devising and implementing new approaches. In Hudson County, this happened.

Second, sophisticated technology was *not* important. The systems used to schedule cases and monitor judges' performance were almost entirely manual. The information collected was very rudimentary, especially by comparison to the sophisticated system developed in Detroit Recorder's Court. It was sufficient, however, to provide essential information about the overall size of pending caseloads, and about dispositions in relation to findings. Most important, the information was used by the court's leaders to identify problems and assess progress.

D. Wayne County Circuit Court: Efforts to Reduce Civil Case Delays

With a 1980 population of 2,337,000, Wayne County is the most populous county in Michigan and ranks fourth nationally. General jurisdiction trial court responsibility in the county has been shared by the Wayne County Circuit Court and Detroit Recorder's Court, with the latter handling all felonies originating in the city of Detroit and the circuit court handling the "out-county" criminal cases and all of the general civil litigation involving claims of more than $10,000.[11] In 1985, the circuit court had 36 judges, of whom eight would at any one time be assigned to hear criminal matters, with all but one of the others devoting full time to civil cases.

Delay in civil litigation is a long-standing problem in Wayne County. The National Center's *Justice Delayed* study, which sampled data on 1976 dispositions, reported a median tort disposition time for the court of 788 days, or about 26 months. For cases that ultimately went to jury trial, the time from filing to the start of trial was much longer—a median of 1,231 days, or 41 months.

By 1977, the situation had worsened, with the court's data indicating that the time from filing to trial was as high as 50 months. The court's approach to the problem, developed and implemented in cooperation with bar leaders specializing in both plaintiff and defense work, was to establish an innovative program that placed primary emphasis on encouraging settlement prior to trial. The key mechanism was a mandatory case evaluation hearing, called a "mediation" hearing, which in most cases was scheduled to be held in the 27th month after the complaint was filed. Cases not resolved at the mediation hearing would be set for trial approximately 90 days later, thus producing a 30-month track from filing to disposition.

As instituted in 1978, the mediation program was designed to fit easily into the existing civil litigation system in Wayne County. Under the court rules then in effect, discovery was supposed to be concluded by the end of the 26th month after the filing of the complaint. During the 25th month, the court's staff would schedule eligible cases (which included all cases involving exclusively money damages or divison of property) for a mediation hearing in the 27th month.

Up until that point, the court would ordinarily have no involvement in any civil case, unless a party filed a motion that required a ruling. Cases would be logged into the court's computer and randomly assigned to one of the 36 judges at the time they were filed. The assigned judge would be responsible for ruling on pretrial motions, but there were no expectations that the judge would take any steps to move the case to speedy resolution. The only monitoring of any sort was done by staff in the court's Docket Management Office, which routinely reviewed case files in all cases 16 months after filing. Those which appeared to involve claims worth less than $10,000 (in which discovery should have been completed quickly), were set for a mediation hearing in month 18. The others would not be reviewed again until month 25, when they were set for a hearing within 60 days.

The system was designed to allow lawyers approximately two years after issue was joined to complete discovery and prepare their cases. The mediation program itself called for payment of a fee ($75 by each side in 1985), required each lawyer to submit a written summary of the case prior to the mediation hearing, and provided for short oral presentations by the lawyers to the three-member mediation panel. The timing and structure of the mediation hearing meant that attorneys would (or should) be aware of the strength and

weaknesses of their cases, so that an intelligent discussion of settlement could occur at the time of the hearing.

Although there have been occasional problems with lawyers
requesting continuances of the mediation hearing date, the program
is well regarded by the bar and has succeeded in producing settlements or other dispositions in a high percentage of cases. Data collected on cases set for mediation in 1982 showed that at least 63%
of the cases were resolved without need for any further court proceedings.[12] There is evidence, too, that the mediation process had a
significant effect in the ultimate settlement of cases not resolved as
a direct result of the mediation proceeding.

Despite the apparent success of the mediation program, however, civil case processing times in the Wayne County Circuit Court
continued to be lengthy. The court's own data indicate that the time
from filing to trial dropped at one point to a low of about 36 months,
but for most of the 1983–86 period it fluctuated around the 40-month
mark. Median tort disposition times improved somewhat from the
1976 figure of 788 days, dropping to 721 days in 1983 and 648 days
in 1985, but this time is still considerably longer than the times in
the faster civil courts in the study. The 75th percentile case, an
indication of the time required for the more difficult cases, took 950
days (32 months) in 1985. The general civil docket disposition times
were also relatively long in 1985, with the median case taking 624
days and the 75th percentile at 943 days.

What explains this relatively slow pace of civil litigation, and
the difficulty of speeding it up? Part of the explanation clearly seems
to lie in the structure of the system and the case management procedures employed. The system itself was designed for relatively complex cases—the sort of case for which the lengthy discovery period
contemplated by the court's rules would be entirely appropriate—
even though cases of this complexity comprise only a small fraction
of the total caseload. With no case monitoring at all until month 16,
and no event to force the parties to prepare and assess their cases
until month 27, there was a general expectation that most cases
would stay in the system at least until the mediation hearing date
loomed on the horizon.

Even after the mediation hearing date has passed, the court has
until recently placed relatively little emphasis on ensuring that trial
dates were firm. Trials would be scheduled for about 90 days after
the mediation hearing, but the main emphasis on the trial date was
settlement rather than trial. At this stage, the individual judge to
whom the case was originally assigned no longer had any responsibility for it, and assignments for trial were made on a master

calendar basis under the direction of the court's Assignment Clerk. Every case set for trial would first be sent for a settlement conference before one of three judges designated to hold such conferences. A significant percentage would actually settle at that point, but many would not, and most of those that did not settle would have to be continued to a date two to four months in the future. Not infrequently there would be another continuance. On the second or third trial date the court would really be prepared to try the case and a continuance would be harder to obtain. Finally, faced with the imminence of an "all-or-nothing" trial, the point would be reached where the lawyers would at last agree upon a settlement.

The organization of the process, with cases assigned on an individual calendar basis until the mediation hearing was held and handled thereafter under a master calendar system, left no one in charge of any part of the caseload from start to finish. The main advantage of the individual calendar system—the ability to hold individual judges accountable for the management of their dockets—was totally lost, since the judges had no responsibility for disposition of the cases assigned to them. And, although a master calendar system can potentially be a vehicle for centralized case management, the combination of the two-year discovery period and the fact that the master calendar system did not really become operational until after the mediation hearing meant that there was no single locus of responsibility for case progress until after the mediation date at month 27.

The structural and procedural factors contributing to delay in Wayne County contributed to, and were in turn reinforced by, the attitudes and expectations of both lawyers and judges. Attorneys expected cases to take a minimum of two years, recognized that the first trial date was not likely to be a true date, and acted accordingly. Judges, believing that attorneys liked the lawyer-controlled calendaring system, were relatively lenient in granting continuances.[13]

Late in 1985, as it became apparent that civil case processing times were remaining relatively lengthy, the court started a new delay reduction initiative. The approach taken was two-pronged. First, an inventory was made of all of the civil cases pending more than 30 months. With the help of visiting judges, these cases would be scheduled for settlement conferences and, if not settled, would be set for trial. Second, a special bench-bar committee was established, charged with responsibility for exploring the possible changeover to an individual calendaring system for Wayne County.

As the bench-bar committee was considering the issues relating to possible implementation of an individual calendar program, a special state-level commission was also exploring the possibility of adopting time standards for the state of Michigan. And, at around the same time, the state's supreme court adopted a rule requiring discovery to be completed within 12 months in civil cases unless extended for good cause shown.

Within the bench-bar committee, there was no clear consensus about future directions. Although there was a shared recognition that many cases could be completed much more quickly then they were taking in 1985, there was also a sense that some cases—particularly the more complicated products liability and professional malpractice cases—needed a period of two to three years. Attorney members of the committee (all of them active litigators) were familiar with the existing system and were skeptical about changing to an individual calendar system that could, in effect, mean that they would have to become familiar with the scheduling practices of 36 different circuit court judges.

The impasse was finally resolved by the court's decision to begin implementation of an individual calendar system on a pilot project basis. The pilot project began on July 1, 1986, with seven judges participating. The initial focus of the judges in the pilot project was on pending cases previously assigned to them for handling of motions prior to the mediation hearing. They would now be responsible for handling all of these cases through to disposition. With the aid of their staffs (bailiff, secretary, and law clerk) they ascertained the status of these cases and set schedules for pretrial conferences and trials. As of January 1, 1987, they began handling a proportionate share of newly filed cases, following approaches designed to enable them to review the status of the case at an early point and set schedules for future events. By April of 1987, the results of the initial docket reviews by the seven pilot project judges could be seen. These judges had already pared down the size of their pending caseloads (average of 851 general civil cases compared to 1,017 for the other 27 judges on the court) and had reduced the number of "old" pending cases (average of 102 cases over two years old, compared to an average of 183 for the other judges). The progress continued throughout the rest of the year, and a second group of seven judges began the transition to individual calendars in October 1987.

The pilot program in Wayne County is an attempt to make a major change in civil case management philosophy and calendar practice in a high volume urban court. Although the early returns are promising, it is much too early to tell what will be the outcome. However, the experiment is clearly one that bears watching.

ENDNOTES–Chapter 7

1. Quoted in David W. Neubauer et al., *Managing the Pace of Justice: An Evaluation of LEAA's Court Delay-Reduction Programs* (Washington, D.C.: 1981), p. 344. The discussion in this chapter of developments in Recorder's Court during the 1976–78 period draws heavily on material in the Neubauer et al. study, esp. chapter 11 (pp. 330–369).

2. State Court Administative Office of the State of Michigan, "Progress Report-Courtflow Improvement II," submitted to the Law Enforcement Assistance Administration, June 30, 1978.

3. Neubauer et al., *Managing the Pace of Justice*, p. 379.

4. *Ibid.*, p. 368

5. The opinion in *State v. Killebrew*, 416 Mich. 189, 330 N.W.2d 834 (1981), held that while sentence concerns are appropriate subjects for plea negotiations, a trial judge's role in plea negotiations must be limited to consideration of agreements between defendants and prosecutors, in order to minimize the possibility of a coercive effect on the defendant. Prior to the *Killebrew* decision, it had been a common practice in Recorder's Court for the judge to be actively involved in discussions about sentence with the prosecution and the defense.

6. Source: Data samples collected from Recorder's Court case records by the National Center for State Courts in 1978 (for years 1975–77) and in 1985 and 1986 (for years 1983–85). All of the data were collected in the same fashion: a random sample of approximately 500 cases disposed of by the court in each of these years. It should be noted that data in the American Judicature Society's study of the delay reduction program in Recorder's Court shows much shorter times (median of 19 days; 75th percentile of 60 days) for cases filed during the period September 1977 to March 1978. The AJS study involved a sample of cases *filed* during this period whereas the National Center's sample was of cases *disposed*, a difference in approach which may help explain these time differentials.

7. The origins, goals, and initial results of the Phoenix Criminal Delay Program are reviewed in Frederick G. Miller, "Trial Delay Reduction: Case Processing in Maricopa County," *State Court Journal*, Vol. 7, No. 3 (Summer 1986), pp. 20–22. This discussion draws heavily on Miller's article.

8. *Ibid.*, pp. 21–22.

9. The New Jersey criminal speedy trial program is discussed in Chapter 8. For a detailed description and analysis of the program's background and first 18 months of operation, including discussion of program initiatives in Hudson County, see Anthony J. Langdon, *The New Jersey Delay Reduction Program* (Denver: Institute for Court Management, 1983).

10. *Ibid.*; see also Edward F. Zampella and Anita Lapidus, "CJP-An Innovative Concept," *Seton Hall Law Review*, Vol. 14 (1984), pp. 520–27.

11. As noted in the discussion of the Recorder's Court program, the allocation of workload changed in 1987. The Recorder's Court now handles

all of the felony cases in Wayne County, and the circuit court handles only civil cases.

12. Kathy L. Shuart, Saundra Smith, and Michael D. Planet, "Settling Cases in Detroit: An Examination of Wayne County's 'Mediation' Program," *Justice System Journal*, Vol. 8, No. 3 (Winter 1983), pp. 307, 313–16.

13. For an interesting description and analysis of the attitudes and perceptions of practitioners in Wayne County concerning continuance policies and calendar control, see David R. Sherwood and Mark A. Clarke, "Toward an Understanding of Local Legal Culture," *Justice System Journal*, Vol. 6, No. 2 (Summer 1981), pp. 200–17. Sherwood and Clarke, analyzing responses to a questionnaire survey of judges and laywers in Wayne County, found that both groups felt that a lawyer-controlled calendar was inefficient and undesirable. The judges, however, thought that lawyers preferred the lawyer-controlled system. The lawyers felt that the judges granted continuances rather readily, thus reinforcing the lawyer-controlled system.

Chapter 8
STATEWIDE PROGRAMS: ISSUES OF STRUCTURE, PROCESS, AND MOTIVATION

As we have seen in the last two chapters, state-level judicial leaders have played key roles in some trial court delay reduction programs. The program in Detroit Recorder's Court, for example, was initiated by the Michigan Supreme Court, which was also instrumental in arranging for additional resources during the backlog reduction phase of that program. Subsequently, the Michigan Supreme Court's adoption in 1986 of a rule limiting the time allowed for civil case discovery also seems to have been a factor influencing the delay reduction program now under way in Wayne County. In Jersey City, civil case delay reduction was entirely a local initiative, but the state's Administrative Office of Courts was very much a partner in implementing the criminal speedy trial program. In Phoenix, state-level leaders were not actively involved in either the criminal or civil case management programs, but the Arizona Supreme Court's approval of the plan for using pro tem judges to handle civil case trials when necessary was an important component of the success of the Phoenix "fast track" program.

All of those programs were, however, essentially locally based. The problems, in the first instance, were regarded as local problems, and in each of those courts local leaders have been instrumental in the implementation process.

What happens when state-level judicial leaders identify delay as a problem of statewide concern and seek to address it on a systemwide basis throughout the state? This chapter provides an overview of the development and implementation of statewide delay reduction programs in three states (Ohio, Kansas, and New Jersey) that have taken distinctly different approaches to the problem. Each of these states has at least one trial court that is included in this study. Our objective here is not to evaluate the effectiveness of specific programs, but rather to describe the strategies used by the statewide leaders and the linkages between the statewide initiatives and program implementation at the trial court level. As we shall see, the impacts of the statewide programs appear (at this stage) to be quite different in different trial courts, with outcomes greatly influenced by the extent to which state-level leaders have been successful in persuading local policymakers and practitioners—both within the judiciary and outside of it—to accept the goals and underlying rationales of the state initiatives.

A. Ohio

Ohio was the first state to undertake a comprehensive statewide delay reduction program. Begun in the early 1970s and led with great vigor and determination by the state's chief justice, the program is widely thought to have produced significant changes in case processing in the Ohio courts.

The basic structure of the present Ohio court system was established in 1968, when voters approved the Modern Courts Amendment, a major revision of Article VI (the Judicial Article) of the Ohio Constitution. The Modern Courts Amendment simplified the structure of the court system, consolidating some trial-level courts and eliminating others. The amendment also gave the supreme court general superintending authority over all state courts, vested it with broad rule-making powers, and authorized the chief justice to act as the court system's chief administrative officer. The supreme court's rule-making authority is subject to only a limited legislative veto, and court rules are recognized as superseding conflicting statues.

The Modern Courts Amendment had its genesis, at least in part, in concerns about the rapid growth of civil and criminal caseloads in the 1960s and perceptions that delays were increasing. The state's fragmented and decentralized court structure was widely regarded as archaic. After the amendment was approved in November 1968, the Ohio Supreme Court moved rapidly to address the problems of delay and administrative inefficiency. In 1970, the supreme court adopted a comprehensive new set of rules of civil procedure, standardizing civil procedure throughout the state. In 1971, after a long process of informal hearings and consultations, the court adopted the Rules of Superintendence, which were designed to define an administrative system and explicitly address problems of backlogs, delays, and judicial ineffiency.[1] The concern about delay—an issue that the state's new chief justice, C. William O'Neill, had come to believe was of critical importance to the effective administration of justice—is set forth at the start of the Rules:

> Caseloads in all our courts are increasing so fast that it is becoming difficult to provide criminal defendants with the speedy trial guaranteed them by the Constitution of the United State and the Ohio Constitution. In an attempt to bring criminal cases to trial promptly, it appears that more judges are being assigned the criminal branches of our larger metropolitan courts. One direct result of this practice is to increase further the number of all civil cases pending in many of these courts.
>
> Delay in both criminal and civil cases in the trial courts of Ohio is presently the most serious problem in the administration of justice in this state. It is to be remembered that the courts are created not for the convenience or benefit of the judges and lawyers, but to serve the litigants and the interest of the public at large. When cases are unnecessarily delayed, the confidence of all people in the judicial system suffers. The confidence of the people in the ability of our system of government to achieve liberty and justice under law for all is the foundation upon which the American system of government is built.
>
> The [Rules of Superintendence] are designed (1) to expedite the disposition of both criminal and civil cases in the trial courts of this state, while at the same time safeguarding the inalienable right of the litigant to the just processing of their causes; and (2) to serve the public interest which mandates the prompt disposition of all cases before the courts.

The process of developing the Rules of Superintendence was a lengthy one. It included a series of informal sessions at which the supreme court heard testimony from a number of judges (including the presiding judges of the common pleas courts in Ohio's eight largest counties), dissemination of initial drafts of the rules to all of the common pleas judges with an invitation for comments, and— at a later stage—consultation with representatives of the state bar association and with groups of medical doctors. By all accounts, the main driving force behind the adoption of the rules was Chief Justice O'Neill.

One of the major areas of dispute in this process was over whether the Rules of Superintendence should require a particular type of calendaring or case assignment system at the trial court level. As in most states, the Ohio courts in 1970–71 were using a variety of different calendaring systems. Two of the largest jurisdictions, Hamilton County (Cincinnati) and Cuyahoga County (Cleveland) were using the master calendar system, and judges from the common pleas courts in both counties were opposed to having any change in their calendaring system forced upon them. However, both counties were experiencing problems of delay and growing backlogs, and there were some judges and practitioners who attributed this to the continued use of the master calendar system. Reportedly, it was O'Neill who convinced the other members of the supreme court that mandatory use of the individual calendar system was essential in order to fix responsibility for handling each case with a single judge.

As finally promulgated, the Ohio Rules of Superintendence laid out in considerable detail an administrative structure and operational program aimed at achieving an expeditious pace of litigation in the state's trial courts. The general approach was to establish centrally the main goals and the mechanisms for monitoring the results, but still leave the trial courts and trial judges considerable authority and discretion over how to organize their day-to-day work to achieve the goals. The judges' independence in conducting trials and deciding cases was not curtailed at all, but their previous autonomy with respect to managing (or not managing) their caseloads was significantly affected.

The mandatory individual calendar system, together with monthly reporting requirements and other provisions of the Rules, made it possible to hold judges responsible and accountable for their performance in managing their caseload effectively. By setting specific time limits in criminal cases and requiring reports to the chief justice on every case that exceeded the time limits, the Rules forced judges to be aware of the passage of time and to schedule events carefully in those cases. The Rules did not establish any specific time limits or standards for processing of civil cases, but the monthly reporting form required judges to list the number of personal injury cases on their docket pending for more than 24 months from filing and the number of civil cases pending for over 12 months. Cases that exceeded those time periods were regarded as "old," with the reporting form noting that the chief justice could require specific information as to reasons for delay in these cases. Other provisions—including the requirements for quarterly review of dockets and dismissal of inactive cases—helped direct judges' attention to their total caseloads and heighten their "docket consciousness."

Once the Rules of Superintendence had been adopted by the supreme court, Chief Justice O'Neill took the lead in seeking to make them effective. A Republican whose experience in state government included serving as Speaker of the House, Attorney General, Governor, and Associate Justice of the Supreme Court, he was a charismatic and highly skilled leader. O'Neill had friends and allies in both political parties, and was adept at working with a wide range of groups including the media. He recognized delay as an issue in which there was at least latent public interest, and used the development of a delay reduction program—built on the foundation of the Modern Courts Amendment and the Rules of Superintendence—as a means of rallying public and media support for a strong, management-oriented judicial system. During this period, he made numerous speeches to bar groups, judges' meetings, law schools, and service clubs, all of them centering on the goals of the Rules of Superintendence and what the courts were doing to achieve them.

O'Neill is said to have threatened to publicize the docket statistics of lackadaisical judges, and is known to have personally reprimanded some judges whose dockets were in especially bad shape. But he never publicly singled out any judges for their failure to comply with the Rules, and he placed most of his emphasis on positive motivators: words of encouragement or persuasion to individual judges, requests to the legislature for judges' salary increases based on statistical evidence of improved judicial efficiency and productivity across the state, and a highly publicized program of "Superior Judicial Service" awards given to judges who reported no cases pending beyond the prescribed time periods. A Youngstown judge summed up O'Neill's approach to implementation of the Rules in these words:

> If some judges were just so far behind in their dockets and in the work they were doing and there wasn't a good reason for it, I'm sure he would have gotten after them. But I'm saying the average run of the mill judge, particularly the ones in the larger cities, I think that he was able to get compliance by encouraging them to comply. The point is that he encourages people to comply, rather than threatens them with what would happen if they didn't.[2]

The Rules of Superintendence, particularly the reporting requirements, were highly unpopular with some judges from the outset. These judges, rejecting the idea that judges should be "administrators," spoke of being "overruled" and "ruled to death." But most judges, in the years immediately following the promulgation of the Rules, were neither enthusiastic proponents nor disdainful skeptics. Few of them had any great enthusiasm for the reporting requirements, but they complied with them.

Although state AOC officials could have audited the reports by checking them against case files, they never actually did so. The reports were, however, spot-checked for mathematical accuracy, and AOC staff members would periodically contact individual judges by telephone when they found apparent inaccuracies.[3] Judges in the trial court knew that the reports were being scrutinized, and that may have helped to ensure broad compliance. As a practical matter, the monthly reports were viewed by state-level officials as being primarily a management tool for individual judges—a regular statement summarizing the status of their dockets.

Operationally, the monthly reports served both informational and motivational functions at the trial court level. In any multijudge court or division, the monthly statistics of all of the judges were collected by the administrative judge, and judges could check their own statistics against those of the other judges. The system evoked both competitiveness and individual pride in effectively managing a docket among many of the judges, as the following comments illustrate:

> You see what's in that report and you know what the other fellows have in their reports and you know, I'd say 10% of my criminal cases are over time and what the hell is wrong here and we would sit down and go over each of them and find out why they are so far out. (Columbus judge)[4]

> The rules have given the judge personal responsibility for cases, triggering a sense of responsibility and pride in disposing of it. I think that judges generally have a feeling that they want to do a good job. Part of the job is what the Rules of Superintendence say. (Youngstown judge)[5]

One of the threshold problems in implementing the program in some trial courts was the existence of a large backlog of pending cases. To help deal with this problem, Chief Justice O'Neill made extensive use of his authority (provided by the Modern Courts Amendment) to assign retired and visiting judges where needed. In Cleveland, for example, additional judges provided under this authority enabled the court to run "double-shifts" for a number of months to help reduce the backlog.

O'Neill also used his position as a member of the state's Crime Control Planning Board (which had responsibility for allocation of LEAA funds) to help obtain resources for trial court improvements and innovation. LEAA funds were used to help support training for judges and trial court administrators, to establish court-annexed arbitration programs, and to begin utilizing new video and audio technology.

Assessing the impact of the Rules of Superintendence on case processing times in three Ohio trial courts in the early 1970s, researchers from the American Judicature Society found that the Rules contributed to speedier criminal case processing in the three trial courts they studied, although the degree of impact varied somewhat from court to court.[6] Our own study includes two Ohio courts (Cleveland and Dayton), neither of which was involved in the AJS study, and it was not designed as an assessment of the impact of the Rules of Superintendence. In looking at case processing in Cleveland and Dayton, however, one cannot help but be struck by the long-term impact of the changes introduced by Chief Justice O'Neill and his colleagues in the early 1970s.

O'Neill died in office in 1978, and his successors as chief justice have focused their attention on other priorities, but the system has remained intact. The Rules are essentially unchanged from what they were in the early 1970s. Trial court judges still operate on an individual calendar system, they still sign and submit monthly reports on the status of their criminal and civil dockets, and interviews in Dayton and elsewhere in the state indicate that most judges are very conscious of the state of their dockets.

Perhaps most important, the Rules provide policy objectives and an administrative framework for strong caseflow management at the local level. As we have seen in Chapter 6, the court in Dayton worked within that framework in developing comprehensive civil and criminal case management programs that have proven to be remarkably effective. In Cleveland, where no such comprehensive program has been undertaken, the court's overall civil and criminal case processing times are generally slower than in Dayton, but the time to disposition in civil cases is nevertheless one of the half-dozen fastest of the 17 courts in the study. The Cleveland court's felony case processing times place it near the middle of those rankings.

B. Kansas

In Kansas, as in Ohio, state-level efforts to attack problems of trial court delay have been closely linked to the politics of implementing a constitutional amendment designed to modernize the state's court system. The issues and personalities involved have been different, however, and so have the approaches and techniques employed.

In 1972, Kansas voters approved a new judicial article to the state's constitution that paved the way for structural unification of what had been a highly decentralized and fragmented court system. When the initial implementing legislation took effect in 1977, the state's probate, juvenile, magistrate, county, and district courts were all consolidated into a single court of general jurisdiction: the district court. The following year the unification effort went a step further; the legislature provided for the state to take over the funding of the personnel costs of all non-judicial employees in the district courts beginning in 1979.

A new chief justice, Alfred Schroeder, took office in December 1977. In the summer of 1979 he named Dr. Howard Schwartz (then the personnel officer in the state's Office of Judicial Administration) as the state's Judicial Administrator. It was Schroeder and Schwartz who would have the task of making the newly unified court system work, a task that was complicated by the fact that the costs to the state of funding all the non-judicial personnel in the court system were proving to be higher than had been forecast by some of the proponents of state financing.

Early in his career, Schroeder had been in the Judge Advocate General's Corps of the Air Force, working in a system that placed strict time limits on the duration of court-martial proceedings. Later, as a trial judge in Kansas, he managed his own calendar and became convinced that judges could effectively prevent delay without impairing the quality of justice. After he became the chief justice, at a point where the court system was facing considerable hostility from the legislature, it was logical for him to focus on delay as an issue around which to rally his forces.

It was not until more than two years after Schroeder took office as chief justice that the Kansas speedy trial program got underway in any formal sense. During those first two years, however, much of the initial goundwork was laid, as the state's Office of Judicial Administration worked to develop the infrastructure of a truly unified court system. One critical problem had to do with the information on caseloads and case processing times. This was an area in which Kansas was actually ahead of most other states because Schwartz's predecessor as state court administrator, Jim James, had begun the development of an information system that enabled the OJA to have a sense of the size and status of trial court caseloads. The available data indicated there were not pervasive problems of delay in the Kansas trial courts, although there were a number of civil cases that had been pending for over two years. The decision was made early in Schroeder's tenure as chief justice to start a delay reduction program before a serious problem developed. During 1978 and 1979, before ever beginning a formal program, the state leadership began quietly working on older cases, using their authority to assign judges across districts to help deal with them.

The first steps toward developing a structured delay reduction program were taken in the spring of 1980, when the Kansas Supreme Court appointed two committees whose work laid the foundations for the speedy trial program. The first of these, called the Supreme Court Standards Committee, was charged with developing means of ensuring just, speedy, and inexpensive dispute resolution. The committee was chaired jointly by Chief Justice Schroeder and Justice David Prager of the Supreme Court, and included among its members two court of appeals judges, seven trial court judges, four attorneys, and three other citizens. Its report, completed in October 1980, and entitled *General Principles and Guidelines for the District Courts*, began by emphasizing that justice, not speed, is the primary judicial goal in case disposition. But it noted that delay "causes litigants expense and anxiety," and called for a pro-active role for courts in ensuring against unnecessary delay:

> No case should be permitted to float in the system. It is the responsibility of the trial judge assigned the case to take charge of the case at an early date in the litigation and to control the progress of the case thereafter until the case is determined.

In addition to stressing that the court, rather than the attorneys, should control the pace of litigation, the report also maintained that case processing time standards should be established. The standards would serve *"as a guide* for the disposition of cases, with the understanding that the system must have flexibility to accommodate the differences in the complexity of cases and the different problems arising in urban and rural judicial districts."

The report recommended that time standards be established for six classes of cases and set forth a recommended median time from filing or first appearance to final disposition for each type of case, as follows:

Type of Case	Recommended Time
Major Civil	
Non-domestic	180 days
Domestic	120 days
Limited Civil	60 days
Probate	365 days
Felony	120 days
Misdemeanor	60 days
Traffic	30 days

The report called for an initial discovery conference to be set no later than 60 days after the filing of a civil case, and said that any civil case pending for more than 180 days should be of special concern to trial judges. Perhaps most critical for effective implementation of a program designed to focus on old cases, the report stated that "when a report of the Judicial Administrator shows that a civil case has been pending for more than two years, such case shall be given priority over all subsequently filed cases and the administrative judge should report the reason for delay in disposition to the departmental justice."

The second committee, known as the Statistical Reporting Committee, was chaired by Schwartz. Made up of trial court administrators and clerks, the purpose of this committee was to develop improved procedures for collecting and reporting the basic information required to manage trial court caseloads. The committee first met in July and completed its work by the end of the year. It developed a standardized set of forms to be used to manage the daily business of the court and, through the use of carbon sheets, simultaneously provide the statistical information to be forwarded to the state Office of Judicial Administration in Topeka.

In December 1980, at about the same time that the Statistical Reporting Committee was completing its work, the supreme court adopted the principles and guidelines recommended by its Standards Committee.[7] The basic foundation of the state's program was then in place: time standards (to serve as *guidelines*, not enforceable outer limits); a statistical reporting system that would enable case processing time performance to be monitored in light of the standards; a new rule (Rule 136) that required district court judges to become involved in the management of civil cases at an early stage; and a clear statement from the supreme court—in its adoption of the Report of the Standards Committee—that judges should be concerned about the expeditious resolution of disputes that come before them.

At the state level, the Kansas delay reduction program got underway in January 1981. At that time, the *Principles and Guidelines* adopted by the supreme court were distributed to all of the district courts and arrangements were made for a series of meetings with the administrative judges, chief clerks, and trial court administrators. At the meetings, the time standards and statistical reporting system were explained in detail, and it was announced that they would come into operation with the start of the fiscal year beginning July 1, 1981. This gave the courts and the OJA six months to adapt their operating procedures to the requirements of the new standards and the reporting system.

The first quarterly report on the delay reduction program was issued in October 1981. The publication of this report is especially significant, as it set some important precedents and established a basic orientation that has held steady in subsequent years. First, the quarterly report contained only a few items of information about each court—the statistical data most relevant to an assessment of the court's performance with respect to the goals of the delay reduction program. These included the number of cases pending and disposed, the median age of cases disposed during the quarter, and the number and percentage of civil cases pending for more than 24 months and criminal cases pending more than 12 months. The report deliberately did not include more detailed caseflow management information such as number of continuances or number of jury trials, on the grounds that these were details of local management and were thus concerns for each court.

Second, the statistics were presented by the OJA as an accurate representation of trial court performance, based on data generated by the trial courts themselves. When some local-level administrators and judges protested that the numbers for their courts were wrong, it was made clear that OJA officials had confidence in the system. It would be up to the trial court clerks and administrators to see to it that the information on cases in their courts was accurate, although OJA would provide technical assistance.

Third, the statistics were published and made readily available to everyone—media, legislators, the governor, and private citizens— as well as to the judiciary. The effect was to make highly visible the linkage between the standards, statistics, and judicial performance, thereby increasing the importance of all three for everyone concerned. As one administrator stated, the purpose was "to raise their [the judges'] level of consciousness. Very early we told judges they should control their courts." Collecting the statistics ensured the information would be available. Making the information public ensured it would be treated as significant. As a consequence, as one administator stated, judges and administrators "can see how they're doing and how Joe Blow, whom they consider comparable, is doing and how the state as a whole is doing."

Fourth, the 31 district courts were ranked on the basis of their success in minimizing the number of old pending cases. The court with the lowest percentage of cases exceeding the outer limits (24 months for civil cases, 12 months for criminal cases) was ranked first, and the court with the highest percentage ranked last. These rankings were published as part of the quarterly report, thus creating a major dynamic for enforcement of the standards—competition among the judges and administators, focused primarily on minimizing the number of old pending cases. The Kansas delay reduction program has never had formal sanctions that could be imposed on a court if it did not conform to the standards, but the comparisons provided by the published rankings are not taken lightly. Howard Schwartz reports that no court has ever ranked at the bottom of the list for two successive quarters.

In subsequent years, the statistical reporting and publication program operated much as it first appeared in October 1981. The statistics are featured in OJA's monthly newsletter, with emphasis on the most positive aspects of the data—e.g. progress throughout the state (and in individual courts) in reducing the percentage of older pending cases, courts that have fast median case processing times, and so forth. When the statistics show a district ranking high or making notable progress, a commendatory letter is sent to the administrative judge. Externally, the program is publicized through news releases, press conferences, and radio and television interviews.[8]

Although the primary approach of the state program has been to provide a structure and set of incentives for local initiatives, the effort also included several types of direct implementation assistance to the district courts.[9] First, OJA staff provided help to local trial courts in handling operational problems such as recordkeeping, personnel administration, and development of caseflow management systems. Sometimes this assistance was provided through formal training programs. More often, it consisted of on-site technical assistance responses to a specific request from the court administrator or administrative judge. Another form of assistance has involved making additional judges (retired judges or active judges in districts where dockets are current) available to help meet a temporary problem such as an unusually long trial or an extraordinary backlog. One senior administrator, discussing OJA policy regarding this type of assistance, commented that "we don't want them having the excuse that they don't have enough resources. [If a local court asks for assistance] I don't second-guess the quality of the request."

On a statewide basis, there is considerable evidence that the Kansas program has been successful. Figures from OJA's quarterly report for December 31, 1986, showed that the median age of felony cases at disposition was 67 days, well within the state's standard of 120 days median time from arrest to disposition. On the civil side, the statewide median time to disposition for general civil cases was 105 days, or 75 days less than the standard of 180 days. More sig-

Table 8A
TRENDS IN SIZE AND AGE OF PENDING CASELOADS
IN KANSAS (STATEWIDE), 1980–1986

	June 30, 1980		June 30, 1982		December 31, 1986	
	Number Pending	% of Total	Number Pending	% of Total	Number Pending	% of Total
Criminal Cases Pending Over 12 Months	825	12.8%	198	4.8%	82	1.6%
Civil Cases Pending Over 24 Months	2,218	5.8%	1,265	2.7%	404	1.3%

nificantly, the proportion of "old" pending cases has dropped markedly since the start of the program, as shown by the figures in Table 8A.

In the state's largest trial court, the district court located in Wichita, the changes have not been as dramatic as they have been in most of the rest of Kansas. For the last two quarters of 1986, the median felony case processing time in Wichita was 112 days, considerably longer than the statewide median of 67 days. The median time to disposition in civil cases, at 110 days, was also higher than the statewide median of 105 days. Indeed, if one looks only at median times, it appears that both civil and criminal case processing times have become longer in Wichita than they were before the start of the statewide program. As Table 8B shows, our samples of terminated cases indicate that median felony case processing time in Wichita increased from 88 days in 1979 to 115 days in 1985. The increases in median times are even more striking on the civil side: from 290 to 411 days for tort cases and from 98 to 160 days for general civil cases.

If median time to disposition were the only criterion for assessing a program's effectiveness in quantitative terms, changes of those magnitudes would raise serious questions about the impact of the program in Wichita. But the median is only one of a number of measures that are relevant to such an assessment, and an examination of data on other possible measures tells a somewhat different story. Table 8B indicates, for example, that the age of the 90th percentile civil case (i.e. the point at which only 10% of the cases are slower), which was at 895 days in 1983, dropped to 632 days in 1985. The percentage of cases requiring over two years to complete,

Table 8B
CASE PROCESSING TIMES IN WICHITA, 1979–1985

	1979	1983	1984	1985
Tort Disposition Times				
Median	290	492	295	411
75th Percentile	512	784	590	670
90th Percentile	720	1,073	848	786
Percent Over One Year	40%	63%	42%	60%
Percent Over Two Years	9%	31%	17%	16%
General Civil Docket Disposition Times				
Median	98	206	166	160
75th Percentile	266	607	413	308
90th Percentile	513	895	687	632
Percent Over One Year	18%	37%	28%	21%
Percent Over Two Years	4%	17%	9%	6%
Felony Case Disposition Times[a]				
Median	88	117	126	115
75th Percentile	153	159	170	156
90th Percentile	240	231	275	205
Percent Over 180 Days	19%	18%	20%	16%

[a]Measured from date complaint filed for 1979, 1983, and 1984; from date of arrest for 1985.

which has been the primary target of the statewide program, dropped from 17% in 1983 to 6% in 1985. At the end of 1986, out of 6,208 civil cases pending in the Wichita court, only 44 (0.7%) had been filed more than two years earlier.

On the criminal side, where the main focus has also been on minimizing the number and percentage of old cases, the 90th percentile case took 201 days in 1985, compared to 213 days in 1979. At the end of 1986, only 13 of the 925 felony cases pending in the court had been open for more than a year. Thus, while median times have increased somewhat in Wichita since 1979, they are still less than the median times called for by the Kansas standards. Perhaps more importantly, the size of the pending caseload has decreased during this period and the number of very lengthy cases has dropped markedly.

While the Wichita court does not rank high among the 31 districts in the Kansas system in terms of its case processing times, it compares very favorably with other courts in our nationwide study in terms of the measures that are of greatest importance under the Kansas standards. It ranks second in terms of median general civil docket disposition times, has the third lowest percentage of civil cases taking over two years, and ranks fifth in the speed with which it handles its 90th percentile felony cases (Tables 2D and 2F, supra).

The impact of the Kansas statewide program has not been dramatic in Wichita, but there can be no doubt that it has had an influence. Prior to the start of the program, the Wichita court was already a "fast" court, as evidenced by the data on 1979 dispositions. However, it had no institutionalized system of caseflow management and very little in the way of regularly collected information that would be useful in ascertaining the extent to which there was a delay problem, identifying bottlenecks, and helping to manage the caseloads.

When the statewide program went into effect in 1980, it met with some initial resentment and resistance in Wichita. As one prominent attorney observed in a 1986 interview, "the bar was not receptive to adoption of the new rules." In fact, the new program and rules did not suddenly change the day-to-day operation of the court. Both civil and criminal case processing still take place under the master calender system, which had been set up in the late 1960s. Over time, however, the court has taken a number of steps to address the old case problem and to set up a system to schedule cases itself, rather than leave scheduling entirely with the attorneys. In civil cases, the effort initially involved a periodic inventory of all of the case files, with court staff reviewing docket sheets to identify inactive cases. In these cases, a notice of intent to dismiss for failure to prosecute was sent to the plaintiff's attorney. If no response was received, a dismissal order would be entered. The procedure resulted in disposition of a number of old cases, and its use provides at least a partial explanation for the lengthy median times shown for 1983 dispositions.

In terms of on-going caseflow management in Wichita, the most important innovation has been implementation of the requirement for an early discovery conference in civil cases, which was mandated by the supreme court rule adopted in December 1980. Much of the effort to accelerate the pace of civil litigation in the 18th District has centered on this conference, which has been put in place within the framework of the court's master calendar system. One judge was assigned exclusively to handle discovery conferences, with the object of moving the discovery process forward as quickly as possible. The role of the judge evolved into being a pro-active manager of cases from filing to the pretrial conference. The judge assigned to the position in 1986 reported using a variety of techniques to move discovery to conclusion. Once a case is filed, a discovery conference is scheduled. The conference is used "to find out what they are doing, kick them in the butt, or set it for pretrial." In complex cases, he works out a schedule of depositions with attorneys, then reschedules a subsequent discovery conference. At each meeting, he asks for a report on what each lawyer has done to complete discovery. He prides himself on being tough but fair, able to distinguish between complex cases that require extensive time for discovery from those in which delay is only a function of inactivity by the lawyer.

The effect of these efforts has been to accelerate the discovery process, but long delays between the completion of discovery and the pretrial conferences are still common. There are often further delays between the pretrial conference and the trial date. In April of 1986, a pretrial conference could not be scheduled until November, with a further wait after that for a trial date. The trial scheduling process has become a primary focus of attention as the court seeks to move toward a firm trial date system.

On the criminal side, there have been no major changes in procedure, but the court has developed its own case tracking system and has instituted a relatively tight continuance policy. At arraignment, cases are set for trial approximately 100 days later, with all discovery and motions to be concluded by the trial date. This "100 day track" is the reason for the relatively long median time in the court. While continuances are still granted in many cases, the system is designed to assure that over half of the cases reach disposition within 120 days (thus meeting the Kansas median time standard) and that all of the rest are concluded within a year after filing (thus meeting the primary objective of the statewide program).

The case management process in Wichita is still evolving, with the court gradually moving toward earlier and stronger exercise of control over case scheduling. It is hard to assess the degree to which the time standards and other elements of the statewide program are responsible for the change, but clearly they have had some impact. The impact is perhaps most clearly manifested in the way the profile of the pending caseload has changed to reflect the goals of the statewide program—median times that are within the program goals (although longer than in earlier years), and a sharp reduction in the number of old cases on the docket.

Statewide, the time standards seem to have gained increased acceptance from the bar. In a 1985 survey of Kansas lawyers conducted by the state's Office of Judicial Administration, 70% said that they favored retention of the standards, though some felt that they should be modified in some respects. In particular, defense attorneys in civil cases felt product liability and medical malpractice cases were too complicated to handle within the guidelines set by the current standards. There was also some sense that some Kansas judges were overly concerned with statistics about case processing time.[10] The results of the Kansas bar survey suggest that the issue for the late 1980s and beyond may not be so much *whether* the courts should manage their business as *how* they should go about doing it. As Howard Schwartz and Leslie Ratliff suggest in an article summarizing the results of the survey, the standards appear to be working for Kansas but may need some fine-tuning.[11]

C. New Jersey

When Robert N. Wilentz became Chief Justice of New Jersey in August 1979, trial court delay in criminal cases was clearly a serious problem in the state. During the 1970s, pending criminal caseloads in the superior court (the trial court of general jurisdiction) had grown steadily larger from year to year, and delays had become longer and longer. According to data collected by the New Jersey Administrative Office of Courts, the median time from indictment to trial had increased from about three months in 1960 to over nine months in 1979. These figures were simply medians: half of the cases were taking more than nine months from indictment. Moreover, there was no regularly collected information that would indicate how long cases were taking between arrest and indictment. In the absence of any reliable data, observers could only speculate about this, but it was estimated that the pre-indictment period averaged about three months.

As soon as he became chief justice, Wilentz pinpointed delay in criminal cases as a top priority problem and immediately began taking steps to reverse the trends of recent years. Robert D. Lipscher, a court administrator who had achieved national recognition for his work in the federal courts as circuit executive for the second circuit, was appointed Administrative Director of the Courts, effective January 1, 1980. Even before Lipscher formally took office, preliminary planning got underway for demonstration projects in two counties that would focus interest on the problem of pre-indictment delay and would provide an opportunity to experiment with new techniques. To help plan a comprehensive statewide program, two task forces were formed in January 1980, one to focus on pre-indictment problems and the other to deal with post-indictment matters. Each task force was chaired by a judge and included representatives of the state's Division of Criminal Justice, the county prosecutors, and the regionalized state public defender's office.

By June 1980, when the state's annual Judicial Conference was held, demonstration projects in Union and Passaic counties had been underway for several months and the two task forces had prepared reports and recommendations. The Judicial Conference—a gathering of nearly 500 judges, county officials, prosecutors, public defenders, legislators, and bar leaders—became the forum for an intensive review of the delay problem and consideration of proposals (contained mainly in the task force reports) for a broad-scale attack on it. While the conference did not give explicit approval to any specific procedural changes, there was a broad consensus that criminal case delay had reached unacceptable lengths and that the judiciary had to take primary responsibility for planning and implementing a speedy trial program. Chief Justice Wilentz, in his remarks at the conference, expressed both an understanding of the difficulties that would be faced and a sense of the urgency about the need to get started:

> The goals of speedy trial will not result automatically from some simple order by the Supreme Court. It is a hope to make progress immediately but it's clear that it will take at least several years to achieve whatever speedy trial goals may be set. . . .

> I am committed to judicial involvement in the management of criminal cases to the date of disposition. To a significant extent, this will be a new responsibility for New Jersey judges. It does not mean that judges of the Supreme Court are suddenly going to make the prosecutors or the public defenders do this or do that. When it comes to the right way to accomplish speedy trials, the only thing we're doctrinaire about is that they won't be achieved without the cooperation of the Public Defender, the cooperation of the Attorney General, and the Public Advocate, and that you don't get cooperation unless you recognize their concerns and their interests. But having said that, there is no question in my mind that the judicial involvement in the management of criminal cases must be much more significant than it has been in the past. . . .

> We do not intend to achieve speedy trials in criminal matters by increasing delay in civil matters. In fact, we hope to reduce delay in both simultaneously.

And last, we see no reason to wait. We see no reason to look for the completed conceptual plan for the perfect program to achieve speedy trials. We see no reason to study further and to plan further. We want to learn by doing and we want to start now.[12]

Within a month after the June 1980 Judicial Conference, the state's supreme court had approved in principle a fairly detailed plan, prepared by the Administrative Office of Courts, for a statewide delay reduction program. The plan adopted most of the recommendations of the two task forces, including the creation of local "delay reduction teams" in each county, chaired by the assignment judge and including representatives of the various agencies involved in criminal case processing. It also set goals: an ultimate goal of disposing of all except exceptional criminal matters within 135 days from arrest and a set of sub-goals framed in terms of maximum time periods for specific stages of the process. The goals were to be phased in over a period of three years, and called for somewhat tighter time frames for cases in which a defendant was in custody.

A separate approach was taken toward cases already in the system. The pending caseload was to be reduced gradually over a three-year period, so that ideally there would be no cases older than 135 days from arrest (90 days from indictment) at the end of the three years. The specific goals, as set forth in a memorandum from the Administrative Director of the Courts, are shown in Figure 8-1.

The plan approved by the supreme court in July 1980 provided for a continuation of the two demonstration programs already underway plus the launching of two new ones, all aimed at accelerating the arrest-to-indictment process. Additionally, the plan called for close monitoring of progress toward the goals (with the trial courts in each county to submit monthly reports to the AOC on filings, dispositions, pending cases, age of disposed cases, etc), designation of a "criminal assignment clerk" in each county who would be responsible for monitoring case progress, and the forwarding of all complaints in indictable matters to the assignment clerk within 48 hours of arrest. Existing rules of criminal procedure were revised to provide for early post-indictment scheduling conferences and close monitoring of case progress by the court. Each local delay reduction team was to develop a detailed plan for achieving the program's case processing time goals and submit it for review by AOC staff and a newly created statewide speedy trial committee chaired by the chief justice. The target date for completing the local plans was November 15, 1980, with implementation to begin in January 1981.

Figure 8-1
NEW JERSEY CRIMINAL SPEEDY TRIAL PROGRAM GOALS

	Arrest to Indictment	Indictment to Arraignment	Arraignment to Disposition	Total Days
New Cases				
First Year (1/81-12/81)	80 days	10 days	150 days	240 days
Second Year (1/82-12/82)	60 days	10 days	110 days	180 days
Third Year (1/83-12/83)	45 days	10 days	80 days	135 days
Jail Cases				
First Year	40 days	5 days	75 days	120 days
Second Year	30 days	5 days	55 days	90 days
Third Year	30 days	5 days	55 days	90 days

Backlog Reduction—First Year: Reduce the backlog by one-third, defined as the number of cases over 240 days as of January 1, 1981.

Second Year: Further reduce the backlog by another one-third, defined as the number of cases over 180 days as of January 1, 1982.

Third Year: Eliminate the backlog remainder, defined as any cases over 135 days.

Source: Administrative Office of the Courts, State of New Jersey, Memorandum to Assignment Judges from Robert D. Lipscher, July 25, 1980. Reproduced in Anthony J. Langdon, *The New Jersey Speedy Trial Program* (Denver: Institute for Court Management, 1983), pp. 271, 276.

In view of the New Jersey judiciary's 30-year history of strong centralized administration, the program's emphasis on local planning was something of a reversal of earlier policies. Given the county-based organization of the agencies principally involved in criminal case processing, however, the reliance on local planning seems not only desirable but probably unavoidable. For a speedy criminal trial program to work at the trial court level, the cooperation of many local agencies, institutions, and individuals would be essential.

Robert Lipscher has aptly described the criminal case process in New Jersey as "multi-leveled, complex, and delay-prone."[13] The problems are particularly acute in the pre-indictment stages of the process, which typically includes initial appearance, bail-setting, and a preliminary hearing in the municipal court, followed by grand jury action. Public defenders are rarely involved at the municipal court stage, but handle most cases once they reach the superior court. County prosecutors screen cases, usually after a complaint has been filed, and decide whether to handle the case as an indictable offense (requiring grand jury action and prosecution in superior court) or "downgrade" it to be handled in the municipal court. The municipal courts, of which there are 529 in the state, varied widely in the speed with which they handled incoming cases. Although nominally part of the state's unified court system, the municipal courts had been subject to little direct supervision, and few of them routinely collected information that would be helpful in monitoring case progress.

Establishment of the broad-based local planning team, chaired by the assignment judge, was conceived of as a way of addressing the problems inherent in this complex process. In many counties, the approach worked very well, with cooperative endeavors producing plans that were creative and effective. The Hudson County program described in Chapter 7 is an example of a clear success: it developed an innovative and highly effective pre-indictment case processing system, and by 1983 had succeeded in reducing the pending caseload and in achieving a dramatic reduction in case processing times. The progress in Hudson County has continued, with case processing times continuing to decrease in 1984 and 1985.

In some of the other counties, however, success has been harder to achieve. One such county is Essex, the most populous county in the state, which contains the state's largest city (Newark) as well as a number of other municipalities. The Essex County Superior Court, which is located in Newark, also participated in the National Center's *Justice Delayed* study, and it is thus possible to develop an overview of trends and developments in the court over a 10-year period.

Table 8C
CRIMINAL CASE PROCESSING TIMES IN NEWARK, 1976–1985

	1976	1983	1985
Total Disposition Time			
Median	209	251	300
Third Quartile	354	405	486
90th Percentile	—	631	882
Percent Over 180 Days	57%	65%	61%
Upper Court Disposition Time			
Median	99	141	124
Third Quartile	179	350	294
90th Percentile	—	612	592
Lower Court Processing Time			
Median	79	135	168
Third Quartile	—	184	234
90th Percentile	—	265	335

Writing in 1978, the authors of *Justice Delayed* described the Newark court as one in which judicial control of case progress was relatively lax. Calendar management was left primarily to the prosecutor's office, but delay reduction and case management did not appear to be elements of concern in that office. The Newark court was one of the slower ones in the *Justice Delayed* study, with a 1976 median upper court time of 99 days, and a median total disposition time of 168 days.

Data from our current study shows considerable deterioration in the situation since that time. Table 8C provides a comparison of 1976, 1983, and 1985 case processing times, using a number of different measures. On every measure, the times are longer in 1983 and 1985 than they were in 1976. Upper court times (from indictment to disposition) show some improvement from 1983 to 1985, but the pre-indictment period—which even in 1976 was considerably longer in Newark than in any of the other courts in the *Justice Delayed* study—has become steadily longer. The 1985 Essex County median pre-indictment period of 168 days was longer than the median total time to disposition in all but one of the other courts in this study.

What explains the strikingly different patterns that have developed in Hudson and Essex over the past decade? In particular, why have the state-level initiatives, which were so important a part of the successes in Hudson County, had such a difficult time bearing fruit in Essex? There are no quick and easy answers to these questions. Our preliminary analysis indicates that there are a number of interrelated factors that may account for the lack of success in Essex.

One factor, frequently pointed to by practitioners in Newark, may be the composition of the caseload. As we saw in Chapter 3, eight of the 18 courts in this study had more filings per judge in 1985 than the Newark court, but only four had a higher total 1985 workload (i.e. 1985 filings plus cases pending at the start of 1985) (Table 3F). Additionally, the proportion of homicides, rapes, and robberies in the total caseload was substantially greater in Newark, where 20% of the 1985 dispositions involved such charges, than in any of the other high volume courts.

Perhaps reflecting the seriousness of the cases (and the potential consequences in terms of severity of sentence or even a plea to reduced charges), the trial rate in Newark (10%) is the second highest of any of the courts in this study. The combination of a heavy workload, high proportion of serious charges, and high trial rate means that demands on court system resources are high. Indeed, given this set of factors, the upper court processing times in Newark—a median time of 124 days, a 75th percentile figure of 294 days—may not seem far out of line. At the upper court level, the Newark median is only four days longer than Jersey City's. The problem appears to be not so much at the post-indictment stage as in the period between arrest and indictment. There, the contrast between case processing time in the two courts is striking:

Lower Court Case Processing Times, 1985	Time in Days	
	Hudson Co.	Essex Co.
Median	54	168
Third Quartile	75	234
90th Percentile	93	335

Essex County is geographically larger than Hudson, and has many more municipalities. Twenty-two different municipal courts handle court proceedings prior to the filing of an indictment. As of mid-1986 it had not been possible to establish a central post-arrest processing point similar to the CJP unit that operates in Jersey City. The structural fragmentation, by itself, is a formidable obstacle to speedy pre-indictment case processing.

In Hudson County, the fragmentation was overcome through the cooperative efforts of the prosecutor and the court leaders. In

Essex County, no such cooperative effort was undertaken during the first half of the 1980s. As in the mid-1970s, delay reduction was simply not a priority for the prosecutor's office during this period. That office actively resisted the notion of court control over case progress during the pre-indictment period, taking the position that pre-indictment case management was exclusively a prosecutorial responsibility. Communications between the prosecutor's office and the court continued with respect to day-to-day operational issues, but there were no significant joint efforts to address the systemic case processing problems in the county. And, as caseload pressures continued unabated, case processing times lengthened (especially in the period between arrest and indictment), and backlogs increased.

In June 1986, New Jersey's annual Judicial Conference again focused its attention exclusively on issues related to criminal case delay, examining the experiences of the preceding six years and the prospects for the future. Looking retrospectively, the evidence seemed strong that a major objective had been achieved: on a statewide basis, the median time from arrest to disposition had been cut by more than half, from over a year (378 days) to 163 days. Active pending cases in the superior court had also decreased, from a total of 17,200 in January 1980 to 14,216 in January 1986. There were also fewer "old" cases, involving defendants indicted more than 12 months earlier: the total of 4,105 in 1980 had dropped to 3,626 in 1986.[14]

When the statewide totals are broken out by county, it is clear that the program has had significantly different impacts in different counties. For example, nine of 21 counties in the state had cut their backlogs of one-year old indictments by 70%, and four others had cut theirs by 40%. Essex and Mercer Counties, on the other hand, had substantial increases in their old case backlogs, and together accounted for nearly 70% of the cases pending more than one year in superior court.[15]

Results of a survey of criminal justice practitioners, conducted in preparation for the 1986 Judicial Conference, indicated differences of opinion as to how the speedy trial program had affected aspects of the quality of justice. By and large, judges and prosecutors felt strongly that the quality of justice had not been impaired, while public defenders and private attorneys were more skeptical. It was clear, however, that all of the practitioners felt that the speedy trial program created pressure to dispose of cases, with both prosecutors and defenders feeling increased pressure to resolve cases through negotiated pleas.[16]

New Jersey's 1986 Judicial Conference was in many respects an extraordinary event—a searching self-examination of a major delay reduction program, initiated by the program's leaders and joined by a broad range of policymakers and practitioners both within the judiciary and in other institutions. Not surprisingly, the results of the stock-taking were mixed. There was clear evidence of success, but also a realization that the program had not achieved even its first-level delay reduction goals in some counties and a recognition that many difficult issues remain to be addressed.

D. Summary

The experiences of the three states whose delay reduction programs have been briefly reviewed in this chapter are directly relevant to policymakers and judical leaders in a number of other states in which delay reduction programs—generally involving development of case processing time standards—are now being planned or are in the initial stages of implementation. State judicial leaders in Ohio, Kansas, and New Jersey were among the first to identify court delay as a serious problem and to initiate major programs to address the problem on a statewide basis.

On the positive side there is clear evidence that the programs have made a difference. In all three states, the programs produced an increased sense of "docket consciousness" among judges and other practitioners and, on a statewide basis, led to significant reductions in case processing times and in the size and age of pending caseloads. In some places (Dayton and Jersey City are good examples) the statewide programs provided a framework and "legitimization" for local-level leaders to develop innovative programs that have proven highly effective.

At the same time, it is also clear from these experiences that successful implementation of statewide delay reduction programs is a difficult long-term undertaking, one that will require cooperation from a great many institutions and individuals. The situation in Newark is illustrative. With no local "buy-in" to the program (and, indeed, active resistance to it on the part of the prosecutor), case processing times in Essex County became longer and pending caseloads increased during the first five years of the New Jersey speedy trial program. Even in Newark, however, there is evidence that persistence may pay off. A new prosecutor for Essex County was appointed in 1986, and as of mid-1987 cooperative planning efforts were underway to streamline the pre-indictment process and attack the backlog of pending post-indictment cases.

ENDNOTES–Chapter 8

1. The Ohio Rules of Superintendence have previously been the subject of a study by researchers from the American Judicature Society. For the full report, see Charles W. Grau and Arlene Sheskin, *Ruling Out Delay: The Impact of Ohio's Rules of Superintendence on the Administration of Justice* (Chicago: American Judicature Society, 1980). A greatly condensed version of the study, bearing the same title, was published in *Judicature*, Vol. 66, Nos. 3–4 (September–October 1982), pp. 108–121. Our description of the background and initial implementation of the Rules draws heavily on Grau and Sheskin's work, but has also taken account of interviews conducted with Ohio judges and lawyers during the course of this study.

2. Grau and Sheskin, *Ruling Out Delay* (Full Report), p. 67.

3. Interview with Douglas K. Somerlot, former Administrative Assistant to Chief Justice O'Neill, May 1987.

4. Grau and Sheskin, *Ruling Out Delay* (Full Report), p. 76.

5. *Ibid.*, p. 77

6. *Ibid.*, pp. 159–166; *Judicature* article, pp. 115–121. The AJS researchers found a marked impact on case processing times in the Youngstown and Columbus courts in the year following adoption of the Rules. In Cincinnati, where the Rules forced a changeover from a master calendar to an individual calendar system, the initial impact was negligible. However, when the state's criminal speedy trial statute went into effect in 1974 (after the change over to individual calendars had been made), there was a significant decrease in case processing times in Cincinnati.

7. Kansas Supreme Court, General Principles and Guidelines for the District Courts, 230 Kan. xviii.

8. See generally Howard Schwartz and Robert C. Broomfield, "Delay: How Kansas and Phoenix are Making it Disappear," *Judges Journal*, Vol. 23, No. 1 (Winter 1984), p. 72; also Howard Schwartz, "Oiling the Wheels of Justice," *State Court Journal*, Vol. 8, No. 2 (Spring 1984), p. 20.

9. *Ibid.*

10. Howard P. Schwartz and Leslie Ratliff, "Delay in State Courts: Are Time Standards an Answer?," *Judicature*, Vol. 70, No. 2 (August–September 1986), pp. 124–126.

11. *Ibid.*, p. 126.

12. Quoted in Anthony J. Langdon, T*he New Jersey Delay Reduction Program* (Denver: Institute for Court Management, 1983), pp. 88–89. Langdon's monograph is a primary source for much of the discussion here about the background and initial implementation of the New Jersey program.

13. Robert D. Lipscher, "Court Rules Have Limits," *Judges Journal*, Vol. 23, No. 1 (Winter 1984), pp. 37–38.

14. 1986 Judicial Conference of New Jersey, Task Force on Speedy Trial, *Report of the Committee on Speedy Trial*, 1980–1986, pp. 1–4.

15. *Ibid.*

16. 1986 Judicial Conference of New Jersey, Task Force on Speedy Trial, *Report of the Committee on Speedy Trial Goals and the Quality of Justice*, pp. 5–6, 59.

Part IV
Future Directions

Chapter 9
POLICY IMPLICATIONS OF THE STUDY

As we noted in Chapter 1, the research discussed in these pages has been action-oriented, beginning with a working premise that trial court delay is an important but not insoluble problem. Perhaps the most important finding of the study is that this premise is solidly grounded. It is clear that a number of trial courts handle their caseloads very expeditiously. It is also clear that where lengthy delays exist it is possible to reduce them significantly and to develop systems that will enable the court to operate efficiently on an on-going basis.

The strong evidence that court delay is a problem that can be successfully addressed has important policy implications. The fact that a reasonably speedy pace of litigation can be achieved in trial courts (including courts that have in the past been plagued with lengthy delays) can no longer be seriously in doubt. The local legal culture *can* be changed. In the urban courts where delay reduction and delay prevention programs have been implemented successfully, practitioner norms, expectations, and patterns of behavior are clearly different from what they had been before the program began. They are also different from what they are in urban courts that still have large backlogs and lengthy delays.

In the courts that have successfully implemented these pro-grams, there is a broad (though not necessarily universal) accep-tance of both the legitimacy and the desirability of caseflow management, and general agreement that delays in litigation should be minimized. No such consensus exists in the other courts. To the extent that delay reduction and prevention are or may become policy goals in a jurisdiction, the primary challenge will be to develop such a consensus. The challenge is thus essentially the same one posed in *Justice Delayed*: how to change the practices, attitudes, and expectations of both judges and attorneys regarding the appropriate pace of litigation and the scheduling of events that take place in the course of every criminal prosecution and civil lawsuit.

For policymakers and practitioners who are interested in having an expeditious pace of litigation in their courts, the main findings from this research should be helpful. They will not provide detailed blueprints, but they contain some useful guideposts and they also suggest areas in which further research can be valuable.

A. Principal Findings

1. Trial court delay is not inevitable. Some urban trial courts handle their entire caseloads very expeditiously.

- The time required to deal with tort cases varies widely, with the fastest courts completing at least half their cases in less than a year and the slowest courts taking over two years. The faster courts deal even more expeditiously with civil cases other than torts.

- Differences in criminal case processing times also vary widely, but a high proportion of the urban courts in this study deal with the great bulk of their felony cases relatively quickly. Eight of the eighteen jurisdictions handle at least half their cases from arrest to disposition in less than three months. All but two of the others do so within six months. The slowest courts, however, take more than five times as long as the fastest ones.

2. Where delays exist, they can be reduced significantly. The study documents dramatic improvements in civil and criminal case processing in several courts in recent years. In some instances, these improvements were made despite substantial increases in per-judge workloads.

- Improvements in civil case processing need not be at the expense of the criminal calendar, and vice versa. Three of the courts in this study—Jersey City, Bronx County, and Dayton—made substantial reductions in *both* civil and criminal case processing times during the 1976–85 period. A fourth court, Phoenix, maintained a speedy pace of civil litigation while greatly reducing its criminal case processing time.

- Data comparing workloads and resources over time are difficult to obtain. However, it appears that the Phoenix court achieved its record despite a 58% increase in civil filings per judge and a 39% increase in felony filings per judge. In Oakland and in Bronx County, too, felony case processing times decreased despite large increases in workloads.

3. The pace of civil and criminal litigation is not clearly correlated with the size of the court, population of the jurisdiction, composition of the caseload, per-judge caseloads, or the percentages of cases that proceed to jury trial.

- Size is clearly irrelevant. The faster courts include some that are large and some that are small. To illustrate, the five fastest civil courts in the study had, respectively, 13, 54, 58, 33, and 21 judges.

- Workload, by itself, does not determine case processing time. For example, Detroit Recorder's Court, which had the fastest 1985 upper court disposition time of any court in the study, had 351 upper court filings per judge and a total per-judge caseload (filings plus cases pending at start of year) of 451. By contrast, the slowest court—Boston—had only 151 filings per judge and a total per-judge caseload of 382.

- On both the civil and criminal sides, the faster courts include some that have a low percentage of dispositions by jury trial and some that have a relatively high percentage of jury trials.

- The fact that none of these structural factors are independently correlated with fast or slow case processing does not mean that all of them are irrelevant. It is possible, for example, that a combination of high case volume, a high proportion of serious or complex cases in the caseload, and a high jury trial rate could cause delays. There is some evidence that such a combination of factors may be related to delays in some of the slower felony courts.

4. The presence of an alternative dispute resolution (ADR) program, whether mandatory or voluntary, is not correlated with speed of civil case processing.

- All but three of the seventeen civil courts in the study have some type of alternative dispute resolution program. ADR programs exist in both fast courts and slow ones.

- While more research is necessary on this subject, preliminary indications are that the key variable is the way cases diverted into the ADR process are managed. Early referral—shortly after issue is joined by the filing of an answer—correlates with speedy overall case processing times. Ongoing management of cases referred to an ADR program, to ensure that the dispute is resolved promptly, may also be important, but was not a focus of attention in this study.

5. The general type of calendaring or case assignment system used in a jurisdiction (i.e. master calendar, individual calendar, or hybrid) does not appear to be a decisive factor determining case processing times.

- Neither master calendar nor individual calendar systems appear to be associated with consistently fast or slow criminal case processing.

- On the civil side, courts employing an individual calendar system appear to be markedly faster in handling their cases than most master calendar courts. However, a few master calendar courts (e.g. Portland, Jersey City, Wichita) are very speedy. This suggests that the key variable may not be the generic type of system, but rather, the way the system is organized and operated.

- The faster civil case master calendar systems are characterized by (1) having a "permanent" master calendar judge who is also the chief judge of the court or the administrative judge of the civil division; and (2) their utilization of techniques of case management, including early intervention and case scheduling.

6. On the civil side, implementation by the court of key concepts of caseflow management is strongly correlated with speedy case processing times.

- The point at which a court begins to become involved in monitoring the progress of litigation and in scheduling future events is important. The faster courts take cognizance of cases at the commencement of a lawsuit, and have mechanisms to enable periodic monitoring and early setting of schedules for future events.

- The faster courts place great emphasis on a court's ability to ensure that trials and other events will occur on the scheduled date. Continuances may be granted, but tend to be limited in number and granted only for good cause shown. Last-minute stipulations by the lawyers involved are generally not adequate grounds for continuances in these courts.

- The slower courts either leave the pace of litigation (including the setting of trial dates and continuances of scheduled trials) entirely to the lawyers or become involved in case management only at the point where the lawyers indicate readiness for trial.

7. On the criminal side, police and prosecutorial practices have a great impact on overall case processing times. Courts with speedy felony case processing times are generally ones in which both the prosecutor's office and the court have a strong commitment to speedy case processing and have worked cooperatively to develop and maintain efficient procedures. Characteristics of the systems in these courts commonly include the following:

- Rapid post-arrest screening of felony arrest cases, conducted by experienced assistant prosecutors.
- Rapid filing of charges in the upper court, in cases where prosecutorial screening has resulted in a decision to prosecute the case as a felony. In jurisdictions using an indictment system (e.g. Dayton, Portland) this process often includes rapid presentation of cases to the grand jury, following the screening.
- Early assignment of counsel for indigent defendants.
- Early disclosure of the prosecution's evidence (e.g. police reports, witness statements, defendant's statements, lab reports). Disclosure is withheld only in exceptional circumstances (e.g. identity of an informer).
- Early filing and early resolution of motions, including motions involving the admissibility of evidence at trial.
- Strong case management by the upper court, from arraignment to disposition, including scheduling of intermediate events (e.g. status conference, motion hearing, pretrial conference) at short intervals and emphasis on ensuring that the court has the capacity to hold a trial on the scheduled date.

8. Jurisdictions that use a prosecutor's information to charge defendants with a felony offense generally handle their felony caseloads more speedily than jurisdictions that use an indictment-based system.

- Median times from arrest to upper court filing, and from arrest to disposition, are faster in most of the jurisdictions that use a prosecutor's information than in most of those that use a grand jury indictment process. However, one jurisdiction that uses a grand jury system, Dayton, is one of the fastest courts in handling felony cases.
- The key factor appears to be not the type of charging system (indictment or information) but, rather, the way in which the overall system is organized and managed by the prosecutor and the court.

9. The size of the pending caseload, in relation to annual dispositions, is strongly associated with the pace of litigation. Slow courts are generally backlogged courts.

- While backlog may not be a cause of delay in itself, reduction in the size and age of the pending caseload is an important threshold concern in the development of an effective delay reduction program.

- The infusion of temporary additional resources can be very helpful in addressing a "one-time" backlog reduction problem, especially if coupled with the development of effective caseflow management procedures that will be used after the pending caseload has been reduced to a manageable level and case processing times are at an acceptable length.

10. The experience to date indicates that caseflow management and delay reduction programs can be institutionalized. Courts that make dramatic improvements will not inevitably slide back into their old ways. However, they must be prepared to resist pressure to retreat from commitments to case management.

- All of the courts in this study that had shown significant progress in reducing delays as of 1983 (by comparison to their situation in the late 1970s) were able to maintain a relatively speedy pace of litigation in 1984 and 1985.

- Even in courts that appear to be very successful in caseflow management, there are recurrent pressures from some attorneys and judges to abandon or relax key aspects of the management programs.

11. The degree and nature of involvement of state-level leaders in addressing problems of trial court delay has varied widely. In some states, the leadership of the chief justice, state supreme court, and state court administrator have been important factors in focusing attention on problems of delay. State-level leadership and support have played critical roles in several successful programs.

- In Detroit, the intervention of the Michigan Supreme Court in the mid-1970s was instrumental in alleviating a crisis situation and initiating the development of a model caseflow management system in Detroit Recorder's Court.

- In Phoenix, the Arizona Supreme Court's authorization for use of pro tem judges was essential for successful implementation of the locally initiated civil case management program.

- In Ohio, the Rules of Superintendence adopted by the Ohio Supreme Court in 1971 have provided a general context and, through a requirement of monthly reports from the judges on their pending caseloads, a specific focus on case processing times. Within that framework, there is room for locally initiated programs such as the highly successful criminal and civil case management programs in Dayton.

- In Kansas, a statewide delay reduction program has been successful in reducing the size of pending civil and criminal caseloads and the number and age of "old" pending cases throughout the state.

- In New Jersey, a statewide speedy trial program focused on criminal cases has been successful in most counties. State-level support for the program in Hudson County—including provision of additional judges to help in a backlog reduction program—has been a key component of the successful delay reduction efforts in the Jersey City court.

12. Ultimately, it is essential to have local-level leadership and commitment in order to achieve case processing time goals and institutionalize effective caseflow management practices in trial courts.

- Even where a successful program has not been the product of a local initiative (e.g. Detroit Recorder's Court in the mid-1970s), it has been the judges, court staff, and bar-leaders at the local level who have made it work. On the criminal side, the role of the local prosecutor's office is especially critical.

- Where local-level leaders have not "bought into" state-level delay reduction initiatives, significant improvements have not taken place. For state-level initiatives to be successful, close attention must be paid to developing local-level leadership and commitment.

13. There is no single model of a successful delay reduction or delay prevention program. Successful courts have used a variety of techniques and have adapted the details of their program to local conditions. The programs have been relatively comprehensive—rather than seeking a "one-injection miracle cure,"[1] they have involved a number of different components and a lot of hard work.

B. Common Elements of Successful Programs

The successful courts examined in this study have used different types of calendaring systems, have had widely varying jury trial utilization rates, and differ considerably in the emphasis they place on encouraging settlements. Alternative dispute resolution programs are an important part of some effective civil caseflow management systems, but not of all. Some of the successful courts have modern computerized information systems that regularly produce all or virtually all of the data needed to monitor caseload status and identify problems, while others make do with rudimentary manual systems. The degree of involvement of the practicing bar, the roles of the prosecutor and public defender, and the nature and extent of the participation of state-level leaders all vary markedly across this group of courts.

However, despite the diversity that exists with respect to specific techniques and approaches used in the successful courts, there are some common themes that can be drawn upon in developing future programs aimed at preventing and reducing delays. The following are the ones that appear to be most critical:

1. Leadership. In their study of corporate innovation and excellence, Peters and Waterman found—somewhat to their surprise—that "associated with almost every excellent company was a strong leader (or two) who seemed to have had a lot to do with making the company excellent in the first place."[2] Much the same thing seems to be true in courts that have been successful in addressing problems of delay. When we asked practitioners in these courts about reasons for a court's effectiveness in minimizing or reducing delay, one of the most frequent responses was a reference to the leadership ability of the chief judge. The specific qualities mentioned in this context cover a wide range, but it is clear that most of the successful courts have had the benefit of leadership by a chief judge with the vision, persistence, personality, and political skills necessary to develop broad support for court policies and programs aimed at reducing delay.

By the same token, the absence of strong leadership concerned about the pace of litigation was frequently cited by practitioners in the slower courts as a prime reason for the lack of attention to the problem of delay. Very often, the leadership problems related not so much to the personality of the chief judge as to the criteria for selection and the "traditional" non-assertive role of the chief judge. In particular, where the chief judgeship is a rotating office that is essentially honorific, with little real management authority and responsibility, there is no strong central core for the development of an aggressive long-term attack upon problems of delay.

Leadership with respect to delay reduction and delay prevention is not exclusively the province of the chief judge. Within a trial court, the trial court administrator or clerk has a key role. More than anyone else, the administrator or clerk must convey the goals of a program to members of the court staff, obtain their input, allay their concerns, and organize the resources necessary to implement the program on a day-to-day basis. Outside the court, bar leaders have vitally important roles. Their active support for delay reduction (or delay prevention) goals, and their involvement in developing a workable program, will greatly enhance the prospects of success. With respect to criminal case processing, the prosecutor's role is crucial. A prosecutor who is committed to expeditious resolution of criminal cases can establish policies and deploy staff resources in ways that will minimize delays.

2. Goals. The development and adoption of time standards for the processing of cases by the Conference of Chief Justices, the American Bar Association, and a number of state court systems reflect a widespread feeling on the part of key elements of the legal community that there are outside limits on how long cases *should* take, at least in the absence of exceptional circumstances. Time standards provide a benchmark—a measure for identifying courts that have a reasonably satisfactory pace of litigation. The experience of courts included in our study suggests that such standards may also have a motivational value. Every one of the criminal courts that we have identified as having made significant improvements between the baseline' year and 1983 had some type of time standards in place. In some instances, the standards had been adopted at the state level; in others, they were entirely the product of local initiatives. Interviews with practitioners—both judges and lawyers—suggest that the standards are generally taken seriously, even if there is no sanction imposed when a case exceeds the time allowed by the standards. Here, the roles of the chief judge and leaders in the court and the bar are critical. Time standards are not self-executing. The more emphasis these leaders place on meeting time standards (and the greater their political skills), the more likely it is that individual judges and practicing lawyers will take them seriously.

On the civil side, relatively few courts (or states) had adopted civil case processing time standards as of 1985. It may be significant, however, that five of the fastest civil courts in our study (Dayton, Phoenix, Wichita, Miami, and Cleveland) operated under time standards that establish outer limits on the times expected to be taken in various types of civil cases from filing to disposition. One of the courts that improved its civil case processing time markedly, Bronx County, also operates under time standards, although these run only from the time a trial readiness document is filed upon completion of discovery.

3. Information. The types of management information systems used in the successful courts vary widely. Some are automated and are highly sophisticated in the types of management reports they produce at regular intervals. Others are entirely manual, and can provide only some of the data that a court manager would ideally want in order to monitor the pace of litigation. In all of these courts, however, some type of management information is collected—and *used* by the leadership of the court—to monitor case processing times and identify problems before they become crises.

Our emphasis on the use of the information is deliberate. One of the somewhat surprising findings of the study is that there are some courts in which basic management information (e.g. size and age of the pending caseload by case type, age of cases at disposition, trial date continuance rates, trends with respect to findings and disposition) is available or can easily be obtained, but is simply not used to diagnose and help devise solutions to problems of delay. Here again, there is a direct tie-in with the critical components of leadership, goals, and commitment to delay reduction. Court leaders who make delay reduction a real priority will want to know whether case processing time standards or goals are being met. Whether or not the court is computerized, they will find ways to get the information necessary to monitor progress.

4. Communications. Delay reduction and delay prevention programs are not undertaken in a vacuum. If there is any one lesson from the research and experimentation of the past decade, it is that good communications and broad consultation—within the court (including both judges and staff), between the trial court and state-level leaders, and with the private bar and key institutional actors such as the prosecutor and public defender—are essential if a program is to succeed. The type of consultation mechanisms used by the successful courts in this study varied widely, but in all of them the channels of communication were open. Some type of formal or informal committee structure—typically involving the chief judge, court administrator, and key practitioners (e.g. prosecutor and public defender on the criminal side; representatives of the plaintiffs' and defendants' bar on the civil side)—was common, although it did not exist in all of the courts.

Our emphasis on communications is hardly surprising, given the centrality of the local legal culture to the pace of trial court litigation. If delay reduction and delay prevention programs are to succeed, practitioner attitudes, practices, norms, incentives, and expectations must be understood and taken into account in designing the program and in making adjustments once the program is underway.

An open communications policy, it should be noted, does not necessarily mean decision making by consensus (or even by majority vote of the judges) in the successful courts that we studied. On the contrary, while comments and suggestions would generally be broadly solicited by the leadership in these courts, many of the key decisions about court policy—and especially about the details of implementing policy decisions—would typically be made by the chief judge or (as in Detroit and Jersey City) by a small de facto executive committee in which the chief judge and court administrator play key roles.

5. Caseflow Management Procedures. Although specific techniques vary considerably, the urban courts in this study that handle their civil cases most expeditiously all monitor the progress of cases from the time of initial filing until the conclusion of the litigation. Their record keeping systems are set up in a way that enables them to flag cases in which progress has not been made within previously established time periods, and most are prepared to take appropriate action (e.g. dismissal for failure to prosecute, imposition of sanctions for dilatory discovery) when this happens. Events in the life of a case are scheduled in consultation with the attorneys, and take account of the attorney's scheduling problems and conflicts, but continuances—even stipulated continuances—are not easily or routinely granted, especially when there is little advance notice.

The successful courts try (and succeed, in a high percentage of instances) to ensure that expectations that an event will take place when scheduled are met. Many of them try to structure their pretrial process to encourage completion of case preparation in advance of the trial date, recognizing that lawyers who know their cases well are more likely to negotiate a settlement—especially if a trial is imminent. The courts in Phoenix and Dayton, in particular, pay great attention to ensuring that the court can try any case set for trial on a particular date, using "backup judge" techniques.

On the criminal side, the same basic concepts of caseflow management—early control, on-going monitoring, a structured process to ensure early discovery and negotiation between prepared lawyers, and a capacity to hold trials on the scheduled date—are relevant, but their application takes different forms than it does in the civil litigation process. One major difference is the presence of an institutional litigant, the prosecutor's office, that can (and often does) exercise a substantial degree of control over the speed with which cases move through the process, especially during the period between arrest and indictment. The jurisdictions in this study that are most effective in handling felony cases are the ones in which both the court and the prosecutor's office are committed to speedy disposition and have worked cooperatively with each other and with others involved in the process to implement caseflow management techniques.

There are a great many techniques for managing cases and caseflow, and this is clearly much more an art than a science at the present time.[3] There is ample room for experimentation, and judges and non-judicial staff in the successful courts have not been afraid to experiment in the search for more effective ways of ensuring fair and speedy resolution of cases.

6. Judicial Responsibility and Commitment. Previous research on delay reduction programs has emphasized the importance of shared concerns, on the part of the judges of a court, about the problem of delay. In the words of one study,

> The most important element in starting and achieving a delay reduction program is a shared recognition in the court of the need to change the pace of litigation and a resolve to achieve that change. If one or only a few judges are committed to reducing the overall time to disposition, the chances of a program being successful are reduced significantly.[4]

Although the degree of judicial commitment to delay reduction or prevention is difficult to measure (and we have not attempted to do so, in any quantitative sense), it is nevertheless clear that such commitment is a key element in successful courts. The commitment manifests itself in several ways. First, there is a commonly (though not universally) shared belief on the part of the judges that the court has the responsibility for ensuring an expeditious pace of litigation. Second, these courts have all adopted procedures and techniques that focus the judges' attention on the age and status of cases, through dissemination of information, attention to docket status and details of case management at judges' meetings, and in a variety of other ways. Third, the commitment is translated into action when the judges hold lawyers to schedules previously set and decline to grant continuances routinely, even when none of the parties object.

7. Administrative Staff Involvement. While the commitment of judges is critical, the judges of a busy multijudge court cannot make a delay reduction program work by themselves. The involvement of court staff members at all levels—from the court administrator through the secretaries and courtroom clerks who handle day-to-day adminstrative duties for the judges—is essential. One of the striking aspects of the operations of several of the successful courts in our study is the extent to which the non-judicial staff members are aware of the court's case processing goals and are actively involved in helping to achieve them.

In Phoenix, for example, the court has prepared a manual for use by all of the secretaries, outlining the court's goals, policies, and procedures with respect to case processing. Since the Phoenix court is on an individual calendar system and each judge's secretary handles much of the scheduling of trials and other matters, the secretaries' understanding of the court's objectives and their ability to handle their scheduling responsibilities effectively are of critical importance in program implementation. Similar manuals have been prepared for use by both administrative staff and judges in Dayton and in Detroit Recorder's Court. The procedures are reviewed periodically in training sessions, and are sometimes revised on the basis of information and ideas provided by staff members. Court staff members are the persons most familiar with the details of ongoing court operations, and attention to detail is critically important in the implementation of caseflow management and delay reduction programs.

8. Education and Training. If courts are to manage their caseloads successfully, both the judges and the court staff need to know why and how to do it. Since the whole notion of caseflow management is of relatively recent vintage, this is not an area in which there is a great deal of knowledge and experience in most courts. Training is essential to familiarize judges, staff members, and members of the bar with the purposes and fundamental concepts of caseflow management and with the specific details and techniques essential to effective case management in the court on a day-to-day basis. Several of the successful courts in this study—notably Dayton, Phoenix, and Detroit Recorder's Court—have placed heavy emphasis on such training.

9. Mechanisms for Accountability. If caseloads are to be managed in courts, someone must be responsible for their management. In the more successful courts, lines of accountability are clear. Of the eight fastest civil courts, five employ the individual calendar system and the other three have master calendar systems in which the judge in charge of the master calendar also has significant long-term management responsibility and authority.

The fixing of responsibility for caseload management upon individual judges is one step toward developing accountability, but by no means the only one. Goals and information also have important roles. To hold individuals accountable, it is essential to have goals that they can be expected to achieve, or at least minimum standards of performance. Information on the age and status of cases is also vital if judges are to be held accountable for managing their case-loads and reducing delays. Other types of information may be useful in gauging the productivity of judges on other relevant dimensions. Non-judicial staff members may also be critical components in a system oriented toward accountability in case processing. There are (or should be) clear roles for administrative staff holding a number of key positions—e.g. judges' secretaries, courtroom clerks, data pro-cessing personnel, and information analysts. The effectiveness with which they perform their duties can be assessed periodically.

Finally, "outsiders"—a state court administrator's office, a con-sultant group providing technical assistance, or an independent evaluator of a program—can have important roles in helping to pinpoint problems, develop clear lines of responsibility, and imple-ment programs effectively. Several of the courts that have imple-mented caseflow management programs successfully—including those in Phoenix, Dayton, Detroit Recorder's Court, and Portland—have utilized such outside "catalysts."

10. Backlog Reduction/Inventory Control. On a year-to-year basis, most courts tend to show a total number of dispositions that is not greatly different from the number of filings. In courts that have a serious delay problem, however, a five-to-ten year comparison of filings and dispositions is likely to show the annual number of dispositions consistently less than the number of filings. The result has been the build-up, over a number of years, of a serious backlog—a large number of pending cases that cannot be dealt with in an acceptable period of time.

The backlog problem is clearly one that must be addressed at the outset of a delay reduction program. Effective elimination of the backlog of cases already in the system is just as important for the success of a delay reduction program as the development of effective means of dealing with new cases. In the short run—until the backlog of old cases is cleared away and substantially all cases are being handled within the time standards adopted by the jurisdiction—this necessarily means that a court committed to delay reduction must dispose of appreciably more cases than it takes in. This is exactly what was done in all of the courts in our study—e.g. Jersey City, the Bronx, Phoenix (criminal), Detroit Recorder's Court—that have been successful in significantly reducing delays. To successfully ad-dress the backlog problem, temporary additional resources may sometimes be necessary. However, unless there is a major long-term upward trend in workload, additional resources should not ordinar-ily be required on a permanent basis.

Where a court is already functioning well and delay is not a problem, control of the inventory of pending cases should still be an important concern. The notion of a "manageable caseload"—a pending caseload size that can be dealt with effectively by the court—is operationally important. Information is obviously a critical element here, but the requisite information is not difficult to collect. If filings begin to exceed dispositions, and if the age of cases in the pending caseload starts to increase, those are warning signals; the court should be prepared to take corrective action.

C. Directions for Future Research

We know much more today than we did ten years ago about the dimensions of the problem of court delay and about ways to attack the problem effectively. Nevertheless, it is clear that much still remains to be learned and that many of the critical issues are ones that involve deeply held values and cut across a wide range of legal system functions. As one observer has noted, delay reduction in the courts is somewhat like profit increase in a commercial organization: it is a pervasive concept, and its pursuit will take managers into every nook and cranny of the system.[5]

Focusing on delay reduction means, sooner or later, focusing on a wide range of philosophical, structural, and operational problems. This section outlines our thoughts with respect to areas in which future research could be especially valuable in improving the ways in which American legal systems deal with the problems of trial court delay.

1. Delays and the Quality of Justice. "Justice delayed is justice denied" is a well-worn phrase that has some grounding in reality, but it is also possible for a judicial process to be so rushed that the doing of justice is an impossibility. As Maurice Rosenberg has cogently observed, "Slow justice is bad, but speedy injustice is not an admissible substitute."[6] Simply moving cases faster, as an end in itself, is not a goal that will attract broad support and commitment from judges or the bar, and a concern with speed to the exclusion of other values will almost inevitably undermine those values. It is important to give more thought and attention to the broad goal of delay reduction efforts: i.e. a better quality of justice for the litigants, witnesses, and others who find themselves involved in civil or criminal litigation. The recent comments of one thoughtful observer who has contributed greatly to developing knowledge about problems of court delay are directly on point.

There is no question that the field [of judicial administration] must remain vitally concerned with efficiency, with productivity, with delay prevention and delay reduction. But most people, especially those who have committed their lives to working in the courts, recognize that courts are about something more fundamental than saving money or operating smoothly and speedily. While expeditiousness is surely a goal to be pursued by courts, few would argue that it is the only goal. (Unfortunately, the attempt to operationalize these other elements of court performance, especially the elusive but critical dimension of procedural and substantive fairness, has proven exceedingly difficult.) Further progress in this area may well be one of the major challenges of judicial administration research in the coming years.[7]

The subject is obviously not a new one, but it arises in a fresh context as trial courts develop management capabilities and techniques that show real promise of enabling them to reduce or prevent delays.[8] While there is undoubtedly a tension between the employment of management techniques to manage cases (and caseflow) and the use of the adversary process to resolve disputes, conflict is not inevitable and the tension can be healthy. Clearly, however, those who are concerned about problems of delay—researchers as well as policymakers and practitioners—must increasingly seek to examine relationships between caseflow management efforts and the broad goals of courts in the society. Some thoughtful ideas about approaches to studying these relationships are already emerging,[9] and this is clearly a high priority area for further attention. Initial efforts might usefully focus on developing a better sense of what we mean by "delay" in the myriad of different kinds of cases that reach the courts and of what may be included in the concept of "quality of justice" in American trial courts. The methodological problems are daunting, particularly with respect to the quality of justice issues, but it is important to begin thinking about how to address these issues effectively.

2. Delays and Resources. There is strong evidence that delay is not caused solely by a lack of resources and that simply adding resources will not cure the problem.[10] But at some point—once the slack is out of the system and courts are using techniques of modern management effectively—the issue of what constitutes an adequate level of resources (judges, court staff, courtrooms, prosecutors, defense attorneys, etc.) will become very relevant. There are limits to what can be done with management techniques alone. Quality of justice questions are important here: the quality of justice that can be accorded to individual cases (or to the total caseload of a judge or court) will ultimately depend on the time, technology, human resources, and other resources that can be devoted to them. As the discussion in Chapter 5 indicates, we are in a very early stage of collecting data on resources and workloads in trial courts. Much can be done to improve our capacity to collect and analyze meaningful data on these factors, across courts. Fragmentary data from this study—particulary the experiences in Dayton and in Detroit Recorder's Court—suggest that the concept of "manageable caseloads" is one that should be explored, with a view to developing methodologically sound approaches to allocating judges and other resources to courts. Such explorations should take account not only of the size and composition of caseloads, but also of the objectives—the quality of justice goals, including expeditious case processing and adequate in-court time for judicial consideration of the merits of cases[11]—that are sought to be obtained through effective court management.

3. Delays and the Economics of Law Practice. As our brief discussion of the Phoenix civil case management program indicates, there is evidence that implementation of delay reduction programs can have significant economic consequences for practicing lawyers. We do not, however, have any reliable knowledge about the actual economic impacts of different types of approaches to caseflow management. On one hand, there are arguments that a fast pace of litigation means that lawyers will get paid more quickly for their work. However, some lawyers are clearly concerned that delay reduction will mean that they will have to take on new associates or handle fewer cases. In fact, it is likely that different types of approaches will have different economic impacts, and that the impacts upon different segments of the bar will vary. This is an area in which research is clearly feasible now, both in jurisdictions that have already gone through change-over to a system of strong case management by the court (e.g. Phoenix, Dayton) and in ones where such a process is just beginning.

4. Delay Reduction and Judicial Leadership. As we have noted elsewhere in this report, practitioners in courts that function efficiently frequently point to the leadership in the courts as a primary factor accounting for a speedy pace of litigation. We have a rough general sense, from the case study work that we have done, about the types of activities that these successful leaders have engaged in as a part of their efforts to implement delay reduction and delay prevention programs. However, we have little systematic knowledge about what they do on a day-to-day basis, about their orienting values and commitments, or about the ways in which they define their leadership responsibilities and approach their tasks.

Given the strong evidence of correlation between strong leadership and organizational excellence, it seems important to know much more about leadership in the judicial environment and about ways to improve the identification, preparation, selection, education, and succession of court system leaders—both judges and non-judge administrators.[12]

5. Caseflow Management Techniques. The findings in this report provide empirical confirmation of the efficacy of applying techniques of caseflow management to reduce and prevent delays. But, while much has been learned over the past two decades,[13] we are still in the early stages of developing knowledge about what specific techniques work well in what specific circumstances. As judges and court staff continue to experiment with different techniques, it would be highly desirable to build in research designed to help answer questions about operational issues. For example:

- What—at a fairly precise level of detail—are the factors that make particular types of calendaring/case assignment systems work effectively (or ineffectively) in specific court environments?

- How can a court develop a trial setting policy that consistently schedules enough cases to enable efficient use of judges' time while also ensuring expeditious resolution of cases, providing attorneys with a meaningful firm trial date, and minimizing continuances?

- What kind of special treatment should be given to the complex "non-routine" cases that make up only a small percentage of the workload of most state courts, but which may require substantial resources and relatively lengthy case processing times?

- To what extent is it possible to identify "complex" cases, or cases that for some reason will require special attention from the court, at the time of filing or shortly thereafter? What sort of case management procedures should be used in these cases?

- How can different types of alternative dispute resolution programs be used most effectively in the context of an overall caseflow management program? What types of cases should be diverted into ADR programs? At what stage in the litigation process? On the basis of what criteria and information? Once diverted into an ADR program, what management techniques should be used to assure that the alternative dispute resolution mechanisms function fairly and efficiently? How does use of specific types of ADR programs alter the outcomes in particular categories of cases?

6. Caseflow Management and Trial Management. Although trial rates vary from court to court, significant amounts of judge time and available courtroom space are devoted to the conduct of trials in most urban courts. However, the amount of time spent in trials of similar cases varies considerably from court to court. One prominent California attorney argues that an important reason why civil trials take a particularly long time in some courts in that state is that in these courts there is no management of cases in the pretrial period. The result, this attorney maintains, is a protracted and expensive period of discovery, followed by a trial that is burdened by many time-consuming issues that should have been resolved at a much earlier stage of the litigation.[14]

If the trial process can be made more efficient in the courts that take a long time to conduct trials, then there is a potential for greatly enlarging the trial capacity of courts without adding new judgeships or other resources. There are clear linkages between a court's ability to manage trials efficiently and its ability to manage caseloads effectively. Efficient management of trials can increase the court's trial capacity and the credibility of its scheduled trial dates, thus heightening the likelihood that cases will settle when faced with the imminence of a trial. Reciprocally, good caseflow management will increase the court's ability to hold trials when scheduled. Both require an orientation to effective management by the court. We need to know more about ways to improve trial management and about the linkages between trial management and caseflow management.

7. The Effects of Time Standards. Although our research suggests that the existence of case processing time standards can have a positive effect in terms of minimizing delays, this is an area in which we are only beginning to develop knowledge. As more states and localities adopt time standards, it is a prime area for research.[15] We need to know more about the process of developing and adopting standards and about linkages between time standards (and the process of adopting them) and the implementation of programs at the trial court level.

8. The Consequences of Alternative Approaches to Caseflow Management. This is a topic closely linked to the quality of justice issues discussed above. Any type of approach to management of the flow of cases through a court—including the abdication of responsibility on the part of courts that choose to leave the pace of litigation entirely to the lawyers—is likely to have consequences in terms of the outcomes of cases as well as the speed with which they are resolved.[16] At a minimum, it is important to be aware of the potential for altering the patterns of case outcomes when a new procedure or management technique is introduced in a jurisdiction. Rather than learn the consequences after the program is in place, however, it would be highly desirable to design some new programs as experiments, with evaluations that would take account of the program's impact on case outcomes as well as on the pace of litigation.

9. Caseflow Management in Other Contexts. Our research, like most of the other research on trial court delay, has focused on general jurisdiction trial courts located in large urban areas. There are good reasons for this focus since these courts are the ones in which problems are most visible. However, they are not the only courts adversely affected by problems of delay. Indeed, in terms of the human costs of protracted litigation, the impacts may be greatest in some of the lower visibility courts such as those dealing with juvenile and domestic relations cases. Fragmentary available data indicate that other types of courts exhibit the same kind of wide variation in case processing times as we have found in the urban courts in this study.[17] However, it would be desirable to know more about both the range of variance in case processing times and the extent to which caseflow management techniques used successfuly in urban general jurisdiction courts will work effectively in these settings.

D. Conclusion

While much remains to be learned about trial court delay and about how to deal with it most effectively, it is not necessary to wait for the results of future research before starting to address the concrete problems that now exist. The needs are plain. Although important progress has been made in the past decade, there are still a number of American state trial courts that have serious problems of backlog and delay. In others, the problems are not pervasive, but are nevertheless real. They include certain categories of cases that take an especially long time to complete, some law firms or individual lawyers who carry large case inventories and repeatedly seek last-minute continuances, a few judges who take no interest in caseflow management and leave case progress entirely to the lawyers, and a lack of senior staff attention to issues of caseflow management.

Data in the tables presented in this study indicate that in a number of courts a high percentage of cases take longer (sometimes much longer) than the maximum time periods set forth in either the standards adopted by the American Bar Association or those endorsed by the Conference of Civil Justice. Clearly, there is plenty of room for improvement.

Unlike the situation a decade ago, however, there is now considerable knowledge about how to reduce delays where they exist, and how to prevent them from developing. There are now a number of trial courts that have developed effective systems of caseflow management. These courts can be models for others, and practitioners in these jurisdictions—judges, court staff members, practicing lawyers, and others—can be valuable resources to those from other jurisdictions who are interested in improving their systems. Workshops and seminars on caseflow management and delay reduction are held regularly at the national level, and special educational programs have been designed for a number of states and local trial courts. "How-to" manuals are readily available,[18] and are reinforced by a growing body of research findings.

But even as knowledge about the utility of specific approaches increases; we are becoming more aware of the complexity of the problem and its relationship to basic societal values. Maurice Rosenberg's words of 1965 remain very apt today:

> The problem of delay may be old, but it is by no means obsolescent; it is complex, but not insoluble; it is stubborn, but not hopeless. In the past we have acted as if we could wage a blitzkrieg against it, but now we see that we must tool up for a long campaign of attrition. The tools we need are persistence, resolution, and a willingness to apply scientific methods of research.[19]

The basic elements of effective action programs are clearly identifiable. There is now good evidence that if these elements—especially, strong leadership, clear goals, timely and reliable information, effective communications, and a few rather simple case management techniques—are present, delay reduction and delay prevention programs can succeed. The challenge for policymakers, at every level and in every branch of government, is to help create environments in which such programs can develop and thrive. For practitioners, it is to utilize the knowledge that now exists, to set goals and implement programs that enable fair and expeditious resolution of cases in their jurisdictions.

Research has played a key role in the development of knowledge about problems of court delay, and, particularly during the past decade, has contributed directly to the development of innovative action programs initiated at the state level and in local trial courts. It should continue to have an important role in the future, with ongoing interaction between researchers and practitioners. As Frances Zemans has observed, serious performance evaluation of courts requires the skills of the research community, while valid and reliable research is dependent upon the cooperation of those in the courts.[20] Researchers should be involved in the evaluation of specific programs, should contribute to refining specific techniques of caseflow management, and, most importantly, should continue to raise and explore questions about the relationships between specific caseflow management practices and other critical aspects of the legal system.

ENDNOTES–Chapter 9

1. The phrase is from Maurice Rosenberg, "Court Congestion: Status, Causes, and Remedies," in Harry W. Jones (ed.), *The Courts, the Public and the Law Explosion* (Englewood Cliffs, N.J.: Prentice Hall, Inc., 1965), p. 56. Reviewing the available evidence as of 1965, Rosenberg was emphatic in rejecting the "miracle cure" notion, noting that only a few of the supposed "delay antidotes" that had gained currency at that time had worked even to a modest extent, and that some had been shown to be counter-productive. He observed presciently that "progress in coping with the old problem of court delay will have to come from marshaling relief measures in groups." *Ibid.*, pp. 55–56.

2. Thomas J. Peters and Robert H. Waterman, Jr., *In Search of Excellence* (New York: Warner Books, 1982), p. 26.

3. The state of the art has, however, advanced considerably over the past 15 years. As two leading observers in the field note, "In 1972, the assertion that the court should take responsibility for active supervision of case progress, while not radical, was far from reality in most trial courts. Today, a growing number of judges and court administrators not only advocate the original concept, but have implemented it through a variety of innovative techniques." Maureen Solomon and Douglas K. Somerlot, *Caseflow Management in the Trial Court: Now and For the Future* (Chicago: American Bar Association, 1988). This monograph, an update and revision of Ms. Solomon's 1973 monograph entitled *Caseflow Management in the Trial Court*, contains a detailed discussion of techniques of caseflow management and related issues. It includes examples of forms and procedures used by specific courts, something that was simply not possible in 1973.

4. Larry L. Sipes et al., *Managing to Reduce Delay* (Williamsburg: National Center for State Courts, 1980), p. 25.

5. Anthony J. Langdon, *The New Jersey Delay Reduction Program* (Denver: Institute for Court Management, 1983), p. 241.

6. Rosenberg, supra note 1, p. 58.

7. Thomas W. Church, "From the Editor," Introduction to Volume 12, No. 1, *Justice System Journal* (1987), p. 6. This volume, a special issue entitled, "Symposium on Judicial Administration Research," consists of six papers presented at an international conference held in Albany, New York, in June 1986, together with comments by other conference participants. As Church notes in his introduction to the volume, one of the principal themes at the conference was a sense that evaluations of court performance have too frequently focused on efficiency-oriented measures (especially delay and judicial productivity), with insufficient attention to other aspects of court operations.

8. For arguments that an over-emphasis on case management by trial court judges is threatening basic values of the adjudication process, see Judith Resnik, "Managerial Judges," *Harvard Law Review*, Vol. 97 (1982),

p. 374; and "Managerial Judges and Court Delay: The Unproven Assumptions," *Judges Journal*, Vol. 23, No. 1 (Winter 1984), p. 9.

9. See, e.g., Floyd Feeney, "Evaluating Trial Court Performance," *Justice System Journal*, Vol. 12, No. 1 (Spring 1987), pp. 148–169; Frances Kahn Zemans, *Commentary* [on the Feeney article], *ibid*, pp. 171–174; D. Marie Provine, "Managing Negotiated Justice: Settlement Procedures in the Courts," *ibid*, pp. 91, 100-110; Geoff Gallas, "Judicial Leadership Excellence: A Research Prospectus," *ibid*., pp. 39–60. A major National Center for State Courts initiative, the Trial Court Performance Standards Project, is now underway, aimed at developing and testing ways of assessing the quality and effectiveness of courts' performance on a number of dimensions, of which timely case processing is one.

10. See, e.g., Chapters 3 and 5; also *Justice Delayed*, pp. 79–80; Steven Flanders, *Case Management and Court Management in U.S. District Courts* (Washington, D.C.: Federal Judicial Center, 1977); David W. Neubauer et al., *Managing the Pace of Justice: An Evaluation of LEAA's Court Delay Reduction Programs* (Washington, D.C.: National Institute of Justice, 1981), esp. pp. 414–432.

11. See Anne R. Mahoney, "Time and Process in Juvenile Court," *Justice System Journal*, Vol. 12, No. 1 (1985), pp. 37–56.

12. See Gallas, supra note 9.

13. See Solomon and Somerlot, supra note 3.

14. See Dale Sipes, *On Trial: The Length of Civil and Criminal Trials* (Williamsburg: National Center for State Courts, 1988). Quantitative data from this study shows a wide range in the amount of time taken to conduct trials in similar categories of cases across the nine courts involved in the study.

15. Within the past two years, several states—including California, Oregon, and Massachusetts—have adopted case processing time standards. The California legislation mandating the adoption of time standards (the Trial Court Delay Reduction Act of 1986) also provides for evaluation of "exemplary programs" that will be designed to implement the new standards in specific courts.

16. See Rosenberg, supra note 1, pp. 55, 57.

17. See, e.g., Barry Mahoney, Phillip B. Winberry, and Thomas W. Church, "Addressing Problems of Delay in Limited Jurisdiction Courts: A Report on Research in Britain," *Justice System Journal*, Vol. 6, No. 1 (1981), pp. 44–72; Anne R. Mahoney, *Juvenile Justice in Context* (Boston: Northeastern University Press, 1987), Chapter 4 "Time Bound Decisions," esp. pp. 54–60; also "Delay in Juvenile, Family and Domestic Relations Courts," *State Court Journal*, Vol. 9, No. 4 (Fall 1985), pp. 29–30.

18. See, e.g., Solomon and Somerlot, supra note 3; Sipes et al., supra note 4; Lawyers Conference Task Force on Reduction of Litigation Cost and Delay, *Defeating Delay* (Chicago: American Bar Association, 1986); ABA Action Commission to Reduce Court Costs and Delay, *Attacking Litigation Costs and Delay* (Chicago: American Bar Association, 1984) (Final Report

of the Commission); Ernest C. Friesen et al., "Justice in Felony Courts: A Prescription to Control Delay," *Whittier Law Review*, Vol. 2, No. 1 (1979), pp. 7–60.

19. Rosenberg, supra note 1, p. 59.
20. Zemans, supra note 9, p. 174.

APPENDICES

Appendix A
METHODOLOGY OF THE STUDY

The research methods used in this study are very similar to those used in the *Justice Delayed* study. The similarity is not coincidental. Like the authors of *Justice Delayed*, we were primarily interested in obtaining and analyzing data on case processing times across a broad range of courts. And, because a second main purpose was to analyze changes in case processing times over a period of years in specific courts, we wanted to obtain data that would enable longitudinal analysis. These purposes were of paramount importance in selecting courts for participation in the project and in making decisions about data collection and analysis.

Site Selection

In selecting courts for inclusion in the study, we sought a mix of urban courts from different geographic regions, all with at least ten judges. Of particular importance, we also wanted to include some courts that met the following criteria:

- Courts that had been the subject of a prior empirical study of case processing times, including both some that were fast and some that were slow. Inclusion of a substantial number of these courts would assure the existence of baseline data and enable comparisons over time. The utility of the earlier data would be greatest if the data collection methodology in the prior study had been similar to the methodology we would be using.

- Courts that had initiated a significant delay reduction or delay prevention effort during the 1977–83 period. This would provide opportunity to examine the elements of different types of programs and to assess their impact.

- Courts located in states in which a significant statewide delay reduction effort had been initiated during the 1977–83 period. This would provide opportunity for analysis of the dynamics of state-local interaction with respect to delay reduction.

Of the 18 courts finally selected for participation in the study, 13 had been involved in the National Center's *Justice Delayed* study. For these courts, we would have baseline data on case processing times for civil and criminal cases that reached disposition in 1976, and would also have some information about their structure, caseloads, and operating procedures as of that time. Some, but not all of these courts had initiated delay reduction or prevention programs in the intervening years.

The five "new" courts were all ones in which criminal or civil delay reduction programs had been started between 1977 and 1983. Three of these programs—all involving felony case delay reduction efforts—were subjects of an evaluation conducted by the American Judicature Society in 1979–1981, and some baseline data would be available for comparison with our own data on case processing times from the 1983–85 period. For the other two courts (Wichita and Jersey City) we would collect baseline data from samples of cases terminated in 1979, prior to the initiation of the delay reduction program in these courts.

Court Record Data Collection

Once the courts had been selected for inclusion in the project, we contacted the presiding judge or trial court administrator to arrange initial site visits by the project staff that had several purposes. First, in these initial visits, staff members would seek to obtain an overview of civil and criminal case processing in the court, through interviews with key judges and administrators. Second, documentary information about the court—organizational charts, management information reports, local court rules, annual reports, and the like—would be gathered. Third, the court's record-keeping system would be studied and, on the basis of this study, the project's court record data collection work would be organized in detail. Tasks with respect to organization of the court record data collection would typically include the following:

- Establishing procedures for drawing random samples of cases that reached disposition in the years being studied.

- Pre-testing the project's "generic" data collection forms and making any modifications that might be required because of a jurisdiction's unique nomenclature or procedures.

- Developing an instructional manual for data collectors to use in selecting the samples and coding data from court records on the project's data collection forms.

- In courts where coding would be done at the site, making arrangements with graduate students or others to do the actual data collection for the full sample.

- Establishing mechanisms for supervising the data collection and coding, to help provide quality control.

The sampling procedures were virtually identical to those followed in the *Justice Delayed* study. We focused initially on cases that reached disposition in 1983, seeking to obtain samples of approximately 500 felony cases and 500 general civil cases that were terminated in that year. The 500-case figure was a rough target that was also used in the *Justice Delayed* study. It is large enough so that, even if there were coding mistakes or other reasons why some cases subsequently would have to be dropped out of the sample, the sample would still be large enough to be representative of the total population of the cases from which it was drawn.

The sample of criminal cases was limited to cases in which the most serious charge in the accusatory instrument (indictment or information) could result in imprisonment for a year or more, and in which the guilty plea, verdict, or dismissal occurred in the year for which the sample was selected. Information on major events between arrest and sentencing was obtained from court records (e.g. case history printouts in courts with automated systems, docket cards, docket books, and case files in courts without automated systems), and recorded on the data collection form developed for each court. Exhibit 1 is a copy of one such form and indicates the types of information recorded. Key items of information included date of arrest (or, where that date was not available from court records, the date a complaint was first filed against the defendant); date the indictment or information was filed; highest charge in the indictment or information; date of arraignment on the indictment or information; date of disposition (e.g. date of dismissal, guilty plea, or jury verdict); type of disposition; and, for defendants who pleaded guilty or were found guilty after a trial, the date of sentence. Some other items of information—e.g. number of defendants, number of counts or charges against the defendant, number of scheduled court appearances, whether or not a bench warrant was ever issued because the defendant failed to appear, trial scheduling data, pretrial custody status, type of attorney, most serious charge at conviction, and sanctions imposed at sentence—were also collected if readily available in the court.

An indictment or information that included charges against several different defendants was treated as a single case for sampling purposes, with one of the defendants chosen for inclusion in the sample by the flip of a coin. Where a single defendant was charged with multiple offenses, either in a single indictment or in multiple indictments, all charges were treated as a single "case" in drawing the samples.

In drawing the civil case samples, we excluded domestic relations, juvenile, probate, and miscellaneous matters such as adoptions, name changes, bar admissions, and the like. The disposition date was defined as the date of verdict (in a case that went to trial) or as the date a judgment or dismissal order was entered. In each court, the information recorded on the data collection form included the date of filing (or service of the complaint, in jurisdictions where that is how an action is commenced), date of disposition, case type, and mode of disposition. Where possible, information was also collected on events such as date of filing of a readiness document, first scheduled trial date, and the last scheduled trial date (see Exhibit 2).

In the courts that have automated systems, our standard procedure was to have the court generate a list of all cases that reached disposition in the year. From that list, a sample of approximately 500 cases would be selected using random selection procedures, and the court would then furnish a computerized case history printout for each of these cases. Project staff located in Williamsburg would code the data, working from the printouts, onto the data collection forms.

In the courts that do not have automated systems, sample selection was a more difficult task, usually involving systematic examination of docket books or docket cards to cull out a sample of the year's dispositions. Coding was also more complicated in the manual systems, often involving examination of several different sources to obtain the desired data for each case. In the non-automated courts the coding was done on site, usually by graduate students working under the supervision of a project staff member or senior consultant.

Once information had been coded on the data collection form, the procedures were the same regardless of whether the coding had been done in Williamsburg or at the court. Samples of the completed data collection forms would be checked against court records for accuracy and consistency and, after entry onto the computer, the data would be subjected to a computer analysis to locate logical inconsistencies. After initial tables showing the composition of the samples and case processing times had been prepared for each court, they were examined by project staff members and then sent to the trial court administrator for review at the court. In the course of this multistage review and verification process, a number of errors were corrected.

Data from the samples of 1983 dispositions were used as the basis for tables and analysis contained in the project's preliminary report, which was prepared for the National Conference on Delay Reduction in September 1985. Following that conference, data collection continued in all of the courts involved in the project, focusing on cases that reached disposition in 1984 and 1985. Samples of approximately 500 felony cases and 500 civil cases were collected for each of those years, following the same procedures used to collect the first samples.

The figures presented in this report on case processing times in the participating courts are based on these samples. Data from the samples of 1985 dispositions are used most extensively because they are the most current; they are also the data that have been subjected to the most thorough and extensive verification procedures.

Original plans called for collecting data in at least 50 civil and 50 criminal cases that resulted in a jury trial in each court, in each year. To do this would have required supplementary sampling in almost every court. Because of time and resource constraints, such supplementary sampling was only done in two courts (Cleveland and Phoenix). One consequence is that the number of cases in our samples that resulted in a jury verdict is relatively small in most of the courts. In some courts, the number of jury trials in the sample is simply too small to be the basis for generalizations about time to jury trial. We have reported the processing times in these cases, but have taken care to indicate in parentheses the actual number of cases tried to verdict (see, e.g., Tables 2A and 2E).

Questionnaires

In order to obtain data on court structure, operating procedures, caseloads, and resources, a questionnaire was sent to each trial court administrator at the outset of the project. Follow-up questionnaires were sent to the court administrator and the presiding judge early in 1986, to update information obtained in the original survey and obtain some supplemental data. In order to clarify some of the responses and obtain missing data, the project staff also contacted the trial court administrator by telephone when necessary.

Information obtained through the questionnaire forms the basis for much of the report's analysis of case processing times in light of court structure, operating procedures, and attitudes toward caseflow management. More generally, this information has been of great value in providing a sense of the context within which litigation takes place in each of the courts in the study. The questionnaires produced basic information on a great many aspects of court operation, including the following:

- Types of subject matter jurisdiction.

- Type(s) of calendaring systems used for civil and criminal cases (e.g. Individual Calendar, Master Calendar, "Hybrid" systems).

- Caseload data for several years—pending at start of year; new filings and dispositions during the year, pending at end of year, etc.

- Number of jury and non-jury trials held during the year.

- Judges and non-judicial staff resources—total number of judges; allocation of judges to particular types of cases; number and utilization of their staff resources.

- Physical facilities—courthouse location(s), number of courtrooms, etc.

- Policies regarding use of retired judges, pro tem judges, etc.

- Perceptions of the seriousness of the delay problems in the court.

- Perceptions of the main causes of delay.

Interviews and Observation

After the first round of court record data collection had been substantially completed, the project staff selected nine courts to which site visits would be made for extensive interviews and observation. The case processing time data for 1983, together with the baseline data from 1976 or 1979, provided a starting point for more detailed inquiry into caseflow management practices in these courts. Our main objective in the site visits was to develop an in-depth sense of the dynamics of case processing in the mid-1980s. In courts where major delay reduction or delay prevention programs had been initiated, we were looking mainly for an understanding of what had happened, what had been tried, what seemed to have worked and what didn't, and how the practitioners in the jurisdiction—judges, lawyers, and court staff—felt about the efforts. In courts where the local-level efforts were linked, directly or indirectly, to state-level efforts, we also sought to gain some understanding of the relationship between the state and local initiatives. In the courts where little or no significant delay reduction or delay prevention efforts had been undertaken, we sought to understand why not, to learn how the existing system functioned, and to elicit practitioners' perceptions about trial court delay and caseflow management.

The length and scope of the site visits varied. Usually, two or three project staff members made a single visit to conduct the interviews, but in several of the courts follow-up visits were made. Structured interview schedules (e.g. Exhibit 3) were prepared and used as a general guide for interviewing, but in practice the scope and subjects covered in the interviews varied considerably. We usually conducted between 12 and 20 interviews in a jurisdiction, and considerably more in a few.

Data Analysis

Only a fraction of the data collected in this project has been analyzed in this report, and the analytic approach has been simple and straightforward. As in *Justice Delayed*, the quantitative data analysis is presented in two dimensional tables in which various measures of case processing times for the courts (e.g. median time from arrest to disposition) are set against independent variables such as number of judges, type of calendaring system, percentage of "serious" cases in the sample, and so forth. Additionally, because we have data collected in a similar fashion for at least three years for all of the courts, we have presented some tables showing changes over time.

The data set is a very rich one, and is appropriate for extensive secondary analysis on a wide range of topics. There is, however, a strong rationale for presenting our descriptive data and initial analysis as promptly as possible. That is what we have sought to do in this report. Hopefully, it will provide a starting point both for future research and for action programs to address the problems that are readily apparent.

EXHIBIT 1

National Center for State Courts/
Institute for Court Management
Delay Reduction Study

Rev. 9/26/85
Maricopa County Superior Court

CRIMINAL CASE DATA FORM

Record 1

(Col. Nos.)

1. Site Identification Number .... | 0 | 8 | (1–2)

2. Case Identification Number .... | | | | (3–5)

3. Sample Type: (CIRCLE ONE)

    General 1   (6)

    Trial 2

4. Court Case Number: (WRITE BELOW)

_____

5. Defendant's name: (WRITE BELOW)

_____

6. Total number of defendants .... | | | (7–8)

7. Most serious charge in information: (CIRCLE ONE)

    Homicide 01   (9–10)

    Rape 02

    Robbery 03

    Assault 04

    Drug-related crime 05

    Weapons possession 06

    Burglary, breaking and entering, trespass 07

    Theft, stolen property 08

    DWI 09

    Other (PLEASE SPECIFY) 10

_____

8. Number of counts/charges against this defendant .... | | | (11–12)

9. Date of arrest .... | | | | | | | (13–18)
                                                  Month   Day   Year

10. Date lower court complaint filed .... | | | | | | | (19–24)
                                                  Month   Day   Year

11. Date indictment or information filed .... | | | | | | | (25–30)
                                                  Month   Day   Year

12. Date of arraignment on indictment or information | | | | | | | (31–36)
                                                  Month   Day   Year

13. First scheduled trial date .... | | | | | | | (37–42)
                                                  Month   Day   Year

14. Number of scheduled court appearance .... | | | (43–44)

15. Was a bench warrant ever issued because defendant failed to appear? (CIRCLE ONE)

    Yes 1   (45)

    No 2

    Don't know 8

16. Date trial started .... ☐☐ ☐☐ ☐☐   (46–51)

                             Month Day Year

17. Number of days on trial .... ☐☐ (52–53)

18. Type of disposition: (CIRCLE ONE)

    Case Dismissed/Nolle Prosequi 01 (1–2)

    Diversion 02

    Plea of Guilty 03

    Guilty Verdict/Judgment After Jury Trial 04

    Guilty Verdict/Judgment After Non-Jury Trial 05

    Acquittal/Not Guilty Verdict After Jury Trial 06

    Acquittal/Not Guilty Verdict After Non-Jury 07

    Other (PLEASE SPECIFY) 08

    _____

19. Date of disposition .... ☐☐ ☐☐ ☐☐ (3–8)

                             Month Day Year

20. Most serious charge at conviction: (CIRCLE ONE)

    Homicide 01 (9–10)

    Rape 02

    Robbery 03

    Assault 04

    Drug-related crime 05

    Weapons possession 06

    Burglary, breaking and entering, trespass 07

    Theft, stolen property 08

    DWI 09

    Other (PLEASE SPECIFY) 10

    _____

    Not applicable 99

21. Custody status immediately prior to disposition: (CIRCLE ONE)

    Bail or ROR 1   (11)

    In Custody 2

    Don't Know 8

22. Attorney at disposition: (CIRCLE ONE)

Public defender 1 (12)
Private attorney 2
Not represented 4
Don't know 8

23. Date of sentencing .... ☐☐ ☐☐ ☐☐ (13–18)

Month   Day   Year

24. Sentence imposed:

	Yes	No	DK	NA	
Fine	1	2	8	9	(19)
Restitution	1	2	8	9	(20)
Probation	1	2	8	9	(21)
Jail/Prison-Maximum of 12 mos.	1	2	8	9	(22)
Jail/Prison-Over 12 mos.	1	2	8	9	(23)
Suspended sentence	1	2	8	9	(24)
Other (PLEASE SPECIFY)	1	2	8	9	(25)

Coder's initials _____

EXHIBIT 2

National Center for State Courts/
Institute for Court Management
Delay Reduction Study

2/7/85
Sedgwick County
District Court
Wichita, Kansas

CIVIL CASE DATA FORM

Record 1

(Col. Nos.)

1. Site Identification Number .... | 1 | 5 | (1–2)

2. Case Identification Number .... | | | | (3–5)

3. Sample Type: (CIRCLE ONE)

   General 1 (6)

   Trial 2

4. Court Case Number: (WRITE BELOW)

5. Name of First Plaintiff: (WRITE BELOW)

6. Date petition filed .... | | | | | | | (7–12)
   Month   Day   Year

7. Nature of case: (CIRCLE ONE)

   Tort—auto involved 01 (13–14)

   Tort—no auto involved 02

   Tort and contract 03

   Contract and commercial 04

   Real property rights 05

   Appeal 06

   Mortgage foreclosure 07

   Tax appeal or tax grievance 08

   Other (PLEASE SPECIFY) 09

8. Number of plaintiffs .... | | | (15–16)

9. Number of defendants .... | | | (17–18)

10. Date trial readiness document filed............ | | | | | | | (19–24)
    Month   Day   Year

11. First scheduled trial date .... ☐☐ ☐☐ ☐☐ (25–30)
                                                    Month   Day   Year

12. Total number of trial settings .... ☐☐ (31–32)

13. Last trial date set .... ☐☐ ☐☐ ☐☐ (33–38)
                                                    Month   Day   Year

14. Date trial started .... ☐☐ ☐☐ ☐☐ (39–44)
                                                    Month   Day   Year

15. Number of court days spent in trial .... ☐☐ (45–46)

16. Manner of disposition (CIRCLE ONE)

    Default judgment for plaintiff 1   (47)
    Dismissal 2
    Judgment without trial 3
    Arbitration 4
    Court trial 5
    Jury trial 6
    Other (PLEASE SPECIFY) 7

    _____

    _____

    Don't Know 8
    Settled 9

17. Date of disposition .... ☐☐ ☐☐ ☐☐ (48–53)
                                                      Month   Day   Year

Coder's initials _____

EXHIBIT 3

NCSC/ICM Delay Reduction Project
INTERVIEW SCHEDULE FOR JUDGES
Civil Case Processing

1. What, in your opinion, are the most serious problems facing the court?
   - Are there any particular problems that we should be aware of with respect to:
   —facilities
   —number of judges
   —salaries
   —court employees
   —volume of business
   —delays
   - In general, how adequate do you believe the court's resources are for purposes of handling its caseload?

2. To what extent is delay in civil cases a problem in this court?
   - What would be considered an "old" case?
   - What is the general policy or attitude in the court about moving older cases?
   —Is there an emphasis on moving old cases?

3. Do the cases that take a long time to deal with tend to have particular characteristics or to fall into particular categories?
   - If so—what characteristics/categories?

4. What are the factors that tend to make a case move slowly?

5. Has the court undertaken any program or project specifically aimed at reducing delay in the past several years?
   - If so—
   —What were the objectives?
   —What changes did the program involve?
   —How successful do you think it was? Why?

6. Aside from a specific delay reduction program, have there been any other significant changes in the way the court handles civil cases over the past several years?

7. Would you predict any problems developing if the court began to move civil cases significantly faster than at present?
   - Who (if anyone) would be upset? Why?

8. Is there any regularized process in the court for monitoring the progress of civil cases?
   - If answer isn't filed?
   - Discovery proceedings?
   - Dismissals for lack of progress?
   - Use of a "trial readiness" document?

9. What (if anything) do you think the court should do in a civil case when it appears the attorneys are "dragging their feet?"

10. Are there screening procedures that allow different types of cases to be treated differently?
    - Complex litigation?
    - Short or routine matters?
    - Injunction, other equity matters?

11. How do you handle pretrial motions in this court?
    - Briefs or motion papers required?
    - In-person hearing required?

12. To what extent do challenges to pleadings and discovery-related motions consume judge time?
    - Are these motions often used to harass or delay?

13. How are trial dates and other court appearances scheduled?

14. Suppose that the court had no problem of a backlog of pending cases. How long do you thing it *should* take—at the most—to complete the handling of a "routine" civil tort case? (For example— a typical "slip and fall" or motor vehicle personal injury action that might involve substantial injuries but not the complexities of a big medical malpractice or products liability suit.)
    - What should be the maximum time from date of filing, if the case goes to a jury trial?
    - What should be the maximum time if it is the sort of case that should be settled short of a jury trial?

15. What role does the court play in encouraging settlement in civil cases?
    - When and how is this done?

16. How are important policies made in the court?
    - Role of presiding judge

- Role of committees
- Role of court administrator, clerk of court

17. What role does the bar have in initiating or modifying court practice?

18. How would you describe bar practice in this court?
    - On defaults?
    - On motions to compel?
    - On requests for continuances?

19. How do you think the various segments of the bar would react to the idea of a program aimed at significantly reducing the time required to handle civil cases?
    - Who would be opposed? Why?
    - Who would favor? Why?

20. How do judges get selected for this court?
    - What role does the bar play?
    - What roles do state and local political leaders play?

21. Are there any particular factors or characteristics of this court that make it unique in relation to other courts of roughly similar size?
    - Nature of the caseload
    - Operating procedures
    - Other factors

22. Insofar as delay may be a problem—in this court or in any other general jurisdiction court handling civil cases—what do you believe would be the most promising approaches for dealing with the problem?

Appendix B
1985 CIVIL CASE PROCESSING TIMES AND JURY TRIAL RATES

	Median Filing To Disposition General Civil Docket (in days)	Median Filing To Disposition Torts (in days)	Median Filing To Disposition "Trial List" Cases (in days)	Median Filing To Readiness Trial List Cases (in days)	Median Readiness To Disposition Trial List Cases (in days)	Median Filing To Disposition Jury Verdict Cases (in days)	Number and Percent of Jury Verdict Cases in General Sample		Percent of General Civil Cases Taking Over One Year	Percent of General Civil Cases Over Two Years	Percent of Tort Cases Over One Year	Percent of Tort Cases Over Two Years	Number and Percent of Tort Cases in Sample		Number and Percent of Tort Cases in General Sample Tried To Jury Verdict	
							N	%					N	%	N	%
BOSTON, MA	789	782	*	*	*	1863	13	3%	68%	53%	70%	52%	197	48%	9	5%
BRONX, NY	*	*	772[a]	586[a]	142[a]	1138[a]	11	2%	*	*	*	*	507	94%	10	2%
CLEVELAND, OH	298	343	*	*	*	551[b]	11[b]	2%	41%	14%	48%	15%	309	49%	6	2%
DAYTON, OH	178	279	*	*	*	332	6	1%	24%	7%	34%	11%	221	43%	4	2%
JERSEY CITY, NJ	379[c]	394[c]	*	*	*	501	10	2%	55%	4%	59%	3%	336	69%	8	2%
MIAMI, FL	186	325	*	*	*	295	9	2%	23%	2%	43%	6%	115	20%	9	8%
MINNEAPOLIS, MN	*	*	603[a]	392[a]	190[a]	822[a]	12	2%	*	*	*	*	107	22%	9	8%
NEW ORLEANS, LA	366	403	560	210	288	745	11	2%	50%	22%	55%	23%	344	72%	9	3%
NEWARK, NJ	623[c]	624[c]	*	*	*	725	14	3%	87%	15%	88%	16%	398	83%	13	3%
OAKLAND, CA	616	637	838	305	420	1617	8	2%	70%	41%	73%	44%	493	89%	8	2%
PHOENIX, AZ	133	292	505	303	210	634[d]	5[d]	1%	30%	6%	41%	8%	144	30%	4	3%
PITTSBURGH, PA	406[e]	651[e]	694	142	438	575	40	8%[e]	51%	23%	69%	37%	168	34%	19	11%
PORTLAND, OR	253	389	*	*	*	694	5	1%	36%	6%	41%	8%	166	32%	11	7%
PROVIDENCE, RI	525	697	1304	86	914	1435	20	4%	59%	42%	65%	48%	269	54%	15	6%
SAN DIEGO, CA	691[f]	719[f]	696	371	261	1064	19	4%	81%	46%	85%	49%	323	61%	17	5%
WAYNE COUNTY, MI	624	648	*	*	*	1314	6	1%	88%	44%	89%	45%	245	56%	5	2%
WICHITA, KS	160	411	*	*	*	1126	3	1%	22%	6%	60%	16%	109	20%	3	3%

*Indicates data unavailable or inapplicable.

[a] Measure is from service of the complaint, not filing with the court. By state law, cases may progress to trial readiness prior to the filing of the complaint.

[b] Processing times for jury trial cases are based on the 11 jury trial cases from the general sample supplemented by 45 cases from a separate sample of jury trial cases.

[c] Does not include cases in which a default judgment, dismissal, or other disposition was reached prior to the filing of an answer.

[d] Processing times for jury trial cases are based on the 5 jury trial cases from the general sample supplemented by 38 cases from a separate sample of jury trial cases.

[e] Sample does not include cases filed directly with the court's mandatory arbitration program, which in 1985 covered all cases involving monetary claims up to $20,000.

[f] Does not include cases that reached disposition prior to filing of certificate of readiness.

Appendix C
1985 FELONY CASE PROCESSING TIMES AND JURY TRIAL RATES

1985 FELONY CASE PROCESSING TIMES AND JURY TRIAL RATES

	Median Arrest To Upper Court Filing (in days)	Median Arrest to Disposition (in days)	Median Arrest to Sentence (in days)	Median Upper Court Filing to Disposition (in days)	Median Upper Court Filing to Sentence (in days)	Median Arrest to Jury Verdict (in days)	Median Upper Court Filing to Jury Verdict (in days)	Number and Percent of Jury Verdicts in General Sample		Median Disposition to Sentence All Cases	Percent of Cases Over 180 Days from Arrest to Disposition	Percent of Cases Over One Year from Arrest to Disposition
								N	%			
BOSTON, MA	*	*	*	332	290	*	332	53	12%	0	*	*
BRONX, NY	20	121[a]	161[a]	152[a]	186[a]	352	318	45	8%	33	37%	15%
CLEVELAND, OH	36	121	164	90	125	175[b]	137[b]	25[b]	5%	32	28%	11%
DAYTON, OH	0	61	85	47	71	112	112	38	8%	19	11%	4%
DETROIT, MI	21[c]	58[c]	63[c]	31	35	128[c]	106	35	7%	21	10%	1%
JERSEY CITY, NJ	54[c]	163[c]	200[c]	115	144	195[c]	145	19	4%	43	42%	17%
MIAMI, FL	20	123	112	108	98	203	169	17	4%	0	35%	16%
MINNEAPOLIS, MN	0[d]	88[d]	*	88[d]	104[d]	134[d]	134[d]	32	5%	28	22%	*
NEW ORLEANS, LA	28	83	84	48	49	135	110	27	6%	0	19%	6%
NEWARK, NJ	168[c]	300[c]	333[c]	124	163	354[c]	208	55	11%	48	74%	37%
OAKLAND, CA	32	87[e]	*	57[e]	*	249	118	22	4%	*	28%	12%
PHOENIX, AZ	15	78	103	58	81	120	114	7	2%	28	12%	3%
PITTSBURGH, PA	23[c]	149[c]	182[c]	120	154	192[c]	160	14	4%	0	29%	9%
PORTLAND, OR	1	55	74	56	77	76	69	33	7%	17	9%	4%
PROVIDENCE, RI	57	122	118	63	58	435	375	12	3%	0	30%	17%
SAN DIEGO, CA	42	77[e]	115[e]	49[e]	89[e]	144[b]	91[b]	23	5%	29	14%	3%
WAYNE COUNTY, MI	30	133	149	64	92	209	165	37	6%	28	39%	20%
WICHITA, KS	0[g]	115[g]	182[g]	115[g]	170[g]	118[g]	118[g]	36	7%	43	16%	3%

*Indicates data unavailable or inapplicable.

[a] In Bronx County, most felony cases are prosecuted under an indictment filed in the general jurisdiction trial court (Supreme Court). However, it is possible to proceed under an information in certain circumstances. In these cases, a plea agreement has ordinarily been reached while the case was in the lower court, the defendant has waived his right to have the case presented to the Grand Jury, and the proceedings in the Supreme Court typically involve only the formal entry of the plea and imposition of sentence. Cases disposed of in this fashion have been included in the calculation of time from arrest to disposition and arrest to sentence, but *not* in the calculation of upper court disposition time.

[b] Processing times for jury trial cases are based on the jury trial cases from the general sample supplemented by cases from a separate sample of jury trial cases.

[c] Measure is from date lower court complaint or warrant is filed, not date of arrest.

[d] There is no lower court stage in Minneapolis. The starting point for all measures is the filing of the complaint in the District Court (general jurisdiction trial court), which ordinarily takes place within 48 hours following arrest of the defendant.

[e] In Oakland and San Diego, it is possible for pleas to felony charges to be entered in the Municipal Court, with an information subsequently filed in the Superior Court and the defendant sentenced in the Superior Court. Cases disposed of in this fashion have been included in the calculation of time from arrest to disposition and arrest to sentence, but *not* in the calculation of upper court disposition time.

[f] Calculations based upon data from net sample of 335 cases; 194 "driving while intoxicated" cases were in the original general sample but have been excluded from the analysis.

[g] Wichita has no lower court. The starting point for measuring time from arrest to disposition and arrest to sentence is the filing of the complaint in the District Court (general jurisdiction trial court), which ordinarily takes place within 24 hours following arrest of the defendant.

Appendix D
1985 COURT WORKLOAD DATA AND JURISDICTIONAL CHARACTERISTICS

1985 COURT WORKLOAD DATA AND JURISDICTIONAL CHARACTERISTICS[a]

	1980 Population	1985 Total Judges[b]	1985 General Civil Judges	General Civil Cases Pending 1/1/85	1985 General Civil Filings	1985 General Civil Dispositions	Tort Cases Pending 1/1/85	1985 Tort Filings	1985 Tort Dispositions	Type of Civil Calendaring System	1985 Felony Case Judges	Felong Cases Pending 1/1/85	1985 Felony Filings	1985 Felony Dispositions	Type of Felony Case Calendaring System	Type of Felony Case Charging System
BOSTON, MA (Suffolk County Superior Court)	650,000	16[c]	8	23,123	7,036	10,832	*	*	*	Master	8	1,548	1,211	1,435	Master	Indictment
BRONX, NY (Bronx County Supreme Court)	1,168,000	44	8	1,839[d]	4,048[d]	3,686[d]	1,630[d]	3,530[d]	3,132[d]	Hybrid(M)[e]	36	2,062	6,700	6,070	Hybrid(M)[e]	Indictment
CLEVELAND, OH (Cuyahoga County Court of Common Pleas)	1,498,000	33	*[f]	15,024	19,524	18,399	7,937	9,143	8,038	IC	*[f]	2,283	9,009	9,377	IC	Indictment
DAYTON, OH (Montgomery County Court of Common Pleas)	571,000	'13	*[f]	2,559	3,973	3,936	794	934	816	IC	*[f]	323	1,840	1,830	IC	Indictment
DETROIT, MI (Detroit Recorders Court)	1,203,000	29	*	*	*	*	*	*	*	*	29	1,849	10,172	10,581	Hybrid(IC)[g]	Information
JERSEY CITY, NJ (Hudson County Superior Court)	556,000	22	5	4,105	5,023	5,370	2,339	2,621	2,768	Master	7	1,963	2,226	2,484	IC	Indictment
MIAMI, FL 11th Judicial Circuit Court	1,625,000	58	30	33,341	32,096	31,035	10,858	7,591	6,914	IC	18	*	14,473	*	IC	Information
MINNEAPOLIS, MN (4th Judicial District Court)	941,000	42	10	2,355[d]	3,770[d]	4,027[d]	*	*	*	*[h]	8	est.800	3,004	3,298	Master	Complaint
NEW ORLEANS, LA (Orleans Parish Civil District Court & Criminal District Court)	557,000	*	10	*	*	*	*	*	*	IC	16	409	4,385	4,374	IC	Information

Court																
NEWARK, NJ (Essex County Superior Court)	851,000	46	11	7,957	8,628	8,585	*	*	*	Master	19	7,048	6,968	6,531	Hybrid(IC)[g]	Indictment
OAKLAND, CA (Alameda County Superior Court)	1,105,000	35	11	3,953[d]	4,476[d]	4,928[d]	683[d]	*	*	Master	12	744	4,475	3,966	Master	Information
PHOENIX, AZ (Maricopa County Superior Court)	1,509,000	50	22.5	22,591	33,146	32,870	7,339	7,461	7,083	IC	13.5	3,421	9,792	8,817	IC	Information
PITTSBURGH, PA (Allegheny County Court of Common Pleas)	1,456,000	47	15	4,713[d]	3,164[d]	3,382[d]	1,830[d]	1,515[d]	1,330[d]	Master	20	*	*	*	IC	Information
PORTLAND, OR (Multnomah County Circuit Court)	562,000	21	*[f]	14,053	19,036	19,573	2,503	2,777	2,820	Master	*[f]	1,575	4,392	4,432	Master	Information[i]
PROVIDENCE, RI (Superior Court for Providence and Bristol Counties)	571,000	13[c]	7	4,686	2,196	1,653	*	*	790	Master	6	1,647	3,195	2,680	Master	Information
SAN DIEGO, CA (San Diego County Superior Court)	1,861,000	48	24	*	42,659	30,049	*	18,085	8,688	Master	12	*	7,422	6,811	Master	Information
WAYNE COUNTY, MI (3rd Judicial Circuit Court)	2,337,000	35	27	31,349	20,506	22,004	18,996	10,867	11,939	Hybrid(M)[e]	8	800	4,165	4,322	Hybrid(IC)[g]	Information
WICHITA, KS (18th Judicial District Court)	336,000	22	9	4,319	14,385	14,142	851	756	839	Hybrid(M)[e]	7	868	1,684	1,844	Master	Information

[a]Sources: Information provided by the trial court administrator's office in each court, except as follows: Information for Boston was provided by the Office of the Administrative Judge for the Massachusetts Trial Court. Information for the Bronx was provided by the Office of Programs and Planning of the New York State Office of Court Administration.

[b]Unless otherwise indicated, this figure is the total number of full-time judges in the court, including those regularly assigned to handle matters other than felony cases and general civil cases.

[c]The figure is a total of the judges ordinarily assigned to civil and criminal business for the court during 1985.

[d]Includes only cases in which a trial readiness document (e.g., Note of Issue, Certificate of Readiness, Praecipe) was filed.

[e]The calendaring (case assignment) systems in these courts combine elements of both the individual calendar and master calendar systems, but are closer to the master calendar system.

[f]The judges in these courts handle "mixed dockets" that include both civil and criminal cases, so it is impossible to determine the number of judges allocated to civil and criminal business.

[g]The calendaring (case assignment) systems in these courts combine elements of both the individual calendar and master calendar systems, but are closer to the individual calendar system.

[h]During 1985, the Minneapolis court was changing from a master calendar system to an individual calendar system.

[i]In process of change to indictment-based charging system.